Hannah's
Art of
Home

A CAPITAL IDEAS BOOK

Practical books that offer expert advice
on key personal and professional aspects of life

Other Capital Ideas titles include:

The Dogs Who Grew Me by Ann Pregosin

Father's Milk by Andre Stein and Peter Samu

The Golden Rules of Parenting by Rita Boothby

Graduate by Kristen Gustafson

A Grammar Book for You and I . . . Oops, Me by C. Edward Good

A Grandmother's Guide to Babysitting by Ruth A. Brown

"Honey, I've Shrunk the Bills!" by Jack Weber

How to Avoid the Mommy Trap by Julie Shields

"Just Sign Here, Honey" by Marilyn Barrett

The Kitchen Answer Book by Hank Rubin

The Man Who Would Be Dad by Hogan Hilling

Our Money Ourselves for Couples by C. Diane Ealy, Ph.D. and Kay Lesh, Ph.D.

The Parent's Guide to Business Travel by Charlie Hudson

The R.A.T. (Real-World Aptitude Test) by Homer E. Moyer, Jr.

Safe Living in a Dangerous World by Nancy Harvey Steorts

UPI Stylebook & Guide to Newswriting
by Bruce Cook, Harold Martin, and the Editors of UPI

Use Your Fingers, Use Your Toes by Beth Norcross

Your New Dog by Susan McCullough

Save 25 percent when you order
any of Capital's fine titles from our Web site: www.capital-books.com.

Hannah's
Art of
Home

Managing Your Home
Around Your Personality

Hannah J. Keeley

CAPITAL
BOOKS, INC.
Sterling, Virginia

Capital Books, Inc.
P.O. Box 605
Herndon, Virginia 20172-0605

ISBN 1-931868-82-4 (alk.paper)

Library of Congress Cataloging-in-Publication Data
Keeley, Hannah J.
  Hannah's art of home : how to manage your home around your personality /
    Hannah J. Keeley. — 1st ed.
      p. cm.
      Includes index.

ISBN 1–931868–82–4 (alk. paper)
1. Home Economics. 2. House cleaning.   I. Title.

TX147.K42 2005
640—dc22

                                   2004008151

Cover photography by Double Image Studios, Richmond, VA.

Printed in the United States of America on acid-free paper that meets the American National Standards Institute Z39-48 Standard.

First Edition

10 9 8 7 6 5 4 3 2 1

To Blair—
In your arms is the only home
I ever need.
To Kelsey, Katie, Kyler, Karis,
Korben, and Klara—
I rock my babies and
they rock my world.

Contents

Acknowledgments

Once upon a time there was a little boy named Charles and a little girl named Mary. They fell in love in kindergarten, and eventually grew up, got married, and had five children. But these were not your ordinary children. They were each endowed with a magical gift upon their births that came into fruition as a result of the love that their parents poured into their lives. They were not only magical, but powerful as well. And their power was stronger as a unit than it could ever be apart. This made Charles and Mary happy, for they knew that these magical gifts would not only protect them in the world, but it would also keep them tied together throughout their lives. The first-born child was the guardian of the family. She possessed the magical gift of legacy. She wove beautiful tapestries that had the ability to tie together generations of the family and protect all who sought warmth beneath them. The second-born child was the rational one of the family. He possessed the magical gift of knowledge. Through his analytical nature and amazing wisdom, he was able to lead the family to positions of great wealth, respect, and admiration. The third-born child was the artisan of the family. She possessed the magical gift of creativity. She wakened the senses of all who came near her so that they could fully experience the wonder and majesty of life. The fourth-born child was the idealist of the family. She possessed the magical gift of hope. All who came within her gaze became more talented, more skilled, and more adept simply as a result of her eyes having rested upon them. And the youngest of the five children possessed the most potent magical gift of all, for she was able to tell the world about them.

Introduction:
I Know Where You Live

No matter where you're living right now, I know it inside and out. I've had shirts starched, pressed, and hanging in the closet the day after being worn. And I have had piles of stinky, mildewed laundry so huge that they blocked doorways and I have been forced to wear overalls because I had no clean bras. I have had kitchen counters cleared and sparkling with a sink shining so brightly that you had to wear sunglasses. And I have had dishes piled up so enormously that I finally had to hand wash a few spoons so I could throw some bowls of cereal to the kids for dinner. So, no matter where you are living right now, I know it. And after years upon years of experience, I have finally figured out that because every person is different, everyone's home management style will be different as well.

You are an incredibly unique person—an artist who is constantly in the process of creating your surroundings. It's time to quit forcing a square peg into a round hole and begin to manage your home around your personality. You will get far more done in far less time and be far happier doing it, if you simply work with the way that you are wired. So celebrate the wonder of who you are! There is no need to change who you are or how you operate. Just travel on the road that is paved to fit your stride, and you can turn that house into your dream home. Live your life—just the way you are!

Please note: The names of my girlfriends have been changed in order to respect their privacy. Family members, however, are on their own.

Part 1

Your Home, Your Personality

Chapter 1

Home, Sweet Home

Some time after you set up your first home in that twenty-by-fourteen-foot studio apartment, you begin to realize that everyone has a completely different way of managing her home. This reality may first hit you when your toddler wipes his nose on your friend's tablecloth, and for some reason that is beyond your comprehension, she is irritated. Or maybe it's when you are helping carpool the third graders to the zoo and one of the kids asks why you don't have french fries and soda cans all over the seat. We are all so completely different and set up our homes in completely different ways. If everyone was the same, it would be more boring than the home movies you had to sit through of your nephew's two-year-old birthday party. We are so lucky to have variety in our lives and in our relationships. If it weren't for variety and differences, two guys like Ben and Jerry would have never made millions whipping up flavors like Chunky Monkey or Cherry Garcia. It would be a vanilla world with vanilla homes full of vanilla people sitting around their vanilla tables eating slices of white bread for dinner. Our differences are the spice of life—the Tabasco in our vegetable stew. It's time we celebrate how intricately unique we all are and quit trying to force ourselves into some preconceived mold that Mrs. Cleaver created the moment she donned that blasted apron and pearls duo.

Our homes, and the ways in which we manage them, reflect the differences in our personalities. In home management terms, there is no one size fits all. As a matter of fact, I don't think there is ever one size fits all unless you're talking about sunglasses. And even with those, everyone's style is completely different.

You may go for the tortoiseshell while your friend prefers to wear something that you would probably see Morpheus wearing in the Matrix. Enjoy your differences, and celebrate all that makes you unique. If you have ever had difficulty managing your home, it may just be because you aren't going in the direction you are wired for. Enjoy this book like you would enjoy a shopping weekend in New York. Try everything on, and find out what kind of method works best with your madness. Instead of trying to mold yourself into becoming the "homemaker" type (whatever that may be), mold your homemaking style around your personality type. Unlike teeth whiteners or juicing diets, these are effects that will last.

As we discuss different personalities, you are going to find bits and pieces of yourself throughout this book. You are going to learn a lot about yourself, how you work, and the best way to manage your home. You are going to turn your home into a haven, because you are going to work with your personality and not against it. There's no need to change who you are. You are magnificent just being you. But you are going to learn how to nurture other parts of your personality to become a more balanced individual. No one is exactly like you. And no one will have the same home as you or manage it in the same way. That is why your home management techniques need to be custom fitted for you only. You will be able to do that as you learn more about yourself and your style throughout this book. You will also find out that you can accomplish amazing things just by learning how you work best. It will be a wonderful and enlightening journey, just like any shopping weekend in New York (unless you get mugged).

Home, Sweet Home

No matter what your personality, we all need a place to call home. We need room to grow and breathe, space to let our hair down and put our feet up, a home where we can turn our sweet dreams into reality. This is home. And I hope you love yours. If you do, it will willingly love you back. It has so much to say about you already. If your walls could talk—baby, oh, baby, the things they would say about you. They would tell everyone how you spend your days, what kind of priorities you set, what kind of mood you are in, how you feel about your life. Basically, if it could talk, your home would speak about your personality. But it can, and it does. Your home speaks more about you than anything else (except your credit report, but that's another book). So, what is it saying about you?

> *You should feel at home in your home.*

Your Haven

Your home should be your haven. Your home should embrace you, comfort you, and sustain you. It should be a big, fat, hug welcoming you in from the hard, cold world. When I was growing up and attending our small country church, one of the best hugs in the entire congregation could be found in the arms of Miss Frances. Her words were always sweet, her soft dimpled skin always smelled of Ivory soap, and her clothes always carried the aroma of sunshine. When Miss Frances hugged you, she would wrap her arms around you and you would feel the cares of the world melt onto the ground below. Now *this* was a hug. *This* was a haven. And this is exactly how your home should feel. When you step through the front door, your worries should simply be able to drift away on a cloud of Ivory soap and sunshine. Your home should allow you to strip off your burdens just like you take off your jacket or put away your purse. A haven says, "Sit back and breathe deep. You're welcome here."

We all carry certain amounts of stress throughout the day, but your home should by all means never be a source of it. Instead, it should help ease the tension. You have enough to worry about in your life without adding homemaking to the list. It doesn't have to be a headache. It should warm your heart instead. I want you to walk into your home and feel peace wash over you. No, this doesn't mean you need to empty your living room of everything except a yoga mat, sage candles, and a trickling water fountain. It can be full and loud and vibrant, but it should still be peaceful and enriching as well. Your home should be a place where your needs are fulfilled and your imagination is inspired, a source of joy and strength. You deserve a home, oh-so-sweet, home. And it can happen when you have the will, determination, and inspiration to make it happen.

Your Pit Stop

A home is also a place where all of your needs are filled. We expend so much of ourselves, constantly meeting the needs of those around us—our children, our careers, our husbands. Not many of us spend as much time as we should nurturing ourselves and meeting our own needs. If you have ever gone two days without a shower because you couldn't manage to carve twenty minutes out of a day for yourself, then you completely understand what I mean. But when we go for a distance without filling our tanks, then every other system in the home begins to run out of gas. In other words, "if Mama ain't happy, ain't nobody happy." We need to stop our motors every once in a while and fill up. Our homes can become a place where we can make that happen. It should be the place where we refuel physically, mentally, and spiritually, where we can stop for a moment and take a breather.

We live in such a high-performance society. It seems we always have to be in a hurry, and that our "to do" list is growing as we sleep. Sure, there is a lot to do. I am the first one to admit it. But, there is such a difference between performing out of pressure and performing out of fulfillment. The first is often a process of scraping the bottom of a parched well. The latter is a process of dipping our bucket into an abundant stream. We can get so much more done in our life if we feel fulfilled and satisfied. We can be a blessing to others as a result of feeling blessed ourselves. Your home should be a place where the waters of fulfillment flow freely, where you can make miracles happen because you know deep down inside that you are the miracle.

I am constantly guilty of running my engine until I finally career off the road. My husband can usually tell when I have worn myself down to a frazzle when he comes home from work and I have my head stuck in a bag of potato chips and the kids are all hiding under their beds. He has to constantly remind me to stop for a minute and take a breather. His philosophy is, "You can't run on

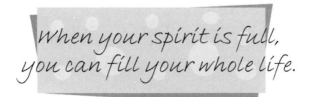

When your spirit is full, you can fill your whole life.

5

fumes." Or maybe that's just his excuse to be able to play video games. In any case, it's true. If you are trying to run on fumes, then you are making yourself and everyone else around you miserable. Your home should be an environment that encourages you to recharge your battery.

I hope your mind is full of good childhood memories. I hope you can remember the feeling of a warm bowl of soup filling your empty belly, a soft bed to snuggle your tired body into, and a tender hand to brush your hair back so that a kiss can fall on your forehead. I hope you can remember these strong feelings because it's important to recreate these feelings of rejuvenation throughout your home. If you don't have these precious memories, then it is time for you to start creating them. Your home can nurture you in so many ways. It can fill your needs and comfort your soul. Up until this point, you may have denied yourself the home that you have always deserved. If so, then it's time to create the kind of home that good dreams are made of.

Your Masterpiece

Your home should also be your masterpiece. Whether you realize it or not, you are an incredible artist. You have a creative spirit within you that is just aching to come out and play. Well, sweetie, guess what. It's playtime! We are going to work with your personality to find out how to best channel that creative energy. You will begin to see your home as a canvas that is longing for the bright colors of your imagination. It will be your ballroom, where you can play dress-up and dance for hours on end. Can't you just hear the band warming up? Put on that satin dress and let's get this party started!

Excuse me? Did I hear someone out there mutter, "I don't have a creative bone in my body?" Au contraire, mon ami. You, my dear, are more creative than you could imagine. You were created in the image of God. And the last time I checked, the Creator is pretty darn creative. We just all have different methods of channeling and displaying that creative energy. You will find the best method, and discover joy in creating that you never knew before. You will learn to listen to that artistic voice inside, and begin to trust where she leads you. Your home will begin to sing for joy at your discoveries and speak of your passions in every room. It will truly be your masterpiece, a beautifully evolving work of art. Just like you!

Give that artist inside you permission to come out and create.

Some Do, Some Don't

So, why does it seem like some people have it made in the shade and others are struggling to catch up? Why can't all of our homes be comforting, enriching, and creative? There sits Suzy Homemaker. She donned her apron this morning, prepared a quiche and hash browns for her hubby and children, dusted the furniture, and started a load of laundry. Now baby is playing quietly while she is preparing her speech for the PTA meeting, waiting for her friends to come over and enjoy some appetizers while they knit sweaters. By the way, she made the appetizers out of the organic eggplant that she grew in her backyard garden. Now here sits Catchup Cathy. She dragged her kids out of bed this morning and threw some cereal bars at them on their way out the door as her baby leaked out of the diaper and all over the living room carpet. Now the toddler is pulling all of the toilet paper off the roll, as Cathy is redoing her grocery list that got misplaced last night.

I am so there, sister! I have been Suzy Homemaker, Catchup Cathy, and just about everything in between. But after this long, I have finally figured out what works and what does not. I have tried to follow another person's techniques to housekeeping or home design, but many times, it seemed as if I were running in quicksand—every effort just dragged me down deeper and deeper. But I realized after years and years of trial and effort that when I develop methods and techniques that fit my personality style, work seems more like play. I can reach my goals because I discover the methods that work best for me. And together, we can discover the best methods for you as well. When you start learning more about your personality, you are better able to set the stage where that personality can really perform.

One-size-fits-all homemaking does not work. Some of us see a program in which Miss Perfect is showing how to best display antique pottery, how to fertilize roses, and how to refinish a dresser, and we are inspired. Some of us watch the same show and we feel completely discouraged because we begin comparing ourselves to an imaginary ideal. Some of us get a book on housekeeping and we are excited about getting started. Others of us open the same book and fall asleep two pages in. One method does not work for everyone, and thank goodness for that. Find out just what works for you.

No two people are exactly alike and no two homes are exactly alike—make yours an expression of you.

You deserve the home of your dreams. But before you can have the home of your dreams, you need to find out how to navigate through your own private dream world. Take Sarah, for example. Sarah hated her bedroom. She felt cramped and stifled. She dreamed of a huge bedroom with an enormous walk-in closet and a reading nook, not her tiny little hole in the wall that she had now. Going to bed at night was more of a chore than a luxury. Laundry covered the bed. Cups, plates, books, and magazines were all over the dresser and vanity. Clothes were crammed in a closet that was bulging at the seams. It was not a pleasant place to spend an evening. Basically, Sarah's bedroom needed help, and it was more than a cleaning service or a home improvement show could offer.

But Sarah began doing some self-discovery. She realized that she was a highly distractible woman. Once she got started doing one thing, she was off to something else. She noticed all of the unfinished projects left around her room—magazines barely glanced through, a quilt rolled up in the corner halfway completed, laundry that remained unfolded for days, five coffee cups with residual gunk in the bottom. She also realized that on an emotional level, she held grudges that ate away at her spirit. Deep inside, she resented the fact that she did not have the bedroom of her dreams, and held a grudge that surfaced every time she would step inside. She chose not to treat her room with respect because she had little respect for herself or her current situation. In addition, she also realized that she had a tendency to hold on to stuff that she no longer needed or wanted because it temporarily empowered her. She did not have many material goods as a child so had the tendency to hoard items as a grown woman. Dealing with some of the issues she carried around and learning about her personality helped Sarah develop methods that work best for her.

Sarah ever so slowly began to part with some of her belongings that no longer met her needs or fulfilled her emotionally. The clutter began to work its way out of her bedroom so that she could feel clarity in the space around her. This compelled her to develop techniques to completely finish tasks. And because of her high distractibility, she designated one coffee cup to be the "bedroom cup." When it was finished, it was cleaned, dried, and put away. The quilt that irritated her every time she glanced at it was packed up and put away for another day and another time. Magazines were placed in a rack in the living room, and only two were allowed in her bedroom at a time. It was like a library—if she wanted to check out one from the rack, she had to turn one in. And when the rack was filled up, they were boxed and taken to her beauty salon or the doctor's office. Eventually, she began to buy one new article of clothing for every five she gave away to a charity. Not only was she learning how to trust her ability to fill her needs, but she also was racking up a pretty hefty deduction on her taxes. Space opened up throughout her room and a positive energy began to flow. She began to respect her room, and even redecorated it and began coming up with some clever design solutions that she implemented. Soon her room felt more like a retreat than a prison. No longer was she dreaming of a huge bedroom. She had created the bedroom of her dreams right where she was.

The home of your dreams does not have to exist in your imagination.

For many of us, these techniques may seem a bit odd. Checking a magazine out of your own supply? A "bedroom cup?" But because of Sarah's personality and tendencies, they were the perfect methods that worked for her. She learned a lot about herself that helped her nurture other parts of her personality to create an enriching environment. And you can do it, too. By learning about yourself you can learn to develop methods that work in accordance to your style. You can also learn to balance yourself by nurturing parts of your personality that have remained dormant. Some people seem to have their acts together because they have personalities that are conducive to the routines of homemaking, and they have discovered what methods work best. Others of us may need to be a little more creative in our techniques because our personality strengths lie in other areas. One way is not the right way. Your way is the right way. And it's time to find it.

All Changes Begin Inside

If you want your home to be comfortable and pleasant, if you want it to be vibrant, nurturing, and fulfilling, then it all needs to begin with you. No matter what your personality type, you have just as much creative ability as anyone on this earth. You have everything you need already tucked away within you. It's time to take it out and let it shine. I don't want you to waste another moment feeling dissatisfied with your home. And if you are satisfied with your home, I want you to feel passionate about it. It can inspire and comfort you and free your spirit, but you have to want it deep down inside, because that's where all real changes take place first—inside.

The reason many methods fail to have lasting results is that they deal with the outside only. I have seen numerous diets fail because they supply a list of foods to eat, prescribe an exercise routine, and leave it at that. They don't take into account that some people may eat to supply emotional comfort. Some eat out of boredom. Some have certain foods, such as sweets, that trigger the urge to eat more. And others simply enjoy the feeling of food in their mouths. There are as many reasons why people overeat as there are personalities. And those extra pounds aren't going anywhere until you deal with the personality issues that underlie the eating behavior. And exercise routines? That's about as personal as you can get. For some of us the only formal exercise we get is holding a squat in a public restroom. And then there are those who live for the feeling of endorphins rushing through their bloodstream and sweat trickling down their back (personally, I can't see myself exercising this fanatically unless someone's paying me a lot of money or chasing me with a weapon). So, as far as personal preferences go, the same is true with managing your home. Until you understand the reasons behind your behaviors, you will never be able to permanently change it.

I just love those television shows where an entire team shows up at your home, empties all the junk out of it, sells it at a yard sale, and then completely decorates and organizes everything inside. At the end of the show the homeowners are completely overwhelmed by the beauty of a clear space and a fresh start. I can't help but wonder how many of these people are actually going to keep it like that. It's kind of like getting liposuction and going back to the surgeon a year later. Before you know it, the shelves are going to be spilling over with all of their stuff, stacks of papers are going to be all over the tables and counters, and junk is going to be stuffed in the closets. The clean fresh house will just be a lovely memory, just like that first kiss or that bikini that you wore when you were in high school.

Sure, you can force some routines and try to make someone else's methods tame your madness, but you will constantly have the tendencies to run back to your comfort zones. We will always choose the path that runs in accordance to our personalities. We are all trying to reach the same destination—a nurturing, comfortable, inspiring home. Instead of trying to change your personality to tread a certain pathway, why not change your pathway to run in accordance to your personality? You will reach the same destination, but this time it will be for good. It's time to quit trying to be something you're not, and start embracing who you already are. Your home is going to be extraordinary because that is just what you are—extraordinary.

Are You in Love?

Have you ever had someone you admire greatly come over to your home for a visit? Do you spend days getting your house ready? When he shows up at your door, the clutter is gone (or at least hidden), furniture is dusted, the kitchen is sparkling, and everything is neat and tidy. It's a good feeling to be able to impress a person you truly respect. But, if there is one person on this earth you need to respect, it's you. Sometimes as we go along in life, we will completely neglect our first love. When you were a little girl, I bet you loved gazing into a mirror. You thought you were the greatest thing since store-bought pickles, and you were right. It's time to gaze lovingly again. You deserve to have a nurturing home. You deserve to be surrounded with beauty. You deserve to be treated with respect. Sometimes the clutter can creep in and we let it surround us because, deep inside, we feel as if we don't really deserve any better. If you may be struggling with this, then I hope this book will give you a glimpse of what a spectacular person you are, and show you that you deserve the best things in life. You will be learning a lot about yourself and your personality, and I hope you fall in love (if you're not already). You are going to create a beautiful home. But this time you are doing it to impress yourself, because you love and respect that woman immensely. No matter what your personality is like, it's your personality. And if you don't already love it, then it's time you started falling head over heels.

Time for Your Prescription

At the end of every chapter, I am going to give you a prescription for your personality type. But since we are not discussing personality types until the next chapter, I have a different assignment for you. One that is even more important and will give you a jump start like you wouldn't believe. You need to get a journal. (No, don't think that I want you to make an entry every day and keep track of your cleaning routine. How boring would that be?!). Instead, it's going to be a sort of workbook to bring your dreams into reality. It's going to be your own personal dream book—your first step to releasing that artist within you. And it's all yours and no one else's! All of my kids know that if they so much as glance within its covers, they are taking the chance of losing a finger! You can use this dream book for anything. Doodle in it, cut it, glue it, write passages, or anything else that leaps from your soul, through your fingers, and onto its clean, white pages.

Here's what you need to look for (and you may have one already). Get a large book with unlined pages. When you have some uninterrupted time, go through some old magazines or catalogs and cut out pictures of anything that appeals to you. It may be pictures of children laughing, old glass jars, a beautiful rose, inspiring words, anything at all. There's no rhyme or reason to this because you are letting your spirit speak, and sometimes it's hard to understand how to speak the language when you have been out of contact for a while. Now with an acid-free glue stick, glue those pictures in a collage all over the cover. When it dries, cover the entire thing with wide strips of clear packing tape so that it overlaps on the inside cover. This helps preserve the condition of your book cover (and it's also handy when your coffee spills on it at 5:30 in the morning). There! You have just created your dream book.

Dream On!

This is the fun part at the end of each chapter. You are going to take out that dream book and put it to work. And we are going to start by taking an analysis of everything that bugs you, and I mean everything! From that leaky faucet to those ugly words your neighbor said. Small issues, big issues, it doesn't matter. All of them stand in the way of releasing your creative energy. When I first did this exercise, I had a few things written down, such as a half-finished patio, a water stain on the kitchen ceiling, ugly carpet, and some others. It took me awhile at first to come up with some things, but as I started writing them down, the list grew longer and longer. The funny thing is, just writing them down began to make me feel better. It allowed me to express my frustration. You don't have to share this list with anyone. Just write it all down. This is an important step, so grab your dream book.

After you have made your list (be it ten or a hundred), give it a good look over, and see all of the things that are pulling from your emotional energy. Whether you realize it or not, your worry breathes life into every one of these buggers. It's time to deal with them, one by one, so that you can free up energy to be used in other more productive areas of your life.

Take each one, look at it, and ask yourself, "Can I fix this with minimal effort?" If you can, then do it right then and there, but only if it requires very little work. Chances are, you won't have very many of these scratched off because if it were a cinch to do, you would have accomplished it by now. Don't fret over it. You will get to them eventually, and I will help you develop methods that work with your personality to get them accomplished. But for now, move on.

Some of these buggers are enormous beasts that keep following you around. Can't you just feel their enormous mass hovering over you right now? Go to your calendar and think of a realistic date that you can accomplish this goal. Now after you get a date, I want you to extend it considerably. The reason is this. You are not going to be under any pressure to fix this big, fat bugger. You will set a goal that does not put a lot of weight on you. If you finish it earlier, then "Yahoo!" Now, write that goal down on your calendar in big letters, scratch it off of your list, and breathe a heavy sigh of relief as you watch that bugger slip away. He can't mess with you anymore. You're the boss now.

Your dream book will begin teaching you how to start loving yourself completely.

Sometimes there is a deeper, more emotional bugger that has been nagging at you for years. Perhaps you need to make peace with someone in your family or resolve an issue that happened long ago. Life is not worth living when you carry around these buggers, and unfortunately, you are the one carrying them around. You are allowing them to pull energy out of you, like a beautiful porcelain tub with a crack in it. But you have lived with it so long, that you don't even notice the drain on your spirit. It's like cruddy old tar that has been wiped all over your ethereal wings. You just remain content walking along the earth, staring up into the heavens with your wings folded along your back, imagining how nice it would be to fly. It's going to be hard to get yourself to resolve these issues. But if you ever want to spread your wings and fly, you're going to have to do it. Forgive someone who sinned against you and tell them about it. Embrace someone who has hurt you and quit holding on to the pain. Take action, and let the tears finally cleanse your wounds. Before long, you will see the beauty coming back to your wings. You will remember the feeling of the wind against your face. You will spread your wings again. And you are going to fly.

Chapter 2

She's Got Personality

We all know what artists are like, right? Absentminded, reclusive, unconventional, perhaps even a bit temperamental. They're the ones who go around smelling of sandalwood, wearing an organic wool sweater knitted by a Tibetan monk, and ordering an escarole salad with no dairy. Well, whether you believe it or not, you are an artist, too. Just don't go changing your name to "Zen," or getting eclectic symbols tattooed on your rear end (at least, not on my account). We are all artists, and all have creative instincts within us. And just as art takes on different forms, all artists have distinctly different personalities. Art can be a beautiful glistening skyscraper, just as much as it can be a marble sculpture in the middle of the park. It can be an amazing computer image, just as much as it can be a breathtaking oil portrait. And trying to compare one artist or art form with another is exceedingly difficult, if not impossible. Comparing Renoir to Warhol is like trying to compare raspberry sherbet to Campbell's soup. Each one is a different style, a completely different flavor and texture—just like each one of us. We all have an extraordinary spirit of creativity flowing through us, but it takes on completely different forms according to our personalities. And the better we understand ourselves, the better we can perfect our abilities, channel our energy, and shape our environments.

So before we traverse the pathway to becoming domestic goddesses, we need to realize just what makes us ethereal beings tick. We need to understand ourselves—our strengths, our weaknesses, our personalities—so that we can harness our capabilities, or perhaps just bring them out of hiding. So much in this world is within our reach, if we only understood how far our arms could stretch. In the immortal words of Cervantes, "make it thy business to know thyself." So let's get busy, baby!

understanding who you are helps you figure out how you work.

Who Are You?

I remember back in my college and graduate school days (yes, if I try hard I can remember that far back), when I took a class on theories of personality, I would be amazed at how many different theories existed and how confusing it seemed to assess and label different individuals. I would read through some characteristics and say, "Wow! That's me!" Then I would read through the next personality type and say, "Wow! That's me again!" Hmmm . . . now that I think about it, maybe that was my abnormal psychology class. But the truth is, each of us is a unique combination of all of our past experiences and everything that has gone into our genetic makeup. Each of us is a one-of-a-kind creation, designed perfectly for this time, this place, to do extraordinary things! And it is extremely difficult to fit into a single category at all times. We can label our personalities, but the truth of it is that we are extremely complex individuals drawing from a lifetime of growth and change. Although our basic temperaments may be set for life, our personalities are constantly evolving in response to our environments. We have a host of strengths and weaknesses that come out to play according to several factors— where we are, how we feel, what we're doing, and especially what events are occurring in our lives.

When you dive into your personality, know that this does not define who you are. Instead, it defines how you operate. For example, I have the personality of a Creative Spirit, who is usually unorganized. However, I have had to become extremely organized because of my lifetime demands, and I did so in a way that worked with my personality instead of against it. My husband is a Mother Hen, always making sure everything is running smoothly and going according to schedule. But because of the risk-taking that occurs in starting up his own business, he has had to develop some "leap before you look" qualities that are not normally found in his personality style. Knowing your personality does not dictate what you can or cannot accomplish. It merely helps you understand yourself better. And if you are going to reach your dreams in life, it's always best to know which pathway most closely matches your stride.

This world isn't big enough to hold the dynamic potential nested within you.

Personality in a Nutshell

Explaining personality in a nutshell is best done with nuts. We are all born with basic temperaments that develop into our personalities. It is the nut that eventually grows into a tree. However, you may argue that some of us remain nuts a bit longer than normal. But, given no genetic mutation comes into play, an acorn becomes an oak tree, just as a hickory nut becomes a hickory tree. All oak trees are different, just like all hickory trees are different. But deep down, all oak trees share the same inborn characteristics that make them what they are, just like all hickory trees share the same "hickoriness." The two types of trees can grow similarly because of how they are shaped through weather and terrain, but they will always be different. The temperaments we are born with stay with us forever. They remain unchanging, even as we develop our individual personalities, continually growing and changing according to lifetime weather and terrain. Basically, we are all a bunch of mixed nuts.

We all know about personality. It is what makes us who we are. It is the reason why one person is picked to chair the building committee and why another person is asked to teach the toddlers. We've even developed our own method of categorizing people such as sticking on the label, "control freak," "brainiac," or "artsy fartsy." We instinctively know about different personalities because we have had to deal with people our entire lives, some sweet, some salty, others a bit on the dry-roasted side.

Personality Through the Ages

Ever since about 400 BC, when Hippocrates was running around Greece making everyone take oaths, personality has been a hot topic. Hippo himself was the first one to suggest that there are four different types of personalities, but he wasn't too complimentary when he named them. He said that personalities were a result of a dominant fluid in the body—if it is blood, then we are cheerful; if it is black bile, then we are solemn; if it is yellow bile, then we are impulsive; and if it is phlegm, then we are calm. Mmm, sounds yummy! About four hundred years later, the Roman physician Galen took Hippo's theories a bit further and labeled the personalities as sanguine (cheerful), phlegmatic (solemn), choleric (impulsive), and melancholic (calm). These dudes in togas certainly knew what they were talking about because these four types have kept on popping their heads up throughout history.

Even the four gospels in the Bible were written by men with four distinctly different personalities. Mark was the spontaneous Creative Spirit, Matthew was the Mother Hen historian, John had the passionate heart of the Starry-Eyed Dreamer, and Luke was the scholarly MasterMind of the quartet.

In the Middle Ages, Paracelsus in Vienna described the same natures of personality, but likened them to the four elements—water, earth, air, and fire. He also couldn't be outdone by Hippocrates in funky titles, so he labeled them nymphs, gnomes, sylphs, and salamanders. I can just see it now, "Hi, my name is Désirée, I like long walks on the beach, a guy with a sense of humor, and, by the way, I'm a salamander."

Many years later in the twenties, a Swiss psychologist by the name of Carl Jung was working on his own theory of personality while eating cheese with holes in it and sipping hot cocoa with little marshmallows. Jung saw that all of us approach life in two different manners—introversion (thoughtful, process information internally) or extraversion (outgoing, process information externally). He also decided that there were two different ways in which we perceive our environment—*sensation* and *intuition*. Sensation is becoming aware of stuff through our physical senses (this blanket is soft and colorful); and intuition is becoming aware of stuff through our emotions (this blanket makes me feel pretty, oh, so, pretty). Now Jung was really on a roll. He also decided that the way in which we process information and deal with things in life could be divided into two categories as well—*thinking* and *feeling*. The thinking process is objective (the head), and the feeling process is subjective (the heart).

As long as there have been persons, there has been personality!

Then the fifties came around and in the middle of the sock hops and the poodle skirts, a lady named Isabel Myers decided to come up with a practical approach to all this psychobabble (just like a woman). She stepped on the personality stage along with her mother, Katherine Briggs (we learn back in kindergarten that we are always much stronger with mama by our side). She and mama added a *judging* or *perceiving* scale to the personality categories to show how people respond to life and make decisions. Those who use *judging,* make choices quickly and run things according to plan. Those who use *perceiving* frequently put decisions off and try to leave their options open. The women took all of this information and came up with a personality index to categorize people according to sixteen different types, and set the precedent for all personality tests to follow. As a matter of fact, the Myers-Briggs Personality Index is still the most widely used test of its kind.

Then in the late sixties, when most psychologists were wondering about the long-term effects of marijuana on memory, a man named David Keirsey caught wind of the mama/daughter team as he was studying other personality theorists and decided this little test of theirs was one of the best things that ever happened to personality theory, kind of like what the Wonderbra did for women's undergarments. He used the Meyers-Briggs Type Indicator (MBTI) in conjunction with the same temperament theory that has been around longer than the Parthenon. But this time he didn't call people salamanders, nymphs, or gnomes. He gave these four temperaments the titles of idealist, guardian, rational, and artisan. And made it as simple as pie by saying that all personalities stem from a basic temperament. His son-in-law, Stephen Montgomery, made papa proud by bringing his temperament theory down to the blonde level (roots don't count) by saying that temperament is made up of what we say (abstract or concrete), and what we do (what works or what's right). Finally! Something everyone can understand! Rationals talk about what is abstract and do what works. Artisans talk about what is concrete and do what works. Guardians talk about what is concrete and do what is right. Idealists talk about what is abstract and do what is right.

Meanwhile, women started leaving home and burning their bras. Then they had unlimited choices and tried to do everything. Finally they decided that home wasn't such a bad place to be after all. And along came Hannah Keeley, who studied psychology, became a behavior therapist, and quit to raise six kids and manage a home. And that's how personality theory and home management courted, wed, lived happily ever after, and wrote a book about it.

Unique, Me-nique, We're All Unique

Ever since that first person was full of phlegm, humans have had the basic knowledge that people are intrinsically different from day one. Some like to sit and ponder, others like to go and do, then there are those who stay up late and watch infomercials. That's what personality is all about! We have our own way of approaching the world, and our own way of dealing with what the world dishes out. So, what are these different personalities that Carl Jung brooded over with his steaming mugs of hot cocoa with mini-marshmallows? Take this quiz and discover who you are.

Put It to the Test

You already know yourself better than anyone in the world and certainly don't need anyone telling you how you operate. But ever since seventh grade home-room class, when we sat in our little cliques filling in the bubbles of the "Does your back-to-school fashion make the grade?" test in our *Teen* magazines, we have known one solid fact of life—quizzes are fun! So grab that pencil and take this little personality test. Drawing little hearts around the letters while you smack on Wild Cherry Bubblicious is completely optional.

1. If I were traveling down the yellow brick road I would be
   a. the scarecrow—what is life without a brain?
   b. the Lion—courage is all that really matters.
   c. Dorothy—there's no place like home.
   d. the Tin Man—you've got to follow your heart.
2. When I implement a new design scheme in my home, it is usually because
   a. the old one no longer functioned adequately for me.
   b. I just followed an impulse and tried something different.
   c. it was featured on one of my favorite home shows.
   d. I just felt like it needed a change.
3. Nothing gets me going like
   a. a new project around the house.
   b. a new activity in my life.
   c. a new membership in something.
   d. a new cause that I undertake.
4. When I start a project around the house
   a. I make sure I have all the right tools and resources and then work at it on schedule.
   b. I roll up my sleeves and jump right in. If something goes wrong, I can always start over.
   c. I follow the directions carefully and chisel away at it until the task is completed.
   d. I consider it for a long time first, and then work on it when I feel like it.

21

5. If I have any problem with clutter around the house, it is
    a. the junk around my desk, but I usually stay on top of it.
    b. the junk left from abandoned projects around the house.
    c. the junk carried in by everyone I live with.
    d. the junk that doesn't have any place to go.
6. Whenever my elementary teacher sent a note home it would say
    a. "She is bored in class."
    b. "She runs with scissors."
    c. "She's my best little helper."
    d. "She daydreams in class."
7. When it comes to cleaning the house
    a. I am always looking for a way to improve upon my methods.
    b. I like to use the latest tools and the loudest music.
    c. I go by my schedules and clean certain rooms on certain days.
    d. I need some serious motivation, like a visit from Mom.
8. If I were an outfit, I would be
    a. a tailored jacket with clean-cut pants (very cerebral).
    b. snazzy overalls with a banana yellow T-shirt (very creative).
    c. an oxford shirt and khakis (very traditional).
    d. soft blouse and bohemian skirt (very dreamy).
9. People would say that my design scheme is
    a. practical and contemporary.
    b. playful and eccentric.
    c. traditional and inviting.
    d. romantic and imaginative.
10. Everyone has needs, I need
    a. mastery over my field and an understanding of how things operate.
    b. freedom to do what I want and make an impact on my world.
    c. to know my place in the world and fulfill my responsibilities.
    d. a sense of purpose and knowledge that I'm working for a greater good.
11. In home management, I excel in the areas of
    a. efficiency. I can usually figure out the best way of doing something.
    b. effectiveness. I can make an impact quickly and noticeably in all areas.
    c. management. I can make sure that all of the systems run fluidly.

22

(d.) relationships. I can see to it that all family members have their needs met.

12. As a home manager, my mood is usually
   a. calm. I go about things in a precise, logical manner.
   b. excited. I am always trying something new.
   (c.) concerned. It is a huge responsibility and I want to do it right.
   d. hopeful. I love nurturing others through what I do.

13. The impetus that usually sets me on track to reorganize something is
   a. the old organizing scheme isn't working out.
   b. I need a change and start a project.
   c. I saw a cool technique in a magazine.
   (d.) to make it a more peaceful area.

14. My friends know that I am the one to go to for
   a. information.
   b. excitement.
   (c.) assistance.
   d. inspiration.

15. When I host a party, I am usually the one who is
   a. programming the audio.
   b. performing at the karaoke machine.
   c. leading the games.
   (d.) talking in the small groups.

16 When I pick up cleaner from the store, it is the one that
   a. performs best. I've done the research so I know.
   b. looks promising. I like to try out new things.
   (c.) I used before. I stick with the tried and true.
   d. interests me the most. I like to judge by smell or labels.

17. The qualities that I most admire in people are
   (a.) willpower and genius.
   b. skill and courage.
   c. hard work and discipline.
   d. integrity and passion.

18. If I were a restaurant I would be
   (a.) fine dining with starched linens and a four-star rating.
   b. a trendy hot spot where the servers get around on skateboards.
   c. a friendly down-home restaurant where I have my regular booth.
   d. an intimate little out-of-the-way dive for good food and conversation.

19. When I pick out some new furniture for the house, I go with
    a. the highest rating and performance warranty.
    b. the coolest design that catches my eye.
    c. the pieces that coordinate best with my home.
    d. the pieces that feel the best. I just know.

20. If I were to become our nation's first female president, it would be because
    a. I have amazing skills with strategy and knowledge.
    b. I know how to get in there and get things done.
    c. I can manage and organize just about anything.
    d. I am a diplomat and listen to what people want.

21. I work best when my home is
    a. innovative. I'm always trying to analyze and improve on some procedure.
    b. stimulating. I like to be surrounded by activity on various levels.
    c. organized. I need structure in order to feel secure and perform at my best.
    d. expressive. To me, it's all about creating a personal atmosphere.

22. If my life were on television, it would be
    a. a Learning Channel documentary hosted by Leonard Nemoy.
    b. an after-hours special on Comedy Central with Eddie Murphy.
    c. a "Good Old Days" marathon on Nickelodeon hosted by Andy Griffith.
    d. a chick flick on the Lifetime channel with Susan Sarandon.

23. If there is one thing that I cannot tolerate, it is
    a. a sense of powerlessness or being unable to understand something.
    b. being bored or feeling constrained in some way.
    c. feeling abandoned or not fitting in.
    d. not living by my own code of ethics.

24. If I were to ever become famous it would be because
    a. I invented socks that were magnetically polarized to their mates.
    b. I came up with the hottest new television show using sock puppets.
    c. I was the only woman in history never to lose a sock.

     d. I was able to lead a crusade to put socks on every cold foot in the world.

25. The motto that I live by is

     a. be excellent in all things.

     (b.) carpe diem (seize the day).

     c. success is 1 percent inspiration, 99 percent perspiration.

     d. to thine own self be true.

what's it all about?

Mostly As   *6*

You are the *MasterMind.* You have the best brain in the bunch! Your home is your laboratory.

Mostly Bs   *4*

You are the *Creative Spirit.* You have the backbone to make a difference! Your home is your stage.

9

Mostly Cs

You are the *Mother Hen.* You have the hands that build the foundation! Your home is your feathered nest.

5

Mostly Ds

You are the *Starry-Eyed Dreamer.* You are all heart! Your home is your dream world.

Celebrate what makes you—you!

The MasterMind

Hippocrates called you phlegmatic, Paracelsus declared you a sylph (whatever the heck that is). According to Keirsey, you are the rational of the group. You talk about abstract ideas and things you can learn or accomplish, and make progress toward your goals in whatever manner that works. You don't have to walk around with a pocket protector if you are a MasterMind. But you may find that you are much more analytical and knowledge-seeking than your average Jane. You have an abstract way of perceiving the world, and respond to that knowledge in an objective way. If you were traveling on the yellow brick road, you would be the Scarecrow, considering the brain the most important possession. As a matter of fact, you value knowledge so much, that it is often your main reason for engaging in activities—to learn from them. The complex doesn't scare you. Instead, it gets you going. You actually enjoy identifying and solving complex problems and issues.

You tend to think in a sequential method, putting step one before two, two before three. When given information in a random pattern, you will immediately try to create some type of order out of it. If you don't already know how to put something together, you will be the first to figure it out. You did pretty well in school. As a matter of fact, you were probably one of those girls who memorized the times tables in two weeks just to make the rest of us look bad. Or maybe you proposed your own version of the electron spin theory while the rest of us were trying to memorize the periodic table. You have a gift. You have the ability to think rationally in almost any circumstance and to be objective about situations,

Putting your brain to the task usually solves 90 percent of the problem!

rather than getting lost in the emotion. You also like to be in control of situations. You know how to do it, and you would rather not be told. You choose to take a job and run with it by yourself any old day.

Your mood is often tranquil or thoughtful, being absorbed in the abstract most of the time. "Calm, cool, and collected" are your three middle names. People may sometimes mistake your contemplation with melancholy, making you out to be the Eeyore of the group, worrying about the weather, worrying about money, worrying about failure, worrying that you worry too much. But you don't see it as worry. You see it as preparation and foresight. When it comes to "looking before you leap," you wrote the book on the subject. You look, measure, and get a topographical map of the layout before you even consider leaping. Sometimes, you get so caught up in the looking part that you forget to take the leap.

Your tendency to attempt to create order out of chaos is one of the biggest reasons that people with your personality make the best inventors and innovators. Problem–solving is one of your favorite pastimes. You could easily get lost in the *New York Times* crossword puzzle while the rest of us are just scanning it for the major headlines, checking out the Dow Jones, or flipping straight to the comics. You are also a determined person, never resting until you have found the most efficient solution with as little wasted effort as possible. As a matter of fact, you hate wasted effort. If you're going to invest your mind in something, you had better come up with a solution that works.

The MasterMind at Home

What does this mean at home? A lot. When you design things at home, you do it with function and practicality at the top of your list. If you get a new comforter for your bed, it's probably because you got a little chilly last night, not because you saw a brilliant fabric that caught your eye. To you, a lamp is a source of light, not an accent piece in your décor. You like to have everything very well coordinated in your home. You probably save up to buy suites of furniture instead of surprising hubby by dragging home a chartreuse armoire that you absolutely could not pass up. When it comes to home decorating, you know what you like, but may have a difficult time executing it. It's hard for you to envision the finished result. And if you're going to make any design changes, you let practicality more than passion direct your choices.

When you do chores around the house, you probably have a set schedule for all of the tasks around the house. However, you put a lot of thought into how you work up your schedules—no haphazard way about it. And you are constantly tinkering with methods in order to improve on them. It also doesn't take you long to clean up because you don't easily get distracted from your job. And you probably run around with a caddy full of cleaners because you put efficiency at the top of your list. But you don't always set a specific time limit for your tasks. Instead, you consider time to consist of whatever amount is needed to complete the job. As a matter of fact, when you are engrossed in something, you will frequently lose track of time.

When it comes to managing your home, you come out shining. You balance yourself exceedingly well. You not only plan, but you perform pretty well, too. You tear the recipes out of the magazines like the rest of us, but you are the one who actually prepares the dish. However, a problem comes up when you make that fantastic dish, but you can't loosen up enough to enjoy it. You sometimes hesitate to have guests over because it puts a kink into your plans. And when you do host a party, you are often so busy picking up and keeping things in order that you don't join in on the fun.

You also take a great amount of pride in your accomplishments, but sometimes you fall into the trap of equating your worth with your performance. It's extremely difficult for you to measure your self-esteem by looking internally rather than externally. You are always concerned with improvement and achievement, and set extremely high standards for yourself, causing you to work harder and harder to reach your goals.

And because you hate getting distracted from the task at hand, you often shy away from beginning new projects, such as decorating a room. And speaking of decorating, opening that can of paint and swiping on a color is not on the top of your list. If you changed the color of your walls, then perhaps your rugs would clash. And that, my dear, would be completely impractical. And speaking of which, because of your affinity toward practicality over creativity, your home has the tendency to be oh, how can I say it—blah? You are creative, as all artists are, but that creativity is often repressed or hidden behind the security of routine. Sometimes, you need a swift little kick in the rear to push you out of your comfort zone and put some spontaneity into your life. Consider this book your swift little kick. Don't worry, it will feel good.

MasterMinds We Know and Love

We've all run across some MasterMinds out there. You may see one every day when you look in the mirror. The professor on *Gilligan's Island* is a MasterMind to the core. He was always coming up with some contraption to solve the prob-

A well-developed strategy puts you well ahead of the game.

lems that one inevitably runs into when stranded on a deserted island. I still don't understand how he could come up with machines that could help Mary Ann bake pies and do laundry, but he couldn't figure out how to make a boat. And while we're talking about professors, Professor Plutonium, the MasterMind behind the Powerpuff Girls, loved nothing more than inventing things down in the bowels of his lab and dipping into the chemical X. However, I still think there must be some reverse-Oedipal thing going on between him and his babes. And Velma was always busy solving the mystery while Shaggy and Scooby remained concerned about where they were going to find their next six-foot-long sub sandwich or why they were always running for four seconds in midair when a monster was right at their heels. Henry Higgins in *My Fair Lady* was definitely a MasterMind, much too involved in his linguistics to "let a woman in his life." And as far as real-life women? Madame Curie was the "Madame of MasterMinds." While other women in France were worried about having someone around to tie up their corsets, she was in the lab discovering radioactivity. Currently, Pat Summitt, one of the most sought-after coaches of women's basketball, is famous for her innovative techniques and strategy development. She brings the brains to the game and is never one to leave well enough alone. As a typical MasterMind, she in continually working to improve her technique, and it shows.

The Creative Spirit

You are the artisan of the group, the person who is not afraid to jump in head first with your back to the wind. You know who you are. You are the one who runs off the side of the road because you thought you saw a cloud that looked like Richard Nixon in a tutu. You think in the here and now, and don't have the time or the patience for thought for the sake of thought. If it's not going to get you anywhere, then forget about it. You talk in down-to-earth terms, none of that touchy-feely stuff. When it comes time for action, you are in the front lines. You jump in with the intent of getting stuff done and doing what works (even if you occasionally have to step on a few toes or bend a few rules to do it). Your window to the world is quite colorful, but sometimes it has the tendency to cloud your vision. Instead of following things in a sequential format, you have the tendency to put things in a more random order—step three seems to be more important, so let's do that first and then we'll worry about one and two (Did you ever start painting a wall before you decided to put down a drop cloth?).

If you were traveling down the yellow brick road, you would most likely be the Lion. You pride yourself on having the backbone to take chances and risks. And speaking of risks, you will gladly leap before even giving it a glance. Nothing gets you going like the rush of endorphins as you throw caution to the wind. Instead of analyzing situations, you usually choose to go by your gut instinct. Pro and con lists usually don't do you any good because you will choose to go by your feelings no matter what the piece of paper tells you. You act on impulse rather than by strategy, like your MasterMind friends. You want your life to be exciting, and you can't sit still for too long. As a matter of fact, once an activity loses its appeal and becomes boring, you are the first to jump ship.

You also work best when the heat is turned up. When the spotlight is focused and the pressure is on, you usually come out shining. Instead of watching the game, you prefer to be the one scoring the touchdown. You don't mind being the center of attention, and you prefer not to have it any other way. No party is complete until you walk through the door because you love making an impact on others and playing the crowd.

And whether it's building a business or composing a song, you have a knack for making the right move at the right time. You are the one who seals the deal, signs the client, and takes the lead. Your eyes are constantly scanning the horizon, looking for some new opportunity. And when you find it, you jump right on it without looking back. If it turns sour, then you just wipe the dust off and, with your characteristic grace and style, move on to the next big thing.

Art in all of its forms just comes naturally to you. You have an intrinsic ability to play with your life, and express yourself through a myriad of different mediums—everything from a beautiful oil painting to a stand-up comedy routine. You just love to shine! Give you the right tools and you can make miracles happen. As a matter of fact, you were the one who did that beautiful charcoal sketch in art class when the rest of us were trying to draw a human figure that didn't look like Hong Kong Fooey.

You have a gift. You have the ability to color your world instead of always seeing things in black and white. You will be the first to pour your heart into your life, no matter what the risk. You truly value your freedom, and exercise it fully. You believe that life is short, and you only go around once, so you may as well squeeze as much juice as you can out of your piece of fruit. You want to taste it all, see it all, hear it all, and feel it all. You live for the moment. Yesterday is gone and tomorrow may never come, so live for today (just remember to take two aspirins before you go to bed to help out with the side effects). As the ultimate Creative Spirit, Ferris Bueller, says, "Life moves pretty fast. If you don't stop and look around once in a while, you might miss something."

Taking a risk every now and then puts roses in your cheeks!

The Creative Spirit at Home

You have no problem bringing color into your world. A can of paint doesn't hold any threat to you. You will swipe on a new color faster than the old shade has a chance to dry. The pieces of furniture that you collect are the ones that catch your eye or soften your heart. It may be an old rocking chair that has the perfect squeak or the china cabinet that is painted in a miraculous shade of violet (so what if it doesn't match anything else?). You have the tendency to be extremely creative and think outside of the box. That's right. You were the chick in high school whose artwork the teacher always used as examples for the rest of us to follow. Now we just get to come over to your house and drool over that awesome faux finish that took you all of thirty minutes to accomplish.

You like nothing more than to roll up your sleeves and get dirty. You don't waste time dwelling on the process when you could just jump in and start taking some action. And because you get a charge out of activity, you can be easily distracted, and may tire of things quickly. Let's take cleaning for example. A simple dusting the bookshelf leads to boxing up some books for a donation leads to emptying a box out of the garage leads to sorting the small hand tools, and on and on. It's as bad as if you gave a mouse a cookie.

31

You are also the first to come up with an unexpected solution when the rest of us get caught up in the problem. Anyone who needs to rearrange her furniture can invite you over—just make sure she does not expect practicality, because you go for the initial impact every time. So what if you have to turn your head at a ninety-degree angle to watch TV or have no place to put your cup of coffee? Just check out that awesome print on the ottoman with the cool shimmering beads! You truly know how to appreciate a beautiful thing, and enjoy nothing more than throwing the windows open on a beautiful day or dining outside under a canopy of stars.

You aren't usually meticulous about your home, but you do need a proper atmosphere to let your wings spread. A corner of clutter or mess is very distracting to you because you are commonly very visual-oriented. You don't necessarily get rid of the clutter, but you at least get it out of the way. You will be the first to make a huge mess, but you will also be the first to put it away because you have bigger and better things to move on to. And when you do the necessary chores around the house, effectiveness is your goal. You want to get the most accomplished for the least amount of effort. This fits into your do-whatever-works philosophy. Always looking for a shortcut, you are the first to try out the new cleaning tools that tout, "less work" or "new and improved." If it works, great. If not, you toss it out and pursue something else.

And sometimes, my sweet free spirit, it is a bit difficult to pin you down to the ground. You frequently appear a bit flighty, but it is only because so much is going on in your head at one time. You are planning to redo your entire closet before you even have your laundry caught up. And speaking of closets—you sure do like to accumulate things in yours. This probably stems from your difficulty to live within a budget. It's like pulling teeth for you. If you see something that pulls at your heart, you must get it no matter what! And you are not known for your immaculateness. Sure, the room will look swell when guests come over, but just don't look too closely, and by no means, open up any doors that are meant to remain closed. You love to have a clean house, but you just have too many

You only go around once, so you may as well have a little fun!

important things taking precedence over a dust rag. You also love a good party, especially hosting one. Oops! You forgot to place the order for the hors d'oeuvres and cake. You put it on a list somewhere, but where did you put that list? Fret not, fair maiden, this book will put some order into your life so that your wings can really take flight!

Creative Spirits We Know and Love

If you are a Creative Spirit, then you are in excellent company. Creative Spirits are usually the first to jump in front of the spotlight. Lucy Ricardo was constantly begging her husband to let her star in the nightclub show, and meanwhile was busy bending the rules and eating chocolate off of conveyor belts. Remember Pippi Longstocking? Mopping the floor with sponges on your feet and riding a horse backward without a care as to what others may think is the essence of a Creative Spirit. It also took a lot of creative thinking to propel Mulan into posing as a man to protect her country from the Huns. Now that took some chutzpah! What about Wolverine of the X-Men? He was one sexy rebel in his black leather, heavy sideburns, and knives for knuckles, always ready to star in his own action flick. He gave the saying, "look but don't touch" a whole new meaning. And for the queen of real-life creative spirits? I'll have to cast my vote for Amelia Earhart. During the same time that most women were living recklessly by raising their hemlines, she was throwing caution to the wind by being the first woman to attempt an around-the-world flight. Madonna also takes the cake for her Creative Spirit ways. This material girl loves the spotlight, and is not afraid of the risk it takes to get it.

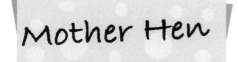

Mother Hen

There's no place like home! Or at least, that's the belief that you and Dorothy hold in common. However, if you wear big blue bows on the ends of your braids and a gingham dress, then that's a whole different issue. You may be taking matters a bit too far. According to Keirsey, you are the guardian of the group, making sure everything is running smoothly and according to plan. You talk about concrete things, what you can see, feel, and touch. And as far as your mode of action, you do what is right. Staying within parameters and following the rules are at the top of your list. You are traditional to the core, holding on to values and principles that you believe to be the backbone of civilization. As a matter of fact, you would probably win the title of Citizen of the Year.

Unlike the Creative Spirit, you are not one to throw caution to the wind. You are very careful about every move you make. And when you are getting ready to undertake anything, you go into it fully prepared and with plans B, C, and D in your back pocket. You are the one who drives around with an American Automobile Association card in your glove compartment, just in case. If it wasn't for people like you, insurance policies would be nonexistent. Some people may view this attitude as pessimistic, but you are just being realistic. Things can and will go wrong, and you don't want to be caught out in the rain wearing cashmere.

When people buck the establishment, you are the one that they are bucking. You know instinctively that there is a right and a wrong, and you see it as your task in life to keep your world (as well as that of everyone around you) on the straight and narrow as much as humanly possible. Because of your deep moral code, you are the first to volunteer to help out and can always be depended upon. Your word is your bond, and something that is not to be taken lightly. When you say you will help decorate the church for the Valentine Sweetheart Banquet, you're there with all of the supplies five hours before party time, frosting the big heart-shaped cake and taping up the red and pink streamers. When you hear the adage, "10 percent of the people do 90 percent of the work," you are the 10 percent. You were the one on the prom committee who came up with the "I Can't Fight This Feeling" theme. You probably spent so much of the day hanging the decorations, that you hardly had time to get yourself ready. You were swiping on the shimmering blue eyeshadow with hot rollers in your hair when tux boy was on his way over to pick you up.

You have a deep respect for authority, and believe in a certain system that you adhere to. You earn your keep, and feel comfortable when you have someone to answer to, whether it's your family, boss, or tribal shamen. You admire those individuals who have put in their sweat equity to achieve titles and positions, and you will be the first to take their expert opinion to heart and follow their advice.

As the cornerstone of any foundation, you are the steady force that keeps it going, the glue that holds it all together. Where would the entire Mickey Mouse Club be today if they had not had the guiding force of Jiminy Cricket telling them what path to take in life? Maybe if mouseketeer Christina Aguilera had listened a little more carefully, she wouldn't be so quick to bare her bod. And as the cornerstone of any group, you love to feel that position of importance. You put a high commodity on belonging, and frequently have the tendency to place too much of your self-esteem in your positions or roles.

You are careful, wary, and cautious to the core, which sometimes results in digging your groove a little too deep. But you draw a lot of comfort from your ruts and your traditions, and sometimes it's just a little too difficult to break out. The unknown sets your heart racing rather than your wheels spinning. You see the beauty of yesterday, when life was much simpler, and feel frustrated when life as you know it is challenged or disrupted by the unconventional.

You have a gift. With your cautious nature, you won't be the woman caught with her pants down. When opportunity pops its head up, you will be the one fully prepared to take advantage of the situation. Everyone else around you is gifted as well, for you are the guiding force in any setting. Because of your involvement, things happen. And when there is any kind of gathering or reunion, you are the one stirring the pot of stew and telling the stories around the campfire—the ones that get passed from generation to generation. You are the traditionalist, the historian, the archivist. You are the strength and the foundation of your family.

> *The strength of any structure lies in its foundation.*

The Mother Hen at Home

Here you are feathering your nest, and honestly, there is no other place you would rather be. You gain a lot of strength and comfort from your home and the routines that you have developed within it. You love creating your home, and pour yourself into it. You just seem to have a knack for the family life, and because of that, everything around you is designed with family in mind. A table that everyone can all sit around, furniture placed strategically for family game night, a play area for the kids, and the perfect picnic table for those weekend barbecues. You love traditions and rituals, and go out of your way to schedule them into your family affairs (clicking the camera the entire time). And talk about scheduling! You leave everyone in a trail of smoke when it comes to your logistical skills. You can outmanage the best of them, making sure everything (and everyone) is at the right place, at the right time, on the right day, with the right stuff. You are not the one who forgets to bring the snack for the soccer team and has to run out to the grocery store while kids are running through drills.

When it comes to your own personal style, you usually prefer to stay traditional (or at least safe). You won't be the one to paint your kitchen in a Day-Glo shade of tangerine, unless of course, you saw it safely executed on a home design show and you already have everything in your home to match it, which is highly unlikely, unless you inherited all of your furniture from Elvis Presley's estate. You have a specific color palette that you rarely stray from. You can see something in a store and know beyond a shadow of a doubt if it will, or will not "go" in your home.

You are the last person to buy a can of paint on a whim and start swiping it on a wall. You plan everything. You count, measure, and weigh your chickens before they hatch. If you are going to change a wall color, then you have already planned the fabric, furniture, and accessories to go along with it. And you've probably already bought them all as well, with money that you have carefully set aside every month.

When it comes to doing your chores around the house, you do things in a traditional manner. You always have mopped with a string mop, so by golly, you always will mop with a string mop. You know what works, and that's what you're sticking with. When it comes to cleaning house, you dance with the date that brought you. You also go about your chores in a very predictable manner, perhaps even planning certain tasks for each day of the week. It works for you, and that's the only thing you're concerned with. As far as trying out the new snazzy products that hit the market, you usually will after a good friend has recommended them to you.

You have the tendency to become a bit rigid in your style. You may love thumbing through the home magazines, but you make your design moves very cautiously, maybe even too cautiously. You have awesome ideas, and are extremely creative. You just need to loosen up a little and put them into practice. Sometimes, when it comes time to making the big leap, you need to put a blindfold on instead of looking this way and that. Consider this your hanky!

Mother Hens We Know and Love

You are definitely not alone when it comes to feathering that inviting nest of yours. Remember Alice, who took care of all of those Brady kids? She was the real matriarch of the family, while Mrs. Brady was laid up in her bed with

> *A love of legacy helps mark our passage through time.*

laryngitis. As a matter of fact, she couldn't even get it on with Sam the butcher because of her sense of responsibility toward the Brady crew (or maybe she was just in it for the free trips to Hawaii). And Darren Stephens was a Mother Hen to the core with the by-the-book way he managed his home—"witchcraft *has* never been done in this home, and it *will* never be done in this home." Excuse me? If I had been Samantha Stephens, I would have been twitching my nose left and right! If he didn't like it, he could have just taken his mortal rear end over to Larry Tate's house for dinner! Cinderella had Mother Hen written all over her tattered rags while she sewed little outfits for the mice in her life (even if that was a little psycho). And for the real Mother Hens of this world? If any woman out there lives by a sense of duty to judge right from wrong, it's Sandra Day O'Conner. She could strut that robe like nobody's business as she upheld the traditions that built this country. And Barbara Walters (Baba Wawa) is constantly performing her moral duty by letting the world know who is on the up-and-up and who is on the down-and-out.

The Starry-Eyed Dreamer

If there is anyone out there who has a heart, it's you. You could belt it out with the Tin Man, "I'd be tender. I'd be gentle, and awful sentimental . . . if I only had a heart." You are emotional to the core, letting it guide you along the paths of life. Kiersey suggests that you dwell on the abstract, and act upon what is possible. In other words, you live in a world of "what if?"

You are the idealist of the group, always seeing potential and goodness in everyone. People love to be around you because of your sincerity and your honest involvement in relationships. In a relationship, you are always the one who says, "Honey, we need to talk," when the honey would rather sit back with a beer and watch the game. You are often ready to have a heart-to-heart, when he may have a hankering for a chip-to-mouth. You can frequently be an intense person, always searching for meaning and purpose. In your opinion, there is always a greater good and you see it as your obligation to unearth it.

You have a still, small voice within you that you are extremely in tune with. You can pick up signals that other people completely miss. It's almost as if you reside in another realm, a realm in which dreams are realities, faith stands firm, and the impossible is well within reach. You live by the adage hope springs eternal. Nothing to you is as it first appears, and you have the vision to look deeper.

You have communication skills that leave the rest of us in your idealizing dust. When you say, "I'm a people person," you mean it. Your best memories are of intimate and personal times together with individuals whom you love and trust. You bring out the very best in people, and that's why everyone flocks to you like bees to a puddle of Kool-Aid. You have an innate ability to see the world through another person's eyes, and have a knack for empathizing with them. And when it comes to your social circles or family relations, you are the ultimate go-between, able to communicate perfectly and ease any troubled water on the horizon. You are the yang of yin and yang, the soul of body and soul, the sweet of sweet and sour (and I have no idea what that last one was supposed to mean).

In high school, you were the one who was arguing against Camus' theory of existentialism when the rest of us were happy if we could get Aristotle, Socrates, and Plato in a one-two-three sequence. You just have a way with the arts. Instead of just hearing music, you feel it. Instead of reading poetry, you sense it. Spirituality is extremely important to you, and you are constantly in search of a sense of self, and where you fit in this world.

Of all of the personalities, you have the gift of living with integrity. Playing a role is not for you. You have to be true to who you are and what you are all about. Living without authenticity is complete agony for you, and you will do everything in your power to mold your life to fit your values. Your vision is within, constantly seeking, searching, discovering, and developing. You do the things you do out of sheer devotion and personal worth.

You are also the hopeless romantic. Valentine's Day is probably more like Valentine's Week, full of roses, chocolate, and maybe a sexy little thong to be discovered later. You will be more than happy to put up with thirteen hours of a wedgie from hell just for two minutes of passion. After all, it takes just seconds for these magic panties to go from being completely exposed to strewn on the floor. We can rationalize it by saying that we wear them to get rid of panty lines, but deep down inside we all know that they are just aphrodisiacs in satin, and potent ones as well.

> *To follow your heart is often the greatest aspiration.*

The Starry-Eyed Dreamer at Home

Of all the personalities, you design your home around your inner sense of comfort. You don't concern yourself with what goes with what as much as you do with what makes you feel at home. Home is a feeling, not a place to sleep at night. If you can't walk through the front door and feel a welcoming embrace, then something is just not right. You are quite the sensual person (we know that from the whole thong episode). The little things bring you the most satisfaction—the intoxicating aroma of a candle, the gentle way a fabric sweeps the floor, the smooth feel of silk against your skin, or just the melody of an autumn breeze whispering through the trees. A day can be glorious for no other apparent reason than because of the way it makes you feel.

Your intuition weighs heavily when it comes to making decisions around the house. You will try out fabrics or furniture placement until it strokes you just right, and you will not stop until you reach that point. You are the first to try out some feng shui or burn some incense.

When it comes to your accessories and decorative touches, everything means something to you. You pour yourself into your environment and your environment reflects that. The sentimental touches mean everything, the plate your son made in the first grade, the picture of you and your hubby on your honeymoon, the teapot that your mother gave you. You love these things, and hold them very dear. Your home is your time capsule, speaking volumes of you in every little nook and cranny.

However, because of your sentimental nature, you are not one to quickly part with your belongings. You often have a tendency to hold on to items until they become lost in the clutter. You finally decide that you are going to do some clearing out, but when you start going through items, you find every single thing has some deep meaning to you. The minimalist, you are not!

You also are not too quick to get to the chores, unless you have planned some event at your home. Because of your constant pursuit toward personal growth and discovery, scrubbing the grout just doesn't rank too high on your list. But you will find that once your environment is cleared out and cleaned up, you will free that beautiful heart of yours to embrace a whole new level of consciousness. Consider this your strong cup of coffee to get you grooving in that direction.

Starry-Eyed Dreamers We Know and Love

You are not alone in your lofty pursuits. How about Jeannie? She was constantly trying to fix everything around her, and always wanting to dive deeper into the relationship she had with Major Nelson. He actually had a problem with this hot blonde at his beck and call. I'm thinking he was probably a little more interested in a relationship with Major Heeley, if you know what I mean. And I still have no idea how Major Heeley even got in NASA. Are their entrance criteria really that idiot-friendly? Pooh is a Starry-Eyed Dreamer down to his wiggly little tail. He enjoys nothing more than sitting in a field of daisies and contemplating his life and his relationships. I wonder if Piglet ever tired of all the talky-talky. Spongebob Squarepants loves to live in his world of "imagination," and his friends mean more to him than anything else in Bikini Bottom. Elle Woods, the legally blonde beauty with a little more drive than ditz, was definitely a Starry-Eyed Dreamer, always ready to serve as a champion for the greater good and Chihuahuas all around the world. And where would we be without our own real life Starry-Eyed Dreamers, making this world a better place to live? We all know that Joan of Arc risked everything to follow divine inspiration and lead the French army against the English. Eleanor Roosevelt, always the optimist, was driven by her sense of justice to leave the world a better place than how she had found it.

When you look through loving eyes, potential exists everywhere and in everyone.

Let's Get Personal

Although your basic temperament is a given, your personality is a product of all of the things that have ever happened to you, all of the personal decisions you have made, and the pathways in life you have chosen. How liberating to understand that for the most part we create the person that we want to be. It just takes a conscious effort—something every one of us is capable of. And it is all about balance. That part of us that can't slow down sometimes needs to stop and enjoy the beauty of the here and now. That part of us that lags behind sometimes needs a bit of a push to get going and catch up. Balance is what we're striving for. It's the yin and yang, the fire and water, the Betty and Veronica. Why do you think it was so hard for Archie to choose between Betty and Veronica? Both of them met his needs, so he needed both in his life to be the Archie we all know and love. So, no matter what your personality is right now, you have the ability to mold yourself into the person who can achieve more than she can even dream.

By understanding and embracing who you are, you can have a better understanding of who you want to be. And when you begin to reshape yourself, it flows throughout your entire home. No longer will you be endlessly attempting to set up some method of organizing your evening meals, stumbling over piles of laundry, panicking if someone calls to say she's on her way over, or staring at blank walls wondering what to stick up there. New dimensions of your personality begin to shine throughout your entire home—bringing order where there is chaos and movement where there is static. Suddenly, maintaining your amazing home is second nature because it is a reflection of you. And you are an amazing person.

You have within you the ability to accomplish infinitely more than you can imagine.

41

Time for Your Prescription

By now you probably have some idea of your basic style, so it's time to stretch it a bit. You are going to develop some aspects of your personality that you may not even realize you have. Think of it as an exercise program for your brain. It's time to get some of those neurons firing. And you may even want to try them all. But it's up to you to figure out the areas that need the most work, and make those your starting point. It could feel a bit awkward at first. All exercise programs do when you first start them. I remember my first day doing a workout class after I had given birth to my first child. I thought I was going to puke, pee, fart, or all three at the same time. Then it was pushed up a notch, and we started doing the step thingy. In horror, I glanced down and realized my breast pads had fallen out of my bra and the snow-white absorbent disks were glaring at me from the floor. What could I do except grab them, run out of the room, and never show my face there again? Hopefully, this won't be quite as traumatic.

Rx for MasterMinds

You need to learn to release some of that creative energy that is lying dormant right now. Find one room in your house and spend a few minutes and rearrange the furniture. I know. You like it just fine the way it is. But, honestly, how long has it been that way? This isn't an exercise in home aesthetics as much as it is an exercise in creative expression. It may be separating a sectional, putting the bed on the other side of the room, or just trading one chair for another. Just give it a breath of fresh air by doing the ole switch-a-roo. There's no telling where a fresh perspective can take you.

Rx for Creative Spirits

So, how is your fridge looking? Would you say it is a clean slate or a bulletin board with the children's art, soccer schedules, and cute little pictures all over it? Here's what I want you to do. Take everything off, and I mean everything. Don't worry. If you miss it terribly, you can always put it back. Take the schedules and record the dates and times in your calendar. Any addresses or phone numbers? Record them in your permanent collection. Now take those pictures and add them to your collection. Just stick them in with all of the others (we'll get to them). Put the artwork in a separate file folder for each child (we'll get to that later, too). Now as for the cute little poems, sayings, quotes, and whatnot—how often do you really read them? They blessed you once, but now they have worn out their welcome. Throw them away if you can, or if you must, store them for later, or pass them along to a friend. When everything is totally off, give it a good cleaning and live with it for at least a week to see how it feels.

Rx for Mother Hens

You have a certain style, but sometimes have a bit of an issue about breaking out of it. Sometimes, you need to put a little more emphasis on following some of your whims instead of staying in your ruts. Somewhere, there is probably a design idea that you have come across but set aside. You probably rationalized it by telling yourself that it would not match a single thing in your home. So what? Maybe you have this vision of jewel tones, but your home is done in pale blues and yellows. Or maybe you saw a magazine spread of an island theme, but you prefer to go more traditional. Get one tiny piece in a design style that you adore, but may not fit in, and put it in a small room. It could be a deep jewel-encrusted picture frame or maybe a basket with shells woven into the rough weave. Put this piece in a small room, such as a powder room or even a laundry room. This little touch of your heartstring will lighten your spirit and put a smile on your face every time you see it. And who knows? It may open the door to an entirely new design style, spreading through your home one little touch at a time.

Rx for Starry-Eyed Dreamers

Now it's time to take action. Okay, you're going to have to trust me on this. All I'm asking for is ten minutes of your time. It's going to be like pulling teeth, but you can do it. Set a timer for ten minutes and take your junk drawer and dump it on your kitchen counter. Now drag the trash can over and start tossing—those pens that don't write, pencils with worn-down erasers, old grocery lists and receipts, yucky ChapSticks, your toddler's chicken nuggets from the picnic last spring—you get the idea. For items that belong someplace else in the house, put them in a separate pile to put away after the ten minutes is up. And when time is up, just get the drawer and shove everything left over back in and put away the other items. Now no more words—just do it.

Dream On!

Okay, ladies! Crack open those dream journals, and find a perfect pen. If you don't have a perfect pen, then I highly recommend that you go in search of one. It makes writing so much more pleasurable. Find one that makes you smile. Perhaps you like the feel of clean metal lines and the smooth flow of black ink beneath your fingers. Or maybe you go for the fluffy pink pom-pom on the end with wiggly eyes. Or maybe you just can't make up your mind and you need the kind of pen with twelve different ink colors, ready to switch out whenever the mood strikes. Find your pen, keep it alongside your journal, and don't use it for anything else. I know you're going to want to grab it for your grocery list when you can't find anything else, but leave that job for the dull pencils and the pens that have pictures of real estate agents on them.

Once you're ready, you are going to do your first dream journal exercise. Find a few minutes to yourself and a quiet corner to hunker down in. Now use your imagination and picture the perfect day. From the minute you wake up until you close your eyes at night, picture every detail as if you were actually living it out. What will you taste, wear, feel, see, hear, and experience? As women, we frequently get so wrapped up in being the caregiver that we forget about being the caretaker as well. It is important that we take good care of ourselves so that we, in turn, can better care for those who depend on us.

Think about all of those things you love to feel and do that perhaps you have pushed so far onto the back burner that they have toppled off the kitchen counter. And money is no object, but remember that sometimes the pleasure we receive from possessions are fleeting. It is the experiences that count. So what will you experience on this day of days? Perhaps you will wake up in a luxury suite and receive a spa treatment before embarking out on your day with a steaming cappuccino in your hand. After spending your morning riding horses along the beaches of the French Riviera, you can dine on a salad of organic greens, crusty French bread, and a glass of wine at a sidewalk café. You may spend the afternoon playing with your children in the hot springs of northern Colorado before embarking on your private jet for Italy, where you accompany a world-renowned chef in preparing an exquisite meal. Ballroom dancing with your honey follows and, of course, you are dressed in a vintage Balenciaga. Exhausted from dancing, you make sensuous love by candlelight before drifting off to sleep under a blanket of stars.

Now write in big letters across the top of the page, "my perfect day," and fill up the page (and the next, if the mood strikes) with details that describe this amazing day. From morning to night, be as specific as possible. After you finish writing everything down, look through the description and ask yourself what variables are preventing you from living out this dream day. What may seem impossible at first, is usually attainable with the proper focus, discipline, and time. But in striving to reach our long-term goals, we cannot forget that it is the daily efforts that matter. Nothing is more valuable than a single day, so start living your dreams today. Time waits for no woman. Figure out what details from your perfect day you can begin incorporating into your days right now.

Perhaps instead of waking up in a luxury suite and receiving a spa treatment, you can get up a few minutes earlier than everyone else in the house, and spend that time wrapped up in a sumptuous robe buffing your nails and sipping on a cappuccino. Maybe you can take horseback or ballroom dancing lessons once a week, or attend a workshop in Italian cooking. Organic greens can easily be grown in a metal tub on your back porch. And as for the hot springs? I've had just as much fun with a plastic kiddie pool and a hose. And as for making love by candlelight? Once again, I've had just as much fun with a plastic kiddie pool and a hose. But seriously, candles are cheap, stars are free, and making love with your one and only is priceless. These daily efforts may not be the whole cigar, but it will be some details that will nurture your spirit. It's time to start treating yourself as the beautiful woman that you are, and this is the first step.

Part 2

De-Clutter It!

Chapter 3

The Chaos of Clutter

No matter what your personality, how huge your home, or what color your under-wear, we all must deal with the same issue sooner or later—clutter. We all manage clutter in different ways, and avoidance gets you nowhere. Before we can create and manage the home of our dreams, we are going to have to figure out how to eliminate the stuff we don't need and focus on the things that we do. That's clutter management in a nutshell. Clutter means all different things to all different people. But if you don't love it and you don't need it then it's probably going to fall into the clutter category. And it is just standing in the way of you becoming all you could be. It's pretty hard to define clutter. Like they say, "one person's trash is another person's treasure." Or at least that's what my husband told me when I wanted to give away his collection of *Mad Magazines*. So maybe instead of defining clutter, I should just describe it.

Clutter Is Contagious

Just like a stomach flu or a moldy fungus, clutter spreads everywhere. What started as a pile of books in the corner soon grows to be an entire corner stacked knee high with stuff. The small amount of dishes in the sink are soon spilling out all over the counter. Let me give you a case in point. I didn't have a chance to fold the load of laundry that I got out of the dryer last Friday, so I set the basket down on the floor next to my bed. I completely forgot about it until I went to bed and was too exhausted to even think about folding clothes. The next day, my husband helped out with some laundry. He saw the pile on the floor and was kind enough to add another clean load on top of it. I did another load, and plopped it right down on top of the mountain. Do you see where I'm going with this? By that evening, the mass of clothes at the foot of our bed looked like the back of a Goodwill donation truck (only without the ugly pleated lamp shade and the singing-fish wall plaque). I needed a forklift just so I could climb into bed. Once there, I knew I was stuck for the night. If I tried to scale the mountain I could easily get lost somewhere in the pile and remain there until someone eventually found me out of necessity—when they needed a stomach filled or a diaper changed.

So, cut off the spread of clutter by trying to prevent it from getting started. Placing a little bit of clutter somewhere seems innocent enough, but the problem exists in the invitation. A little bit of clutter invites more, and before you know it, the problem has become unmanageable. Think of it this way, if you enter a home and the living room is completely clear and clutter-free, you would probably ask where you could place your purse or jacket. However, if you enter a home and the sofa is piled full of laundry and there are stacks of books, papers, and toys all over the floor, you feel completely welcome to rest your purse and jacket right on top of it all. It is a subconscious act. You don't even have to think about it. The absence of clutter requires permission. The presence of clutter offers an invitation. One is guarding your home against unwelcome intrusion, the other invites it right in. If you are going to stop the disease of clutter, you need to start by getting rid of the virus and emptying out the contaminants. In other words, fold the laundry as soon as it comes out of the dryer!

Clutter Is Stagnant

I can't stand stagnant air. It reminds me of stuffy elevators or hospital rooms. If the weather outside is the least bit conducive, I will throw open the windows and let the air flow through our house (with six children, it needs all the airing out it can get). Whenever I have had to stay in the hospital, I would hate looking outside at a beautiful day and not even be able to open the windows. I've even tried to do so before, until the nurse came in and caught me pushing at the window. I don't know which surprised her more—a patient trying to open the hospital room window or catching sight of the rear view (which, if I may add, was quite startling given that I was wearing one of those breathtaking hospital gowns).

49

So, imagine that it is a beautiful spring day outside (and you're not wearing a hospital gown—unless you're just in to that sort of thing). The birds are chirping, the flowers are blooming, and a light breeze is blowing through the newly budding trees (we will just pretend that pollen does not exist for this little exercise). Well, you throw open the windows to let the fresh air through your home. If your home is clear and clean, that breeze can blow through your home and invigorate it. If it is cluttered and messy, the breeze just causes the dust to start flying through the air. The clutter that has built up on the shelves and in the corners is like a magnet, drawing the fresh air in and then absorbing it so it no longer circulates. The mess and clutter causes the flow of energy to stop and stagnate. It refuses to let anyone benefit from the beauty of natural flow. The clutter is heavy and dense, pulling everything into it. The inhabitants are often edgy, distracted, or perhaps feel the need to escape. They want to accomplish exceedingly much, but feel that they can't even get their thoughts straight. Their spirits, just like their environment has begun to stagnate.

Even if there is no breeze, a home that is free of the clutter invasion allows a flow of positive energy to circulate. It has a light and free aura that enriches those who inhabit it. It is an environment of creativity. It is stimulating and invigorating. Don't you deserve a home that lifts you up and encourages your development? Look around and find the innocent clutter that has been weighing you down, and get rid of it. It can even be good clutter, the basket of soaps your mother-in-law gave you, the precious bedroom slippers that your son used to wear. The point is, these items have begun to pull energy out of your spirit instead of building you up. Its purpose is finished, it's outlived its welcome, and it's ready to go—just give it a little help.

Clutter Is Disorganized

You can stack it. You can file it. You can box it up or put it in quaint little baskets. But you are never going to get it organized. Clutter absolutely refuses to be organized. It goes against its very nature. For example, you may have a year's worth of magazines lying around. You remember seeing some fantastic home decorating ideas that you intend to try (once you get the house straightened up). The problem is, you never will. Whatever you saw that appealed to you has already been filed away in your brain, and you will naturally be drawn to these ideas at a later day and create an environment that is all yours. And anyway, when you

Dump the junk
and feel your spirit lighten!

finally get around to it, that look may be completely dated and you will want to try something new. Meanwhile, the magazines will continue to arrive every month, and will continue to stack up. They will also continue to bother you, reminding you that if you were a really good wife and mother, you would have decorated your home like the glossy pictures they hold inside their covers. They are beginning to fill your environment with negative energy and are no longer fulfilling their purpose of being entertaining and informative. You can file them by month and year, and put them in labeled storage boxes, but they will continue to take up valuable space in your home and demand your attention.

Don't waste your precious energy trying to come up with an organizational system for clutter that you no longer need to hold on to. Your life is way too important to have this intrusion. Just let it go. But, I will say one thing about organizing clutter. No one is perfect. You are going to have the residual junk lingering around even after you have cleared out every corner of your home. Have a spot for this and don't beat yourself up about it. A junk drawer in the kitchen is a perfect example. You need a spot for all of the little doodads that make up life in the kitchen (e.g., matches, pens, scissors). There's your spot. Throw it in, and let it go. If it makes you feel any better, I have two junk drawers. One got so full that I had to remodel my kitchen and create another one. So if you're looking for perfection, then you had better look someplace else. By the way, if you do already have an organized junk drawer than you are the woman of the year. Put this book down quickly before it begins to contaminate you!

Clutter not only refuses to be organized, but it also prevents organization of other items. Have you ever been unable to locate something because of clutter? Have you ever been unable to find your keys when it's time to go, and could not get your hands on some paperwork that you needed it? You knew you had it, but you just didn't know where. The problem was the clutter that surrounded it prevented it from being found. That contagious disease of clutter is at it again, inviting you to set items down anywhere that is convenient, even if you do have a

*Don't bellyache about the clutter—
stop the clutter from bellyachin'!*

specific spot for it. For example, you place all of your children's permission slips into a zippered pouch in your day planner. However, when you get the permission slip, you are in the car, and it is much easier to just throw it on the floor with the other junk. Now when little Cindy has to explain to her teacher that the reason she doesn't have her permission slip is because her mother lost it in the car, who's going to look like the bad mama of the year?! Take a few minutes and put it where it goes. It will save time in the long run (as well as public humiliation).

Clutter Is Selfish

The clutter you have allowed in your home has grown up to be spoiled rotten brats—demanding your attention every minute of the day. You try to sit down for some coffee in the morning and that pile of craft materials screeches at you, "What do you think you're doing just sitting there?! Are you ever going to work on me? Don't you care at all about finishing what you start?"

You try to spend some time reading books to your children, and that stack of books starts yelling at you, "Excuse me! But you were going to read *me* today! You bought me over a month ago, and haven't even opened me up!"

It's time for this selfish clutter to shut its trap! The longer you ignore it, the worse it's going to get. Its selfish nature just keeps nagging at you, morning, noon, and night. It's time to take some serious disciplinary action. You are an amazing person, with an even more amazing purpose in your life. You will only reach your goals and dreams when you begin eliminating the roadblocks that stand in your way. The clutter demands way too much of your energy. It constantly needs to be tended to, and you don't need to be bothered any longer by the intrusion.

It seemed so innocent at first, all of their little whispers. There they all sit, telling you what to do with your life—"Dust me! Vacuum around me! Move me someplace else! Organize me!" You need to start becoming vigilant about the

52

demands that are placed upon you—is it positive or negative? Do you enjoy how your things serve you, or are you frustrated at how you constantly serve them? If you find that the little piles of clutter have become little pains in the butt, then get rid of them. That doesn't mean act on all of them. It simply means get rid of them. That scarf you were knitting was fun when you started, but now it is just sitting there reminding you that you have no sense of commitment. Box it up, label it, and put it away. You can always get it out later.

Clutter also makes its presence known constantly. You can put in a brand new countertop in the kitchen, but if there are stacks of clutter on it, guess what people will notice? You got it, the clutter. You can get a brand new set of furniture for the living room, but pile a stack of books on the sofa, and guess what people will notice?—the clutter. You notice it every time you glance there also, but you have grown so accustomed to its existence, that you no longer realize the energy it pulls from you. It has robbed you of enjoying the beauty of your surroundings, and it's time for that to change. You deserve to enjoy the best in life, and to quit being distracted by the selfish odds and ends of clutter.

Clutter Is Sick

And I mean this literally. Clutter is a dirt magnet. You can try to clean around it, but you haven't removed the filth that is within it. You may wonder why your nose is congested whenever you stay in your home, and the condition goes away every time you leave it. You may wonder why you cough and wheeze at home, but never when you're out shopping. You cannot clean clutter. Even if you do manage to take all the time and effort to clean it, it gets dirty within minutes. Think of all of those bottles of soaps and bath gels that are sitting around your bathroom. How much time do you think it takes to remove and wipe off all of the bottles and then clean the counters and bathtub, compared to the time and energy it takes to spray a couple of times and swipe the counter clean?

Clutter can cloud your vision of true beauty.

53

Cleaning is a breeze when an area is free of clutter. It takes just seconds to dust furniture that doesn't have loads of junk all over it. But when you know you have to take off every little doodad, clean the doodad, then clean the surface area, you'll never want to pick up a bottle of furniture polish. It's hard enough to get motivated to clean, so don't make it tortuous. Quit trying to clean the clutter, and just get rid of it.

I remember thumbing through one of those magazines with the word "Country" somewhere in the title. I usually love all of the beautiful design concepts and get a wealth of ideas from them (I never knew butter churns or wooden spools had so many uses). In this particular issue, I saw a two-page spread of a living room that made every hair on my clutter-free neck stand on end. Every surface in the room was packed full of odds and ends from one end to the other. A mug full of colored pencils, a row of thimbles, little figurines, candle holders, wooden finials, framed pictures, and, in the words of Karen Carpenter, "we've only just begun." When I saw this spread, I wasn't thinking "cute and country." I was thinking, "torture to clean." The way I see it, I can spend an hour cleaning a dresser, or I can do something with that time that I actually enjoy. If you just love to dust and have an extra two hours to spend, then go for it. But if not, then clear it out. You will feel so much better later! Both your body and your mind will be relieved, because sickness is also a result of stress.

The stress that clutter creates can definitely take its toll on your total health, and create a whole host of symptoms that you may be living with—headaches, stomach problems, fatigue, you name it. They could all be caused by stress. You are on an incredible journey through life, and you don't need to be weighed down by junk—books that you are never going to read, clothes that you are never going to wear, to-do lists that you have no intention of actually doing. Focus on what really matters, and let the rest go.

Clutter Is Useless

We've all done it. At least, I hope we all have done it. I would hate to feel like the only one who was guilty of storing items that were of absolutely no use to me or anyone else. A pen doesn't write well, so we put it back in the drawer and go search for another one. The skirt looks hideous, so we take it off and stick it back in the closet. The clippers don't trim the bushes well, so we put them back in the garage and get another pair. For no other reason than to take up precious space within our homes, we stick completely useless stuff in drawers, bags, closets, and

Decluttering is good for the body and for the soul.

garages. Kids are notorious for this. If I didn't police the bathroom every once in a while, they would have enough toilet paper tubes to make pinto bean maracas for the entire first grade class all stacked up on the counter (it beats all the effort of changing the tube and sticking it in the trash). I've even witnessed them taking the last stick of gum out of the kitchen junk drawer and then sticking the wrapper back in the drawer when the trash can was less than two feet away!

And kids aren't the only culprits. I remember one birthday party for my oldest daughter. She decided that she wanted a campout, even after I had tempted her with a myriad of other more exciting (and more mom-friendly) ideas. So, out came the huge tent, and out came the twin-size air mattress. Someone had to sleep with the girls to chaperone them. My husband was out. I figured the parents would have a bit of a problem with a grown man sharing the sleeping quarters with their preadolescent girls. That, and the fact that he would enjoy camping out in the front yard as much as he would enjoy getting his chest waxed. I was pregnant at the time, so I insisted on at least having an air mattress to cushion my expanding abdomen.

At around midnight, while the girls were chattering so loudly that it made the tiki room at Disneyworld seem like a meditation chapel, I began to notice that my hips were ever so delicately grazing the earth below. Given the size of my hips, this came as no surprise to me. Then around 3 A.M., as the girls were just beginning to wind down, my enormous body was digging into the ground with such gravitational force, that I felt as if the earth was going to swallow me up, hips and all. Rocks that felt as big as bowling balls were creating caverns on my backside, adding to the intricate assembly of texture that was already there. My air mattress was now just a thin layer of vinyl between me and the ground. Try as I might, I could not get into a position that was comfortable. With enough fidgeting around, I finally dozed off to sleep between 4:15 A.M. and 5:30 A.M. with my left buttuck cheek perched on a smooth patch of earth, my right leg twisted over my left, my left shoulder nestled within a hole that I had burrowed through

Scrape off the clutter and look at how brightly you can shine!

the cushiony soft vinyl, and both hands trapped between my thighs. It was not a good night. When the black sky birthed a hint of early morning grey and the first bird chirped, I darted for the warmth and comfort of my bed. I climbed in next to my husband, waking him up. He looked at me, bewildered.

"There is a hole in the air mattress!" I whispered vehemently.

He closed his eyes, rolled over, pulled the covers over him and mumbled, "Oh, yeah. That's right. There is."

Evidently, my husband, who is the grand pooh-bah of packing and unpacking the camping gear had knowingly put away a defective mattress. Needless to say, he was the one who was cooking pancakes for a dozen girls that morning. Do yourself a favor. When you come across something that is useless, get rid of it. Don't store it with the idea that you're going to throw it away later. Use the space for something else, like pancake mix.

Clutter Is Dangerous

This can be the biggest reason of all to get rid of the clutter. If the situation is bad enough, then clutter can cause accidents and inflict harm. How many times has someone tripped over a pile of toys and gotten hurt? Or what about breaking something after the stacks reached mammoth proportions, causing an object to fall off the shelf or counter? What about getting caught in the shower without a towel handy because all of the laundry is stacked up so you run out of the bathroom naked, slip on the wood floors, and get a scratched-up knee and a big red splotch on your thigh? (Or was that just me?) Anyway, the point is, clutter can be dangerous. It not only causes accidents, but it can also prevent emergency preparedness. What about not being able to locate a phone number in the event of an emergency? Not being able to find jumper cables when your battery dies? Misplacing medication when you or a loved one is dependent upon it? The list goes on and on. We never know when life can spring these unpleasant surprises on us, but one thing is for sure—they are going to happen, and they will always happen when you are not prepared for them! Consider getting rid of your clutter as insurance against these unfortunate events. You know they won't happen when you are actually ready for them. But even if they do, you will be.

Clutter Is a Freeloader

And we all know how much we love a freeloader! All of the clutter that one way or another has found its way into your home is now just taking up residence. It has outlived its purpose, but lives on anyway. Everything that entered through the doorway had a purpose to begin with. Perhaps that spoon rest was exactly what you needed when you had a different decor in your kitchen, or those jeans were exactly what you loved wearing when they were actually in style, or that wall hanging your sister gave you looked great in your last home, but there they just sit—never used or admired, just taking up space. You need to get rid of the guilt associated with dumping out these freeloaders—they have no thought, meaning, or energy, other than what you attach to them. For example, the dress your mom gave you is never worn. You don't need to keep the dress just because she gave it to you. It holds no love of hers or possesses any energy associated with her life. Your mother loves you, not the dress. You love your *mother,* not the dress. She gave you the dress as a display of her affection toward you. She thought of you when she saw it, and gave it to you to show her love. The action was beautiful, not the object. You need to see the beauty for where it really lies—the love behind the gift, rather than the gift itself. And because she loves you, she would never want you to carry around the stress associated with holding on to an object that no longer enriches your life. Let the item go, but keep the love.

If it is still difficult to let those freeloaders go, imagine how much rent you are paying for them every month. Your money that is invested in your house is sucked up by all of the objects that are housed within its walls. I am more than happy to pay the room and board for my computer because I use it all the time and it is a tool that I am employing to reach my goals. However, that old dresser in the basement is not doing anything for my life right now, yet part of my house payment goes to paying the square footage that it takes up. Part of my electricity bill goes to keeping it cool in the summer and warm in the winter. It is, therefore, a freeloader. It's time to claim your home, and take back what rightfully belongs to you.

Clutter Is Embarrassing

Here you are at home, and a good friend pops by for a visit. Your husband is home and is lying on the sofa watching a football game in his underwear. Your friend glances over at him, and he makes no move to get up and go change. You are mortified and your friend is embarrassed for you as well. You try to grab a couple of chairs together in the kitchen, but she can still see your rude husband out of the corner of her eye. The two of you are unable to talk freely because of this intrusion so the conversation is somewhat hampered. He then strolls into the kitchen throws open the fridge and belches at the top of his lungs—a long, deep, rolling one ending with some juicy tones at the end. Your friend decides that perhaps another day may be better to come visiting, and she will be sure to call first. Your husband walks the two of you to the door, picking his nose the whole way. Sounds unbelievable? Well, you don't know my husband (just joking). But in all sincerity, clutter behaves in the same way.

Clutter relishes opportunities to embarrass you and damage your relationships with your friends and family. It draws attention to itself, and speaks volumes about you before even giving you a chance to speak on your behalf. I don't recommend you give your husband a one-way ticket out of your home, but I greatly encourage you to do this for the clutter that has invaded your life. You are too beautiful and worth too much to be humiliated by the clutter that surrounds you. Let it go, and you will find peace and satisfaction that you didn't even know existed.

Clutter Is Out of Sight, Out of Mind

A funny thing about clutter is that when it's gone, you never, ever miss it. Many of us are surrounded by clutter that we don't even perceive as clutter. How many articles of clothing in your closet do you actually wear? How many toys do the kids actually play with? Now don't get me wrong. Just because you have forgotten about it, that doesn't mean you can categorize it as clutter. During our last move, I was spending my days unpacking box after box after box. Needless to say, I was getting sick and tired of the boxes. Finally, after we had already been living in the house for three months, I still had several to go. I decided that if I had not had a need for it by now, I probably never would so I was determined to

Empty your home of clutter and feel the positive, refreshing energy begin to flow within its walls.

give it away. Before I stuck it in the Salvation Army stack I opened them up and glanced inside. One box was full of our wedding pictures! It's okay to be a bit zealous about getting rid of clutter, but try not to get carried away.

You may be completely surrounded by clutter, and not even be aware of it! Everyone who moves says the same thing, "I had no idea we had so much junk!" Packing up box after box of stuff eventually drives you crazy and you're tempted to swear off material possessions for good and go live in a monastery somewhere. That's one of the problems with clutter—when you don't see it, you don't think about it. But eventually down the road somewhere, you're going to have to deal with it. Why not deal with it now? By emptying your home of some of the clutter, you may very well free up cabinets, closets, even rooms that you could use for some other purpose other than a holding tank. For example, if you haven't done a major fashion overhaul within the last five years, you may desperately be in need of one. One clue is if you open your closet door, and say (usually in a nasal tone), "I have nothing to wear!" It's not that you have nothing to wear. You probably just have nothing to wear that actually looks good on you and you feel comfortable in. Get rid of anything that says, *Saved by the Bell* or *Golden Girls,* and give it away or use it for fuel the next time there is a power outage in the middle of winter. Get some clothes that feel good and look good. You don't need clutter, and you definitely don't need to wear clutter.

Clutter robs you of the joy and peace that could be surrounding you all the time. You do not need these things. Perhaps you needed them at one time, or perhaps they are part of a person that no longer exists. For example, that jewelry that you collected when you had a different career is still sitting in your jewelry case, never being worn. You are not the same woman anymore. The woman who used to wear heavy gold bangles now opts for simple understated rhinestones. You let the woman go, now let go of the items that you associate with her. It would make beautiful gifts or excellent tax-deductible donations. As soon as it is gone, you will never even miss it.

You deserve to be clutter-free.
No more clutter!

When you let go of the clutter that lives in the past, you are also allowing yourself to let go of any negative energy associated with it. It's important to live in the present. Fully living in the present ensures us of blessing in the future. Hold on to some few things that bring special memories (we will talk later about good strategies to do this). But for now, truly analyze the clutter. Does it make you smile? Does it make you a better person? Does it create energy instead of destroy it? You may be surprised at how quickly this clutter is forgotten once it leaves your world. Holding on to clutter is a way of pouring energy into the past. Letting go of clutter frees up that energy to be used in the here and now. It will truly surprise you. Peace and energy will begin to pour into your life.

Clutter Is Inevitable

In case you don't know it by now, clutter is one of those givens in life that we will never be able to completely eradicate, unless you want to take an oath of poverty and live in a monastery somewhere (which sometimes seems like a good idea when you have to lock the bathroom door and slip on some headphones just for a few minutes to yourself). We will constantly have a parade of clutter marching through our homes. But just remember to keep the parade marching. You don't want it marching in to your homes and then stopping there. Repeat it as you would, "wax on, wax off"—"march in, march out." You can bolt the doors and paint all of the windows shut, but it will continue to slip in, completely undetected. It's like the people under the stairs—the clutter is there, hiding, invisibly gaining strength and power until it's ready to take over the entire house and cause some really gory special effects. You don't want to clean up a mess like that, so just keep the innocent little parade marching in, and then marching right back out.

Don't freak out and try to completely get rid of the clutter because you're just going to be fighting a losing battle (kind of like if I ever tried to play video games against my son). Instead, just learn how to effectively manage it. You can completely get rid of clutter, but I am assuming that you actually have a life and don't walk around with a feather duster in one hand and a can of antibacterial wipes in the other. Live your life without the stress of completely obliterating clutter or being completely consumed by it. It's all about balance. Live fully enough to let clutter in, but love yourself enough to push it back out.

Time for Your Prescription

There's a new day dawning, and you can see the glow on the horizon. I know for many of you, clutter is a big problem, especially if you have children. We all know that kids and clutter have a codependent relationship. It's like bees and honey, spaghetti and meatballs, Simon and Garfunkel—one can hardly exist without the other (especially if they do a reunion concert in Central Park). But the main thing that I want you to realize about clutter is that it robs you of so much in life. It stresses you out and junks up your life, and you deserve so much better than that. Each one of us has our own tender parts when it comes to junk. My husband is an emotional junkie. Anything that our children have ever touched, he wants to save to look back on. I can just see him now, "But, honey, it was the first tissue that she ever blew her nose on!" As for me, I'm a useful junkie. If I think we may have a use for it, I have a tendency to pack it away. I constantly need to catch myself and let things go. So, where are your tender parts? Likely it can be found somewhere in your personality.

Rx for MasterMinds

You aren't usually one to collect a bunch of clutter. But if you do, it is usually brain-related in some way or another. But you don't have to save every piece of paper that crosses your desk. You like security, and you appreciate knowing that somewhere in there, a check stub or statement is neatly filed away. You probably couldn't access it if someone paid you, but even if you could, does it really need to be there in the first place? Most companies have all of your information in their computer files. So if you needed to find out exactly how much you owed on that washer and dryer, you could do so easily with a phone call. Tax information should be saved for seven years, but after that you can feel free to toss it. Be vigilant about what crosses your desk and if you can toss it without negative repercussions, do it. For right now, empty off your entire desk and clean it completely. Now designate a place for everything and make a new rule—don't put it down, put it away. Try going through at least five of your file folders while you're sitting there and empty them of everything that you no longer need.

Rx for Creative Spirits

I know, I know, something catches your eye, and it has to be yours. Whether it's a lovely stained-glass picture or a richly woven fabric, you love to stalk it, claim it, bag it, and carry it home. You can try to resist the purchase, but then you just go home and stare at the spot where you were going to put it and fantasize. It's time to step out of your fantasy world for a minute and strive toward making your fantasies a reality. Go ahead and long for the objects of beauty. It may drive you to empty out some of your home in order to make room for other things. Just remember to purchase them only if you have made twice the room. Are you just dying for that new suede jacket? Then find two that you already own and give them away. You've just got to have those vibrant cotton four-hundred-thread-count sheets, right? Then find two sets that you can do without and pass them on. This will validate your purchase. For right now, find ten duplicates of items that you currently own and give them away. It shouldn't be that difficult. Try your closet.

Rx for Mother Hens

You are homemaker material. Because of that, you often try to keep your clutter in check. I'm not saying you don't accumulate any. You just may not give the impression that you do. If you do happen to horde a bit here and there, then it is usually "use" related. You may want to use that fabric one day for curtains. You may want to use those pictures to make a collage. You may want to use that crystal bowl for a centerpiece someday—always someday. Forget about the someday that you have stuck in your mind, and try to focus more on today. Get rid of the extra stuff that you have accumulated so that your todays are clearer and more focused. Go through all of your craft and sewing supplies. Figure out what you are saving for an actual use, and what bits and pieces are just resulting in a stress headache. With your personality, you receive comfort by being prepared for anything and everything. Even if the price of comfort may often feel like mass confusion. Make a conscious decision to push yourself out of the comfort zone and let go of some of those items that you have been holding on to. You will probably never use them. If the need does ever come up, then consider the money that you will pay for a new or used replacement a small price for the space that you have freed up and the peace of mind that you have embraced.

Rx for Starry-Eyed Dreamers

Just because it was your anniversary dinner does not mean you need to save the menu, the napkins, and five books of matches from the restaurant. You have the tendency to attach a lot of emotion to objects that have no way of returning your affection. If you don't believe me, take a look at your photo collection or all of the greeting cards you have saved. It would be okay if you actually did something with them, but most of it is just packed away gathering dust. Either that, or it is on display somewhere in your home doing the same thing—gathering dust. You may not be emotionally ready to part with these objects, but you are very ready to part with all the clutter. Here's what you need to do. Get two large cardboard boxes or plastic totes. One of these will be for items to give away. And don't beat yourself up if you only have a couple of things in there. There are probably very valid emotional reasons why you are not ready to part with many items yet. The other box will be for items to put into storage. The next time you sit down to watch television, get up during the commercials and find one thing you have sitting around that you no longer use and no longer enriches your life (that candleholder from Grandma, that music box your child used to wind up all the time, books you don't read). Now toss it in one of the boxes and forget about it. When the storage box is full, label it, and put it away. When the giveaway box is full, drop it off at a local charity. Keep doing this and it's likely to become addictive.

Try this little exercise in your dream journal. Walk into a room and look all around. Think about the activities that take place within that room and all of the items that are needed. Now leave the room and grab your journal. Before any thoughts can leave your mind, write down all of the items that are absolute necessities to have in that room. The objects of beauty are essential as well, because they perform a duty within that room. When you believe you have exhausted that list, take your journal and go back in the room. Now look around at all of the items that you have in that room that are not necessary to its functionality. Do you see how much you could get rid of?

Think about how you could use the space you create when you do dump all of the clutter—perhaps an area to exercise or do yoga; room for that perfect chaise lounge that you have always wanted, but never had the room for; or maybe even an area to put a beautiful arrangement of fresh flowers. Draw out the items that you would love to see in that space (or just draw the space itself—for empty space can be just as lovely). If you don't feel comfortable drawing, you can always cut pictures out of a magazine. This can be your incentive to create a new environment. For example, I could never rationalize getting new towels because I had such a vast assortment of them. When I finally bagged up all of the ugly old towels and got rid of them, it finally gave me permission to invest in a few that I really loved. Now it is a joy to reach for my clean, thirsty, white, cuddly towels rather than those ragged ones that tickled my legs with their stray threads. I don't have nearly as many towels as I did before, but now I really enjoy the ones I have (and I like the extra room in the linen closet as well). Get rid of the junk you have because you deserve better. Give yourself permission to enjoy the finest things in life. You don't need a lot of it. As Mary Poppins said, "Enough is as good as a feast!"

Chapter 4

Preparing Your Canvas

We all know what clutter is, and we all know that it's pretty much unavoidable. But some of us have a tendency to invite a little more clutter into our homes than we know how to manage, sort of like that time I decided to let fourteen girls spend the night together in the living room (I didn't really like that lamp anyway). Clutter comes in our house, and sometimes doesn't make it back out. Pretty soon, closet doors won't shut, drawers won't close, and you trip over stuff when you get up to use the bathroom in the middle of the night. If you seem to have a case of the clutters, then we are going to attack that area before we can begin any place else. You are an artist, and now is the time to clear out your studio so that you can begin creating that masterpiece called home. Just think of it as opening the windows after your husband gets out of the bathroom so that you can go in and get yourself ready for the day.

The Power Principle

Stuff makes us feel so powerful. Big stuff, little stuff, it doesn't really matter as long as it's a lot of stuff and it belongs to us. One reason that we keep a lot of clutter around us is for the feeling of power that we associate with possessing items. I guess it just stems from the days of, "I have a bigger animal hide in my cave than you do, so nya-nya-nya-nya-nya." Whether we really like something or use something is completely unimportant. The only thing that matters is that we possess it, and that makes us feel important.

Your spirit will take you on incredible journeys once you start letting go of those weights that pull you down.

Have you ever experienced one of those "life sucks so I'm going shopping" kind of episodes? It's the feeling of conquest—whip out that credit card, strut your bad mamma jamma self out of the shop with your arms loaded down, and, girl, you are power-full! I can just feel the adrenaline flowing now! We are all guilty of buying things we don't need at one time or another. If we only bought things we needed, then how could a product like the rotating pizza cooker actually exist? For the most part, it's the feeling of power we're after, not the product itself.

And the thing with emotional purchases is this—emotions are fleeting. Buying that item fulfills your emotional need, but only temporarily. Almost before you can start making payments on it, you need to go buy something else. Instead of putting a Band-Aid on an emotional boo-boo, it may be time to search for a cure by figuring out what that woman deep down inside is really after. And I will tell you this right now. You are already a powerful woman. Perhaps you just need a little help finding that strong voice within you. And when you do find it, you will be able to give that stuff its marching orders.

Creature Comforts

If there was one place we would all like to live, it would be in our comfort zones. Another reason we have a hard time letting go of clutter is because it provides us with comfort in one way or another. We all find comfort in so many different things. That's probably because so many different things stress us out.

You MasterMinds out there get completely stressed out when you feel as if you have no power over a situation, or that you do not have enough knowledge or competence to handle a situation. You obsess over things until you move on to a new project or figure out a solution to the problem. You Creative Spirits freak out if you're bored, constrained, or you feel like you are not being noticed.

66

Eventually though, you move on to a new activity and do something that no one can ignore (people are still talking about that lighter trick you pulled at last year's Oktoberfest that left scorch marks on your Calvins). You Mother Hens get upset if your authority is challenged or you feel alone, or if you just don't fit in anywhere. You usually remedy this by including yourself in what's going on around you or joining something. You Starry-Eyed Dreamers feel stressed when you sense any insincerity or that you have been let down in some way. You have a way of allowing the healing words of others to serve as a balm to your spirit. You also can seek wholeness by aspiring to new goals.

Evidently, we all have our own comfort zones. I prefer macaroni and cheese. But that's just me. We all have different ways of dealing with stress and soothing our spirits. And what we seek as comfort often has a lot to do with what types of clutter we allow in our homes. As different as we all are, one thing that we all have in common is that feeling comfortable often requires stuff. If we don't feel loved, then in the back of our minds, we often feel that we can buy items that will give us this feeling. A MasterMind may buy some new computer device to solve her problem. A Creative Spirit may buy a tool to enable her to take action. A Mother Hen may buy gifts for her home or her children, those things she identifies with or watches over. A Starry-Eyed Dreamer may buy emotional objects that confirm her integrity.

The problem with buying comfort is that the comfort usually doesn't last. And as much as we love objects, they will never love us back. Instead, it often works the opposite way. The initial feeling is euphoric, but then our blues get even worse and leave an acute emptiness that we try again to fill with more stuff. And what does all of that stuff become? Clutter. And we become comfortable festering in the clutter we have created.

And that feeling of comfort is exactly why it is so difficult to make big changes. As much as it stifles our energy, aggravates our emotions, represses our spirit, and hampers our peace of mind, clutter makes us comfortable because it is a world that we have created and we have grown accustomed to. It gives us a reason to do less than we are capable of and it gives us an excuse for our own shortcomings. If we started clearing out and cleaning up, then we may be expected to accomplish more in other areas of our lives. But sometimes, change is good. We often find that when we are expected to do more, we miraculously do more than expected. Getting out of your comfort zone may not be too comfortable, but it can be exhilarating! Dump the clutter and make room for amazing things to happen in your home.

The Inevitable

Ladies, it's time. Swallow that fear, grab those trash bags, and let's go! We are going to begin emptying out your treasure box so that the riches of heaven can begin pouring into your life. As I said before (and I'll say it again and again), you are an artist. And an artist is only as good as her supplies. Before you can begin creating, you need to begin preparing. And this is just as much a part of the artistic process as anything else, for it is truly a form of creative expression to clear out and let go. As you begin pushing clutter out of your life, you will begin creating clarity, serenity, and peace within your spirit, and this will echo throughout your home. So are you ready to stretch that canvas and enlarge your spirit? Get on some heavy-duty working clothes, 'cause we're going to get nastier than a halftime show at the Super Bowl!

Tools for the Task

Here's what you are going to need for the job. Yes, I know it's a long list, but bear with me:

- a trash bag
- a box or paper sack
- two laundry baskets

Okay, did you get that? Now, I'm sure you have heard this by now, because this trick is one of the oldest ones in the book. It's an oldie, but a goodie! You are going to use the trash bag for trash (duh!). You are going to use the box or paper sack for items that you want to give away (it looks nicer than a trash bag). And you are going to use the laundry baskets for items that you are going to put away or store away in another location. We're not going to worry about cleaning right now. That comes later. Right now we are just setting our sights on conquering clutter. Note: If the trash bag, paper sack, and laundry basket is too much work, then just make four piles or grab four grocery sacks. The only reason I have to gather up containers is because I always have at least one toddler who is interested in grabbing things off of the floor and putting them in his or her mouth.

Throw Away

Now the question is, what are you going to throw away? Everyone is so different, and we all have various things that we like and don't like. But, by and large, the criteria that you are going to use to judge whether it makes the cut are two simple questions:

Do I use it? Do I love it?

You need to be completely honest with yourself. If you don't use it and if you don't love it (and you can't imagine anyone else using or loving it) then toss it in the trash. And if the answer is, "but I could be using it," then you are just asking for something else to clutter up your life (either through time or space). Perhaps you are not using it because you don't have the time to use it, and getting rid of it will not only open up the space for more useful energy in your home, but it will also relieve you of the guilt that weighs over you every time you see it. You know that juicer that sits on your pantry shelf? Yeah, you could be using it, but the truth is you're not. Just give it away. Perhaps one day, you will have the time and energy to devote to juicing. And when that time comes, you can always run to the store and pick one up. The price you pay for it will be a small amount considering the clear space and peace of mind you have received.

And if the answer is, "but I should be loving it," then you are also asking for clutter. Guilt should not have any effect on the load that you carry through life. Many times we are given a gift that is not exactly us. I'm sure you know what I mean. Kellie, one of my girlfriends, never drinks a drop of alcohol and she has a wine rack, wine glasses, and a corkscrew stashed away in her attic. It was given to her as a gift, and she has not had the gumption to pass it along to someone else. If we have a gift that we know we will never use or want, we often feel as if we have to serve a penance to the thoughtful gesture by storing it for a certain amount of time before we get rid of it. Here's the deal—the gift was an act of love, and your grateful acceptance was a response to that beautiful act. You serving time to the gift by storing it is not listed anywhere on the official guide to gift exchange etiquette. Your mother-in-law meant well when she gave you the crocheted Christmas sweater with the "Ho! Ho! Ho!" buttons. Storing it in your closet doesn't mean you love her any more, and giving it away doesn't mean you love her any less. And if you are actually wearing it, then I strongly suggest some nightly doses of the Style channel.

No Ifs, Ands, or Buts

When you do begin filling up your throwaway bag, don't second-guess it. Toss it in, and forget about it. When you fill up the bag, tie it up, and throw it in the trash can (outside preferably). That way, it is far away from you and you have already cleared it out of your life and your home. (I've been known to rummage through trash—so putting it far away is a protective device.) Now, there is one more thing that I want you to keep in mind when you are throwing stuff away. This is no time to be an environmentalist. I am sure everyone who knows me personally is shuddering right now. I recycle like a fiend, donate to environmental charities, and even alter my diet to support a more earth-friendly approach. But keep this in mind—right now, you are saving your sanity—not the world!

Sure, you could drag a lot of that stuff to a recycling center, but you have got to get your home in order before you can do anything about the environment. Think of it this way—do you want to throw all of that stuff into a landfill or do you want your home to become a landfill? Either way, it is unused and unloved junk, and it belongs in the trash. Just put it where it belongs and get the trash out of your home. You don't want to live in a dumpster! You can start up a recycling and reduction program later. Right now, the only environment you need to be concerned with is the square footage of your home.

If it makes you feel better, think of how environmentally unfriendly clutter is. You have to make repeat purchases of items because you can't find them—more to add to the landfill. You store junk in your home—more expense in heating and cooling cost. You have more stuff to clean—more chemicals flushed into our environment. You hold on to items other people could use—less recycling. Okay, some of these are a stretch, but the point is de-cluttering your home is actually eco-friendly!

Give Away

This is one of my favorites. I love giving stuff away for two reasons—money and happiness (and no, those two do not necessarily go hand in hand). If you are deliberating about giving away some items, perhaps that incentive will help you as well. I love to see the look on people's faces when I give things to them. It is so true—the giver is always more blessed then the recipient. And when you start giving things away, the happiness you feel becomes addictive. You want to give away everything! Once, I heard about a young lady who was pregnant and did not have the money to get many things for herself or the expected baby. I bagged up all of my maternity clothes—the gorgeous velvet dresses, the cute little short sets, everything. I was planning on having more children, but it was a step out in faith. I took three boxes of clothes to her, and the image of her happiness will always be imbedded in my mind. She was so grateful. And it's so true that when you start pouring out blessings to others, more and more blessings will pour into your life. A year later I got pregnant again. Without my putting out any requests, clothes began to appear left and right. My sister-in-law dropped off two huge trash bags full of very nice clothes. Friends would bring boxes and bags of clothes to church and leave them in my car without my even realizing it. I had so many maternity clothes that I honestly had to start turning some away because I didn't have the room in my closet! What a blessing!

So, dare yourself to give it away and bless someone, and you will find that the blessings just keep on coming. But do me and everyone else a favor, don't give something away when it really belongs in the trash. You know that dozen pairs of underwear with the worn-out elastic and skid marks in the crotch? Do you honestly think anyone is going to want to put on those skanky drawers? You're not blessing anyone with those things. When I was pregnant with my first child, a friend dropped off a box of maternity clothes. I opened it up, and found a whole assortment of very nice clothes folded neatly away. However, (I'm hoping it was by accident) at the bottom was also a neat little pile of folded-up maternity

Step out in faith, and you will soar in the winds of prosperity!

underwear—and I won't bother you with details. Let's just say that they were not so "gently" used. So, if you are thinking that some of your belongings may have a better place in the trash can, then you are probably right.

Turning Trash into Treasure

Now the other thing is money. You can get money for your unneeded belongings in two ways—sell them or deduct them. An excellent way to sell them is to have a yard sale, place an ad in your local paper, or do it online. Yard sales are great if you have a bunch of big and little odds and ends. You can get rid of a lot of things at one time, and have some extra cash in your hands. Placing ads in your local paper works well if you have a few things that are big and expensive. Furniture, for example, will probably fetch a better price if you place an ad and sell it that way. And remember to be honest, that sofa with a purple Kool-Aid stain is *not* in "excellent" condition. If you do any false advertising, it is just a waste of everyone's time—they won't buy it, you won't sell it. Price it honestly, and advertise it honestly.

Selling things online is a whole different thing. I know many people who make a lot of good money doing this. However, before venturing into the wide world of cyber selling, you should probably find some friends or resources that can help you, and make sure that you have the time and the energy to devote to it. I do not sell things online because I do not have the time. Between six kids, two businesses, and homeschooling, I can't run to the post office every other day to mail a package. However, if you do have the time, it would be well worth it. You can often get a better price because you have a larger audience bidding for it, and the money can automatically go directly into your account.

Yard Sale Time

Here are some things to remember when you are going to hold a yard sale:

- Advertise for it. Place a small ad in your local paper, but just include the street and not your personal house address. Otherwise, you will have people sitting in your driveway at 5 am.
- Put lots and lots of colorful posters up (especially at every turn). Make the words big and bold and clearly mark the direction to follow. Put these up the night before so it will be one less thing to worry about that morning.
- Get money to make change a day before the sale. Make sure you have plenty of ones, some fives, and lots of loose change.
- Cash boxes are great if you have someone sitting in front of it at all times. I have better luck with a fanny pack that I can keep strapped on.
- Don't price things unreasonably. You are trying to get rid of stuff, not run a boutique. If it's in good condition, price it at about a quarter of what you paid for it.
- It is easiest to group things by price. Have $1 tables, $2 tables, $5 tables, and so on.
- If you don't have a rack for hanging clothes, then string a clothesline through your garage and hang your clothing on it. It is easier for people to look through hanging clothes than to throw your neatly folded clothes all over the place (and believe me, they will). They will also sell quicker and for a better price.
- Use all of the tables you can find—people don't like to bend over. If you can't find a bunch, set up boards on cement blocks and cover them with blankets.
- Have an electrical outlet handy so that people can plug in your items and make sure they work.
- This is a great opportunity for the kids to earn some extra money selling baked goods and drinks. Encourage them also to sell their belongings (and let them keep the money).

- Don't think that you just have to sell things. You may want to use this opportunity to pass out items. One time we had a huge box of strap-on cow noses that was left over from a promotion. We gave one away to everyone who made a purchase—people thought it was hilarious. And nothing draws a crowd like two adults wearing cow noses! Unless it's two adults wearing nothing but cow noses!
- This is also a great opportunity for you to bless the lives of others. Be quick with a smile and a friendly word or two.

Sweet Charity

The final way to get money for your belongings is to deduct them. I do this more often than anything else. It is quick and easy (two things I consider very important in my life right now). As you put items in your giveaway box or bag write them down on a sheet of paper. I have had two-page lists before! Now when you fill up the box immediately carry it to your car and put it in there. This will empty it from your home, freeing up space. It will also decrease the chances of you scrounging around in it afterward. Take the list that you have completed and stick it in your day planner so that you will have it with you. Next time you are in the area of a charity drop-off center, take in the boxes, show them your list, and get a receipt (how easy is that?). At tax time, you simply price all of the items at approximately a quarter of what you paid or whatever their current value, and deduct it from your taxes as a charitable contribution. If you are in question about the value of your contributions, there are excellent resource books and computer programs that can help you. By doing this, you are blessing others and yourself!

Store Away

In the first laundry basket, throw everything that you love and are not quite ready to part with forever. Some of you may not even need this basket because you are ready to get it out of your life for good. However, for many of you, especially you Starry-Eyed Dreamers, one look at that kitty cat figurine that your daughter painted at her six-year-old ceramics studio birthday party, and your heart just melts. You don't want to part with it, but you need to de-clutter and remove some items. Just stick it in that laundry basket designated for items that you are going to put into storage. I came across this problem recently when I redecorated my living room. I had a beautiful picture that a friend gave me that just did not fit with the current decor. However, I did not want to part with it because I truly loved the picture and knew I would display it in another place at another time. So, into storage it went.

When your basket is full and it is time to go into storage, I want you to do it in a way that will prevent it from getting lost in the deep, dark, dusty, storage abyss. Get sturdy boxes or plastic totes. And if you still have pack-rat tendencies, get a lot of them. There are two ways you can handle your storage. The first way is for those of you who gravitate more to the Mother Hen/MasterMind side. For you people, you also need a small file box and a set of index cards in addition to your boxes.

As you fill up one box, write the contents down on an index card, and try to store like items together if possible. For example, you may want to store hubby's baseball cap collection and his old high school trophies all in one box (unless you're planning on just throwing them out and never telling him). After you have the box loaded and the contents written on an index card, all you need to do is number the card and number the box (big, bold magic marker). This helps when you need to access something. Instead of rummaging through a ton of boxes, all you need to do is glance through your index file and then find the appropriately labeled box.

To make sure you stay on top of it all, a good idea is to schedule a time to go through it at a later date. Go to your calendar, look four months ahead, and write down a date to look at that index card. When you get to that date, read the card, check the contents, and see if there is something that can finally leave your home. By that time, you may have come to an emotional point where you are ready to get rid of those miniature bobble heads.

If this sounds like way too much work, then you may gravitate more toward the Creative Spirit/Starry-Eyed Dreamer side. You need a method that works with you. Dump your stuff in the box, slap a label on the side, seal the lid, and stick it in your basement or attic to deal with the next time you move, or when you feel that you are emotionally ready to weed through it. Not ideal, but realistic. One of my daughters has the softest heart you could ever imagine, and can't bear to part with a single thing. When it comes to managing her corner of the world, she is definitely a Starry-Eyed Dreamer. I remember a few months after our seasonal switch-out of clothes, she had only given away enough of her outgrown clothes to fill a small Barbie suitcase and was faced with drawers that couldn't close and a closet that wouldn't shut. After threatening, cajoling, pleading, and demanding, I finally dragged in a huge plastic box, and wrapped my arms around her as she stood there, evidently upset over the condition of her room and the frustration it was causing.

"Sweetie," I told her, "Why don't you take one drawer at a time, put half of your very favorite clothes back in the drawer, and just throw the rest into this box. We can just store them in here until you want to wear them again. I'll even put a big label on the side with your name on it."

Relief immediately swept over her face.

"You mean I don't need to get rid of them?" she asked.

"No way, baby," I said, "They're yours."

She began to de-clutter her room with a renewed energy. In less than fifteen minutes, she came bounding downstairs.

"Mama," she said, with excitement in her voice. "Come upstairs and see my room!"

I went upstairs, and saw a clean floor, a clean bed, clean drawers, a clean closet, and a huge plastic box with clothes heaped up and spilling over. She looked up at me, as I stood amazed at the transformation, and then said something I'll never forget—"Can't you just feel the fresh air?"

The clutter may be frustrating, perhaps even suffocating you, but somewhere deep inside is a little girl who is not ready to let go. And that's okay. There may be a good reason why you are having difficulty getting rid of things, so instead of fighting it and beating yourself up, be kind. Wrap your arms around that sweet little girl inside, and let her know that she is safe. She doesn't have to hand over her security blanket, not yet, maybe not ever. But she deserves to have her own beautiful space to grow. Just pack it up and place it somewhere else. It still belongs to her, and she can get it anytime she wants. But it's time to give her room to breathe. Her spirit needs to feel the rush of fresh air.

Put Away

As for the other laundry basket, it is going to be for items that you want to keep but need to put away someplace else. For example, if you are de-cluttering a toy chest and you run across your red satin bra, you would toss that in this basket because it obviously belongs somewhere in your closet or bedroom and not in your child's toy chest. And if it does belong in your child's toy chest, then I would definitely keep that information within the family.

After you finish de-cluttering the space, you are then left with a basket full of items that you need to put somewhere else. Whenever I do this, I usually tell each one of the kids to pick out X number of items and put them where they belong. After all, that's why we had kids, right? If you don't believe in slave labor, you can always pay them 5¢ for each item they put away. However, you may want to do some serious consideration before agreeing on a payment schedule. If I paid my kids 5¢ for every item they put away, in a month I would probably need to take out a small loan.

As you are putting items away, you may be confused initially about where they belong in your home. Don't stress yourself out. We will cover more about creating appropriate places for items in the organization chapters. Eventually, if you continue to de-clutter and organize your home, everything will begin to fall into place. For right now, just toss the objects into the basket to put away in another part of the house and use your best judgment as to where they belong.

Tiny Little Chunks

As you begin weeding through your home, you need to go easy on yourself. Take it one little baby step at a time. You did not get into this mess in a day, and you're not going to get out of it in a day. It is going to take time and patience. Remember that you are doing this to create a fresh and new environment for your creative spirit to take flight. There is no room in your life right now for the critic. You know who it is, that evil little monster that follows you around the house muttering things like, "How could you let this house get this way? You are an awful mom— just look at how your kids are living! You will never be able to get this home into shape, so don't even try." I bet you hear his voice a lot, especially if you are like me and try to take on the world. Well, you no longer have room in your life for him. It's time to show the critic the front door, and politely kick him out of it.

You are enough right now, but it is time to allow yourself to have more and be more.

Learning to Let Go

If you are anything like me, then you may be having difficulty getting rid of stuff. That is totally understandable! Whether we realize it or not, holding on to things actually empowers us in one way or another, depending on our personality traits. However, hoarding things becomes unhealthy when it begins to impede upon our time, energy, money, and peace of mind. For example, how much time do you waste searching for matching socks, car keys, old receipts, or even a decent pen to write with? How much energy do you use up taking a trip to the grocery store only to forget some necessary items or implementing an organizing strategy that turns out to be more difficult than the previous bedlam? How much money do you waste running out to the store to buy things that you already have—hand tools that you can't find or a new coat when a perfectly good one is stashed in the attic somewhere? And what about peace of mind? Sure, you have spare batteries and extra fuses, but are they readily at your fingertips when you actually need them?

If any of these predicaments sound familiar to you, then welcome to the club! I dealt with this (and still do) on a daily basis. I would keep magazines around for years because I liked a design idea in it—of course, when I had the opportunity to implement it the magazine was lost somewhere in my household abyss and the idea had slipped right out of my mind. Still, I held on to them—my knee-high stack of magazines. When I started having children, I would hold on to every little piece of artwork that their fingers created—and I mean *every* little piece. This was fine when I had one or two. But more came along, and I soon realized that I had to make some serious changes before our entire family went floating away in a sea of construction paper, glitter, and Popsicle sticks. And I did make changes. I developed strategies that worked with my personality (as I hope they do for you), and took control of the clutter crisis.

So, if you are having trouble letting stuff go, don't beat yourself up about it. Build yourself up. This is vitally important because you will eventually become whatever you believe yourself to be. Before you get out any trash bags, boxes, or baskets, it is imperative that you understand the reason for clearing your home and life of clutter. You deserve the best because you are a wonderful person—believe this with everything in you. If you are stuck in a pool of negativity, then you need to change that thought pattern right now. Find a mantra that you can make completely yours. Write it down. Stick it to your mirror. Repeat it as you are driving down the road. Find some words that speak to your soul and fill you with positive affirmation. Perhaps it could be one of these:

I love myself.

I am fantastic.

I am blessed.

I am a blessing.

My life is wonderful.

Find one and make it your own. A thought pattern can do amazing things. It not only has the power to change you, but also to alter the thoughts of those around you. It works like magic.

There was a famous artist in France during the late 1800s named Henri Rousseau. His art was amazing, but what was even more incredible was his imagination. He would become so wrapped up in his creations that he would actually believe that these imaginary places were real. And his fantasy was infectious. People around him would begin to adopt the same beliefs that he held. His passion was contagious, just as your passion is contagious. It affects you as well as your family and friends. What you believe about yourself and your home will be what everyone around you believes as well. Do you want people to begin treating you with respect? Then respect yourself. Do you want your home to be a loving environment? Then love your home. As you develop belief patterns, those around you will begin to reflect your zeal. Make a decision to be passionate about yourself and your home and your life—today!

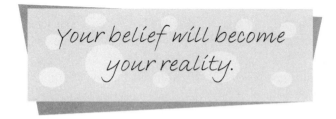

Your belief will become your reality.

Time for Your Prescription

For some of you, reading through all of this talk on clutter is just a walk in the park. You are way ahead of me. You have your holiday decorations stored in matching boxes and there's nothing under your bed. Then there are those of you who, right now, can hardly see the words on the page for all of the critical thoughts in your heads. You figure, why bother? It's such a mess, it would take a gallon of kerosene and a box of matches to clean this place up. Be easy on yourself. It is going to take little steps, but you can do it. Those little steps will put you miles ahead of where you are right now. But most importantly those little steps are teaching you that you deserve better and helping you learn to respect yourself and the home that you live in.

Rx for MasterMinds

Now it's time to start stretching that creative muscle a little bit here. Look around at the items that you use in your kitchen and come up with one design solution that will increase the convenience of preparing food, but make it something a bit more animated than you are used to. It may be to take all of your big wooden spoons out of the drawer and place them in a skinny metal bucket beside the stove. Now try the same thing with your office desk. Do you need something to hold all of the in and out mail that crosses your desk? Instead of two trays, why not try something different, like an open tool box? What about something clever to hold your pens and pencils? Don't go with the same ho-hum pencil holder. Look around and find something a bit unconventional for your taste—a little flowerpot? A miniature beach pail? It's a stretch, but you can do it. Check out the aisles in stores for items that share the same characteristics as the ones you need, but are a bit on the whimsical side.

Rx for Creative Spirits

How many things have you purchased to make your life easier? Do those work-out DVDs really give you firm abs? Does that new mop really cut your mopping time in half? Before you reach for something to throw in the cart, ask yourself if you are buying this to make you think you are closer to reaching a goal rather than actually helping you reach it. You are constantly looking for ways to cut corners. Unfortunately, a lot of these products are just sitting around making you serve them rather than serve you. Before you read the next chapter, go through your cleaners and pick out the few that you actually use and get rid of the rest. Don't beat yourself up about the waste. You've been wasting too much of your life allowing it to intrude and make you feel guilty. You also need to go through your software (including your children's software) and do the same thing. If you get so compelled, all of those lotions and potions that you have tucked away in your bathroom are waiting for the same weeding out process. You probably already know if that anticellulite cream works or not.

Rx for Mother Hens

You love to start projects around the house, but every now and then you bite off a little more than you can chew. You get something up and running, and then your life pulls you begrudgingly in another direction. Before you know it, that project you started is just sitting on the back shelf, hollering at you every time you pass by. You need to reward yourself for the effort, shut the door on the project, and realize you always have the option to open it up at a later date. Find one thing sitting around nagging at you. It could be some curtains you started sewing but never finished or perhaps that mosaic tiled mirror. You bought all the stuff to make it, but never began the project. My suggestion? Pack it up. Label the box. Forget about it. The day will come when you're shuffling around the house in your plaid robe and terrycloth bedroom slippers with your reading glasses in one hand and a cup of Metamucil in the other, wondering how to pass the time until *Hollywood Squares* comes on. You can always get that box out then and continue on your project. After all, you will need something to do with your time. So, consider packing up some home projects as insurance against making your son leave work to drive you to Target to pick up the foot massager that you saw advertised on TV.

Rx for Starry-Eyed Dreamers

I know you don't want to part with the clutter. But, what good is it doing for you sitting on that shelf? You don't have to drop-kick it out of the front door just yet. Of course, if you are ready to, by all means, put on your kicking shoes and pump up the volume. If you're not, then at least put it away. Try the storage box technique to begin clearing your area and clearing your mind. Pack them up in a box, label them with a corresponding index card, and store it. But, please, don't forget to go back at a later date. I think once you realize how well you did without it, you will be more than happy to toss it permanently. Of course, if you can't get yourself to toss it, then just store it away for a rainy day. Those elementary school yearbooks may come in handy when they want to feature you on a VH1 special.

Dream On!

Here's how we are going to halt the biting words of the critic in your mind. Open up your dream journal to a nice, clean sheet and let the wheels of your mind begin turning. Of course, if you're like me, you can't ever make them stop. I love the way some people so blithely tell others to "let their mind go blank." This is absolutely impossible for me. I remember in yoga class, the pretzel twist while balancing on my little toe was no problem. But the meditation? That was excruciating! The yogi would say, "Now exhale all thoughts from your mind, and let it go completely blank." I would concentrate so hard on trying to empty my mind that I would tense up all over! So, forget the pressure. The mind is always active—encourage it! With a pencil, pen, or incredible colored marker, begin to make a list on the paper of all of the words your critic mutters to you. I have no shame, even at times when I probably should. So I will share some of my list with you. Things that come to my mind are:

I'm a lazy homeschool teacher.

I don't finish half the projects that I start around the house.

I don't exercise enough.

I don't keep up with the laundry.

If you will make the list, you will also discover where your sensitivities lie. Your critic already knows this, that's why he goes after your soft spots. Evidently, my sensitive areas are homeschooling, housekeeping, and my body.

Now, here's how we are going to shut that critic up! Turn the page, and find an even more incredible colored marker. Now, take that list you came up with, and you are going to attack it one item at a time. Look at the first thing your critic told you, and try to step outside of yourself and look at it realistically (it helps if you pretend you are just one of your friends, or even get a close friend to help you).

Now write down from the voice of realism something positive to turn that statement around. For example, "I'm a lazy homeschool teacher" can be turned around to "My kids are smart, confident, happy, and well educated." "I don't finish half the projects that I start around the house" can be turned into "I am creative and brave enough to see opportunities and take action." I can turn "I don't exercise enough" into "I run up and down the stairs a few times during the day" (okay, that one was a bit pathetic). But anyway, you get the idea! Now get crackin'! Down with the critic!

Chapter 5

Methods to Tame the Madness

Here we go. Now you know why you need to get rid of the clutter. You know how you get rid of the clutter. But it's time to get a little deeper. For many of us, we are accustomed to letting the clutter come into our homes without making it leave. Clutter management is a balancing act. You let some stuff come in, and then you push some stuff back out. Just letting it pour into your life without opening up the outlets to let it pour out is living out of balance. It's like going to IHOP and ordering a Root 'n' Tooty, Fresh 'n' Fruity but hold the "Fresh." You want your home and your life to be fresh and balanced—not just a bunch of roots, toots, and fruits. And if you have a lot of little ones running around, then you probably already have your fair share of toots. Manage the clutter by keeping what comes in and what goes out in balance.

But change is never easy, and going from accumulating to paring down can be quite an adjustment. But there are some key methods for taming the clutter beast that work with your personality. Some methods will work better because they play right into your style. And just like anything in life, progress is a matter of discipline. You need to discipline yourself into turning some of these methods into habits that you practice daily. At first, it could be extremely difficult. For some of you, it may be going against everything you have ever known in life. Be patient, be disciplined, and be determined. You deserve the peace and comfort of a de-cluttered life. But it's up to you. Let some of that "fresh" flow into your life.

> *Empty space is often slammed full of creative thought and positive energy.*

The Positive Side of Negative Space

Many of us are constantly tempted to fill empty space. Whether it is an empty wall, an empty corner, or even an empty day. We fill it with stuff—good stuff, bad stuff, it doesn't matter, as long as it is filled. I want to encourage you to appreciate the beauty of negative space. Some of the best art in the world is a study of negative space. In Van Gogh's *Starry Night,* we are taken by the beauty of a night sky, not by the clutter of homes in the village below. The famous painting, *Christina's World* by Andrew Wyeth has an incredible impact because of how the artist uses the negative space of an enormous wheat field and a clear white sky to communicate a feeling of expansiveness. The use of negative space can create very positive emotions. It gives us room to stretch, grow, and dream.

See your home as an art form. Look around and see how much room you have allocated to negative space. The eyes need a place to rest every now and then. And the spirit needs room to breathe and relax. Look in your cabinet. Are there cups piled on top of cups? Do you really drink from them all? How relaxing would it feel to open up the cabinet and find neat rows of the finest cups that you own? And what about your closet? Is it a pleasure to open up the door and find neat rows of the clothes that you love and wear regularly? Ready to whip off the hanger and make you feel magnificent? Or does it deplete your energy just glancing at all of the junk that is stuffed in there—dresses that are out of style, shoes scuffed and thrown all over the floor, clothes that you will be able to wear "someday" (Just between you and me—I have found that when I finally do fit in them, they are grievously out of style.).

The first method to taming the madness is having the reason and the will to do it. And sometimes the beauty and impact of negative space is reason enough.

*Negative space allows energy
to move throughout your home
and your life.*

If you don't believe, try it for yourself. Take one shelf in any closet in your home. Pull everything out, sort through it and find out what you can give away or throw away. If it is really cluttered, try to get rid of about one-fourth of it all. Then put it all back neatly. Don't get caught up in the whole closet, just do that one shelf. Now step back, take a deep breath, and assess how it makes you feel. Can you feel the energy flowing just a little better? Can you feel your spirit stretch just a little farther? Now imagine if your entire home flowed like that. It can happen. But like I said earlier, it takes reason and will. You have a reason. Now let's work on the will.

Put the Emotion in Motion

Oh, you Starry-Eyed Dreamers out there—I understand your struggles. You take one look at something and your heart just melts. I can hear you now, "I could never throw that away. It was Jeffrey's first picture of a house with four windows. All of the other ones he drew only had two." Let me just put it this way—most of us keep way more than we will ever be able to appreciate. And when we do hold on to too much, we can't appreciate what we have. It's like fudge—a few pieces and you're in hog heaven. Half a pan and you're sick as a dog.

Many things come into our lives with positive emotion attached to them. It could be a painting our child did or a card from a dear friend. When we receive them, they give us nice warm feelings. Because of this positive emotion, we have a tendency to hold on to them, hoping for that warm feeling again. Some items do give us those warm feelings over and over again. But some items—we never look at again. The problem is, many times we refuse to part with any of it. Then the items that no longer fill a need in our lives leave them congested so that we are

> *Store tokens of affection in your heart, not in stacks, drawers, bags, and boxes.*

unable to benefit from the items that still do. A good example is cards and letters. If we kept every piece of paper that someone sent us, we would never be able to appreciate the letters and cards that we will look back on later. See the gesture for what it was—a token of love and friendship. Instead of piling it in a box somewhere, file it in your heart. Let it serve its purpose by strengthening your relationship with that person instead of cluttering your life.

R-E-S-P-E-C-T

By saving too much we also don't treat the few things that really matter in our lives with the respect that they deserve. Can you quickly locate the beautiful pictures of your children that you took last Thanksgiving? Are they preserved and well displayed? What about the video that you taped of that first soccer game? Is it labeled and stored appropriately? When they are stuck away in a box somewhere with a pile of other junk that we will never look at again, they are not being respected or appreciated. Cut away the clutter and then the things that you truly hold dear will once again be able to serve a purpose in your life.

Our children's schoolwork and artwork is a perfect example of saving so much of something, that we lose our appreciation for it. If we truly respect something, we give it a special place with special meaning. Sometimes it's extremely difficult to part with the good stuff so that we can keep the best stuff. But it is imperative that we do so if we are ever going to truly respect and appreciate what we have. Enjoy your finest possessions and your most precious memories. Treasure these by focusing on them and letting the rest go. Keep those few perfect sweaters, and pass along the ones that you never wear. Capture the essence of your child's accomplishments by archiving a sampling of artwork and schoolwork and tossing the rest out. Respect the beautiful furniture you have by building a room around those special pieces and getting rid of the items that are just taking up valuable space.

> *Let your memories enrich your life instead of congest it.*

Let's start treating those things that matter in our lives as they deserve to be treated. Let the kids enjoy looking back at their artwork by weeding through it all and saving the pieces that really mean something. Otherwise, it will all be lost in the clutter. Let's start appreciating the precious cards and letters we receive by keeping the few that warm our hearts or put a smile on our faces when we look back at them. Otherwise, we will never get that opportunity. The pictures, the videos, the memorabilia, the keepsakes—weed through them so that you can fully appreciate them.

Get in Missile Mode

My mother was famous for this. She was affectionately nicknamed the "cruise mis-sile." Whenever she had a goal to meet, she would zero in on her target and nothing could veer her off her pathway. One of us kids could be pinned under a car and she would chirp, "Let me finish bringing in the groceries and I'll give you a hand." Okay, maybe she wasn't that bad. But she certainly has this principle down pat. And that's probably how she manages to accomplish so much (Hey, she was able to raise me, and that was no easy task). Getting in missile mode will help you tremendously. You will reach your goals, set new strides, and accomplish more than you imagined you could. Missiles reach their targets. They don't get distracted and they don't stop until they have accomplished their missions.

If you don't realize it by now, distractions are a way of life. If you don't believe me then get on the phone with a good friend and see how many times one of your kids comes in the room needing immediate help (usually having to do with blood, throw up, or torn clothing). My kids seem to have an internal sensor to detect when I am on the phone (especially if it is an important business call). I remember one afternoon I had scheduled a call with the processing facility that manufactures my baby spa products. I had just finished milling some wheat for bread, the entire house was quiet, and I assumed it was a safe window to make my call (That was my first mistake). So I settled down in the dining room to discuss things like unit prices, delivery times, and raw supplies. I was five minutes into the conversation when my two-year-old wandered into the kitchen and turned on the grain mill that was sitting on the counter. If you have not heard an electric grain mill, just imagine standing on the runway as a 747 takes off. This deafening noise pierced the solitude in the house as my toddler came running out of the kitchen with eyes as big as saucers and a cloud of flour following him. Needless to say, the conversation was cut short. Anyway, I was laughing too hard to discuss anything serious.

Distractions are a part of life, and you've got to learn to roll with them (and laugh at them as well). That's why it is so important to get in missile mode. Focus on your task, and keep it at the front of your mind even when you get distracted from it. Missiles can change directions and bypass objects on their way to hitting their targets. And unless you are trying to hit Maverick in his Top Gun fighter jet, missile mode will ensure that you hit the target (we all know that if he slams on the breaks, it will fly right by).

The Attraction of Distraction

When you get in missile mode, you have to realize that you are going to veer off target every once in a while. The goal is to get back on as soon as possible. All too often one distraction leads to another distraction leads to another distraction. Before we know it, we forgot what we were doing in the first place! Now there's no way you can ignore a skinned knee or spilled juice. It's just a part of life. Homemaking is one career that has very little parameters in the way of structure. We have to be ready to fill any need that arises at any given moment. For this reason, it is vital to build structure as much as possible. So the first step to reduce the number of distractions is to structure the task at hand so that you are not inviting even more distractions.

One of the most important steps to structuring your tasks is to set realistic goals. Don't try to take advantage of little Suzy playing with her dollhouse to start cleaning out the pantry. You are going to get halfway through one shelf and Suzy is going to fall out of love with the dollhouse. She is going to want a snack, want a new toy, or just want a little attention from you. And you? You are going to get frustrated, abandon the task, or try to speed up the process and make a bigger mess than before. If it was me, I would probably try to hurry up so that I can finish the job and in my haste spill a pound of dry spaghetti noodles and drop an entire jar of kalamata olives. You don't want that. The smell lingers for days!

Take my advice, and set realistic goals. If Suzy is playing with her doll-house, now may be a good opportunity to clean out one shelf in your kitchen cabinets. You may want to start on the pantry, but that would require too much time. However, a shelf is a good step and you will be left feeling energized and pleased with your accomplishment. If you try this for a while, you can get pretty good at judging the time span of certain tasks. For example, one child sitting on the potty learning to go poop equals two shelves in your bathroom medicine cabinet. One boy playing Star Wars with a neighborhood friend equals yesterday's mail or until one boy gets poked in the side with a light saber. One husband watching a football game equals four garages, two attics, and everything under your child's bed. Okay, you get the point. Judge your tasks and grab them at the appropriate times.

Clear the Playing Field

Another key to being in missile mode is to begin your de-cluttering projects when there are no other ones lying around begging for your attention. If you are face to face with a big fat stack of holiday decorations that need to be put away, it is not the time to start going through your old photos. You are going to keep looking at those decorations and the scrapbook is going to get one measly picture in it before you abandon it. Sort through the decorations and put them away, clear your thoughts, and then you can sit down and devote some time to your pictures. Clear the kitchen counter before you begin making dinner. Put away baby's laundry before you sort through her clothes to find out what she has outgrown. Beginning a project while there are a million other ones lying around is just asking for a distraction. They are like little whiny children begging for attention. They are impossible to ignore, and before you know it you're going to be going

A missile always hits its target eventually, so fire away.

around wiping their snotty little noses, going nowhere fast. Tend to the distractions before they have the opportunity to distract you, then you can begin your project.

The Complete Picture

The last step to being in missile mode is to form habits of completion. This is a hard one to learn for many of us, but it is one of the most useful steps to maintaining a calm and de-cluttered home. When a task is begun, make a conscious effort to complete it. This may at first appear to be common sense, but we often abandon tasks without even realizing it. You may have some forms to be filed and you stack them on top of the filing cabinet instead of taking the extra effort to open it up and file them away, or the shopping bags get placed by the back door on your way into the house instead of being emptied and put away. Completing a task is not something that just comes naturally to many of us because we often choose the path of least resistance. Although finishing a task completely will give us less work and less confusion in the long run, we often don't see the big picture until it is tumbling down around us.

It takes a conscious effort, a physical push, to continue the effort until the task is completely done. Think of it as repeating a mantra over and over—complete it, complete it, complete it. You have to have the determination to be your own dominatrix. And you have my permission to wear a black leather bustier with thigh-high boots. I wouldn't bring the whip out until hubby gets home and the kids are asleep in bed. But whatever works, use it. You're going to have to ride your own back until the form is filed away or the shopping bag is emptied. I will often catch myself placing an empty cup on the counter instead of putting it in the sink, and will have to ride myself to take the extra step necessary. I will dump laundry on my bed and my inner dominatrix will have to give me a kick so that I just spend the extra few minutes folding it all up. It will seem like a pain at first, but change is never easy. But it is so worth it!

Five a Day

No I'm not talking about fruits and vegetables, that's another book. This is one of my favorite steps to de-cluttering a home because it is so easy (and the kids actually think it's pretty fun, too). It's a tiny step. But just like all small steps, when you

> *Once you start clearing out the clutter, the process takes on a power of its own.*

do it everyday, you will be shocked at how quickly the clutter begins disappearing. Once you start practicing this method, it practically becomes addictive. And that's just what you want it to become—a habit. So, are you ready for this one? Five a day means finding five items that you want to throw away and five items that you want to give away—every day! Do you think I'm crazy? Well, yes, I am, but that's not up for dispute. When you begin to let go of items that you no longer need or want, you will be surprised at the stuff that you have hidden away in the nooks and crannies of your home. The kids enjoy this one, too. We set a time limit, put on some music and every one has to find at least two items—one for each give-away or throwaway bag. It's a blast! Okay, so maybe we don't get out much.

But try this one out and watch the clutter leave out your front door. Whenever you have a minute (and it really takes just a minute), grab two bags and throw five things that you can give away in one and five things that you can toss in the trash in another. Throw the trash in the can outside, and throw the giveaway bag in the back of your car to leave at the local charity drop-off center. This is so easy. For example, when you're putting on makeup, find five old items of makeup that you can throw away (Think old mascara and that hideous shade of blush that makes you look like a walking apricot). Now look through your cabinet and find five things you can part with (Think of that "Where's the Party?" beach towel that you've had since spring break back in college, and those butterfly clips that were only meant for women who are young enough to know Batman as George Clooney and not Adam West in his sexy blue tights).

Start the Momentum

Sometimes you're sitting there, looking around your house, and you just don't know where to begin. Relax. It's not so important to know *where* to begin as it is to know when to begin. And the when is right now. So, if you are going to get your home de-cluttered, one of the most important methods to employ is just to

> *You can stew on it, fret on it, complain about it, attempt to escape it—or just do something about it.*

get up and get started. For many of you, it's going to go against every hair on your head to just take action. But the talking and the planning and the wishing and the willing can only go so far. There eventually comes a time when you need to put feet to your dreams if you are going to get anywhere. The best way to get moving is to avoid looking at the entire task to be completed. If you need to clean out the garage, then for Pete's sake, don't look at the entire garage. Look at the garden tools—that's it, no more. If you set out to do the whole garage, then you will probably never get started. As a matter of fact, you may have a coronary just thinking about it. Don't think about it. Just pick one task and start.

Momentum has a way of working in our favor, but it is up to us to start it. You will probably get a lot more accomplished than just the garden tools, because as you begin to see the results of your efforts, you won't want to abandon the task. Put energy and effort toward reaching a manageable goal, and watch the fruits of your labor ripen before your very eyes. Don't set out to paint an entire room, just tell yourself that you are going to start on one wall. Before you know it, you're done. Don't sort through your entire closet, just do your sweaters. Before you know it, you have sorted through your sweaters, your dresses, and your shoes in the time that you allotted to just do the sweaters. It works. Trust me. A little bit of energy applied toward a goal has the ability to multiply the effects. In no time at all, you will have the job done in the time it would have taken you to surf through some channels and find something decent on TV. Actually, in the time it would take you to find something decent on TV, you could probably do your entire home!

Set a Timer

At first, this may appear to be something that you would only do in your child's preschool class, but if it works for the little ones, it will work for us, too. One reason that we may not get as much accomplished during the day is because we overestimate the time that it takes to get things done. Try this little exercise. Get all of your supplies ready to do a routine task around the house, such as wash dishes or mop the floor. When you are ready to perform the task, check to see what time it is. Now when the job is finished (not counting the interruptions, please), check to see what time it is again. You will probably surprise yourself. Setting a timer compels us to begin taking action, it gives us a stopping point, and the "tick, tick, tick" doesn't hurt either. It's like a race—you against the machine (In our fantasies we can be anything, even James Bond pushing a vacuum and sorting lights from darks.).

Setting a timer will also help if you cannot get motivated to start on a project. When you know that you are going to be working for fifteen minutes and that's it, it's easy to open up that storage cabinet and start weeding through your stuff. Try weeding through the kitchen cabinets for fifteen minutes (ugly dishes, Christmas mugs you never use, that sandwich cooker that just sits there gathering dust). Then when the timer goes off, immediately move to your living room for another fifteen minutes (framed pictures that you can put into storage, that potpourri that no longer has a scent, those ugly coasters). Next comes your bedroom for another fifteen minutes (figurines that are just there to clean around, that candle you never light, the silk plant with leaves that are now gray from all of the dust). Now when the timer goes off this time, take a break for the last fifteen minutes. Sit back, kick your legs up and enjoy a light snack or good book. Just trust me on this. Give yourself that one hour of time and use a timer to help motivate you. You will be pleasantly surprised at the results.

What Goes In Must Go Out

This is a good one, and it really helps us keep a check on how much stuff we have the tendency to accumulate in our homes. Plus, it's super simple, which we can all use a little more of. The trick is, whenever you bring anything new into your home, get rid of an older one before you store it away. For example, if you buy a new blouse, get rid of an old one before you hang it in your closet. If you buy a new CD, find one you can pass along before you add the new one to your collection. If you buy some pots and pans, pass along some old ones. It's so simple, and it works so well. You can even turn this into a habit by putting an old item in the shopping bag as soon as you take the new one out. This way, all you have to do is switch out the contents and then take the bag out to the car to drop off at a local charity. See? I told you it was simple.

You Can't Bless Yourself

We're on the road now, letting go and paring down. There is a big difference between a life that is full and a life that is all filled up. You are clearing off your canvas so that you can create your beautiful masterpiece of a home. But there is one more thing that you need to understand. You cannot bless yourself. You can embrace yourself. You can love yourself. You can enrich yourself. But you cannot bless yourself. A blessing is a supernatural event, a miraculous occurrence that we cannot plan or predict. It is a result of opening up and letting go, and it can only exist beyond our reach. A blessing is received, never taken. And when you try so hard to fill up your life with stuff, you leave no room for the miraculous.

It takes trust—a belief that God is good and that He wants to love you and bless you immensely. Once we understand this amazing spiritual truth, we can begin to let go and know innately that more will pour back in (and in more wonderful ways than we could anticipate). It is as tried and true as the theory of gravity, but with a twist. What we pour out of our lives comes right back to us—but in larger proportions than our current lives can encompass. Our lives begin to grow and expand as our willingness to let go increases. We can try and try to fill our lives, but our lives will truly not be full until it comes from the hands of God. So give away, pass along, fill needs, and step back and watch a miracle occur.

Many artists will speak about feeling possessed or taken over by a powerful force while they are in the throes of creating a masterpiece. Instead of being the artist, they feel as if they are more of a channel for a creative spirit that is greater than they are. Perhaps that is what art is all about. It is about opening up and letting go so that a greater force can work a miracle through you. You are a miracle! And a masterpiece is being created through your life. Pour yourself out so that the blessings can pour in.

Time for Your Prescription

Rx for MasterMinds

You are extremely skilled with strategy development. You can look at the big picture, and be able to work out a strategy to accomplish it. Use this skill to your advantage. Break large projects down into the bite-size chunks that you feel more comfortable with, and start eating away. Develop the strategy, but don't dwell on it. Set the small tasks that you need to do, and then begin taking action. As you do accomplish the smaller goals, remember to practice "what goes in must go out," so that you won't feel overwhelmed. Also remember to keep lists of your giveaway items for tax-deductible purposes. You can come up with a good strategy for organizing this—perhaps a sheet of paper that you keep in your day planner or glove compartment. Also, when you begin to de-clutter, a strategy that may work well for you is to take one room at a time, break the entire room down into a list of small projects, and set a goal to do one of these projects every day.

Rx for Creative Spirits

You need more room for your creative spirit to soar. But you need to create it. It will probably be necessary to set certain parameters for you to follow so that you can get some stuff done around the house. For example, try setting a timer to get yourself going. Also, you are really going to have to ride yourself. Remind yourself to finish your job completely so that you won't be creating more work for yourself later. A strategy that may work well for you is to get dressed for the part—all the way down to your socks and shoes. And remember to have all of your supplies on hand. This will ground you and get you focused on the task at hand. This may seem a little peculiar at first, but trust me here. If you set the stage and assume the role, then you are less likely to get lost somewhere in the dressing room.

Rx for Mother Hens

You have the ability to manage clutter pretty well. But make sure you remember that clutter is not just the stuff that you can box up and stick in the attic. Sometimes, you can clutter up your life with far too many obligations and responsibilities. You take pride in the fact that people depend on you, but sometimes you need to be enough for yourself as well. Try to focus on cutting back on some of the clutter in your life. You don't always need to fill up the empty spots. Sometimes, the empty spots can be the biggest blessing of all. Before you take on a new position or make a new purchase, ask yourself if you are allowing room for miracles in your life. Are you cramming it too full for anything else to flow in? Repeat after me—"I am enough. I do enough. I have enough." Managing clutter in your life is the same as managing clutter in your home. You've got to learn to let go of the *good* obligations so that you can make room for the *best* ones.

Rx for Starry-Eyed Dreamers

Parting is such sweet sorrow, isn't it? I feel for you sweetie, and I wish I were there to give you a great big hug and help you sort through all of that precious memorabilia of yours. We could share a pot of coffee and just make a day out of it! But, don't fret. Go ahead and brew a pot, because I know that there is the desire in you for clear, uncluttered space, and you have the ability to make it happen. Don't overwhelm yourself with five shoe boxes of old photos. Instead, just tackle one manageable stack at a time. Try doing five a day. That way you don't feel so threatened by the thought of getting rid of everything all at once. A good strategy for you may be to ask yourself these questions when you pick up every little piece—"Does it make me smile?" (Go ahead and put it in the save pile). "Have I looked at it within the past two years?" (You may want to think about trashing it, unless it is a very special keepsake). "Do I have a place for it?" (Create a spot if you don't). "Will I be just as happy as I am today without it hanging around?" (Chances are, you will, so get rid of it).

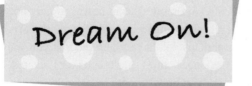 

Are you ready to go shopping? Put away your credit cards and get out your imagination (and your dream journal). Now, bring out all of those catalogs that you hold on to. You know the ones I'm talking about. They are probably covered with drool marks, or the pages are so dog-eared that they look like one of those Christmas trees I used to make as a kid. My mom used to hand me a huge catalog and say, "I bet if you fold every one of these pages into a triangle, you could make a beautiful Christmas tree!" (Translation: "If you don't sit still for a few minutes, one of us is going to need to be tranquilized.") Well, don't start folding pages and getting into the holiday spirit just yet. Instead, you are going to find all of those beautiful things that make your eyes glaze over with lust. Cut them out and glue them into your dream book. Maybe it is a beautiful bed or a gorgeous leather skirt. Across the top of one of the pages I want you to write a positive affirmation such as, "I deserve the finest things in life." You need to believe this about yourself because it is so true. You are a superior woman, and you deserve superior things. But before any of these things can come into your life, you need to have a superior attitude.

This imagination shopping is your incentive to begin clearing out all of the clutter from your home. Can you imagine that beautiful bed in your current bedroom? What would need to be cleared out in order to give this gorgeous item the appropriate atmosphere? How about that leather skirt? Could you really imagine it hanging in your closet among the worn jumpers and out-of-date belts? Start clearing out the space in anticipation of these items in your life. Sell the old furniture and earmark that money for the purchase of the new bed. Add up the deduction you can take for those clothes you donate and start a fund for that fabulous leather skirt. As you are preparing their homes, keep looking back in your dream book, anticipating their arrival. And if you do drool, just wipe it off before you shut the book. It will make the pages stick together (not that I've ever done that, of course).

Whatever you do, don't strain yourself financially to purchase these items. Give it a good long time. As you mature and develop emotionally, you will find that your tastes change dramatically. Six months from now, you may not want that bed anymore because, with all of the clutter and mess gone, your room is exactly the way you want it. Or perhaps you have found out that you want something better instead. I remember saving pictures of a home that I wanted. I thought about it, dreamed about it, even bought some holiday decorations in anticipation of being in it. When we finally found the perfect house that fit that description, I realized I didn't want it anymore. I had started a business, and decided that I wanted to stay where I was so that I could put more mental and financial energy into getting the business off of the ground. You never know where your blessed path will lead you.

Part 3

Organize It!

Chapter 6

Why Organize?

The Big O—Organization

As contrary to popular opinion as it may be, organization does not mean that you have matching bins in every closet with cute little labels adhered to them. Let it be known that on the average day, my home does not look like it stepped out of the pages of *Real Simple* magazine. As a matter of fact, it usually looks more like the "what's wrong with this picture?" page in *Highlights* magazine. What few people understand is that organization is not about bins, boxes, folders, or labels. Organization is about systems that work. And organization has very little to do with cleanliness. A home that at first may appear to be messy, could very well be quite organized. The difference is the underlying system of the home's operation. An organized system is one in which everything has a place, and you can locate items when the need arises. That's all there is to it. However, the place that you give your things, and how you go about locating them is completely up to you (I smell personality entering the plot.) And no matter what your home's style, size, or activity level, it is important that it be organized. Why? Well, have a seat, while I get out my soapbox.

Organization Reduces Your Stress Level

I know what it's like to feel stressed out. You're running late to karate practice, the baby has leaked out of her diaper, your two-year-old dumps a shoeful of sand onto the carpet, your daughter has lost the scrunchie that matches her top, you can't find your keys, a weird noise is coming from the washing machine (that you just bought), and you haven't even eaten breakfast yet. If you are anything like the millions of other women out there who constantly juggle the responsibilities of managing a home, then you know that there is absolutely nothing consistent about the job. You can set your schedules and time lines, but the reality of home soon hits you. You have to be ready to swing at whatever pitch you're given. Some days go as smoothly as Sade singing in a smoky lounge. Then there are those days that more likely resemble Pee Wee Herman over a Wal-Mart intercom. We need to know how to take the situation we are given and run with it.

On the inside of my kitchen cabinet, I keep a little corkboard where I post items that I often need for reference. Right smack-dab in the middle of all the phone numbers and schedules, is a piece of paper that reads, "Never give up. Never surrender." I'm not saying that our home resembles a war zone, but there are some days that feel as if I am fighting with my last line of defense and some-one replaced all of my artillery with Tinkertoys. By being organized, you are ready for those days. Organization makes the chaotic days easier and fewer. And ten to one, whenever a tough day rears its ugly head, it is almost always a result of disorganization.

Lack of organization can keep you living in chaos. If you are attempting to manage a home, then the last thing you need is more chaos. Take the situation that I gave you earlier. If you are running on schedule early (which I highly rec-ommend), then the chances of being late are slim to none. Now, I know, some-times running late is unavoidable. There are those days when the dog poops all

Make room for joy in your life by getting rid of the stress that is hogging the space.

over the new rug in the living room, but on closer inspection of your "potty-trained" child you realize it was not the dog. Poop happens, and it always seems to happen right as you are walking out the door, and there is nothing you can do about it. You cannot predict these things. Therefore, you should always make it a habit to be early. More often than not, running late is a result of a disorganized home and a disorganized schedule. Being organized will usually get you out of the door in plenty of time.

The two-year-old dumping sand onto the carpet usually doesn't happen if he knows that his shoes should come off immediately when he enters the house. Your daughter's scrunchie and your car keys would not be lost if there was a place for everything and everything was in its place. You wouldn't be worried about your washing machine because you have the receipt filed away somewhere. And breakfast would have already been on the table if you got up on time and your schedule was organized. And these "smooth as a mochaccino latte frappe" days can actually happen—and more often than once every lunar cycle.

Living in an organized manner may at first appear time consuming, but it actually saves enormous amounts of time. It takes less time to prevent your battles then to fight them all day long. Do yourself and your emotional health a favor and start today to organize your home and your life. Getting up thirty minutes earlier than usual to organize one small aspect of your home will do wonders for your stress level, and will also set the tone for the entire day.

Organization Saves Time

Like I said earlier, being organized saves enormous amounts of time. All home managers could use a little more time in the day to get stuff accomplished. Organizing does just that. It lets you do more stuff in less time. Think about all the time it takes to look for lost items, backtrack your steps, or repeat your efforts. Sometimes when I am preparing food and my kitchen is disorganized, I will repeat steps two or three times without even realizing it. For example, a bowl is dirty, but the sink is full of dishes. I may move it to the sink, then move it to the counter to clean out the sink, then move it over to another counter because I need that counter space to do another task, then I may move it back to the sink to wash. What a waste of time and effort! On the other hand, if I keep an organized kitchen while I prepare a meal, I can get some food in the oven and toss together a few side dishes in record time. Your time is too valuable to spend it in fruitless

> *You have better things to do with your time than to spend it in chaos.*

effort. Think about all you could be doing with that extra time—play with your children, run for office, take bagpipe lessons!

You may not even be aware of how many times you repeat efforts or backtrack your steps as a result of disorganization. How many times do you pick up that pile of mail to go through, set it down, then pick it up again? How many times do you run in a room to get something and then forget what it was you needed? How many times do you get in the car, start down the driveway, then have to run back in the house because you forgot your purse, the grocery list, or your children (now that's bad)? If you have any or all of these symptoms, you may be suffering from a condition known as "runningincirclosis," and as far as I know the only medication you can take for it is a hefty dose of organization. Even if there were medication, it would probably cause heinous side effects— cramping, bloating, flatulence (but only in public), singing "Ave Maria" in Korean, chewing on your husband's socks, and wearing your bra on the outside of your shirt. I think if I were you, I would just put an end to the situation and get organized.

Organization Saves Space

Just as being organized lets you do more stuff in less time, it also lets you keep more stuff in less space. And speaking from the viewpoint of the old woman who lived in a shoe, there is definitely a premium on space. Very frequently, when we allow our homes to become disorganized, we do it layer by layer. When seasons change, we just layer new clothes on top of the old. When we buy groceries, we layer the items on top of the ones we already have stored away. We buy new jewelry and layer it on top of stuff that is no longer in style. This can carry on for years and years until we are so surrounded with layers that it takes a pickax and an excavation kit just to get to the bottom of it all. A geologist could come in our homes and document our entire family histories just by slicing off fragments of the layers. Sometimes we let the layers build up until we have no idea what is tucked away underneath it all. We lose items or forget about them entirely. There is a flathead screwdriver somewhere in that storage shed, but you can't seem to find it anywhere. What do you do? Just buy another one and layer it on top.

By pulling the layers apart and separating them into the items that we currently use and love and the items that need to be stored or tossed, we not only realize what we already have, but we also make the best use of the space that is available in our homes. Imagine opening up a dresser drawer and finding only the clothes that you love and wear tucked neatly away. All you have to do is reach in and pull out anything and you will be happy with your choice—no digging or shoving. And you won't have to spend time modeling in front of a full-length mirror asking your husband if the outfit makes you look fat. And between you and me, are you really looking for an honest answer?

Organization Is Aesthetically Appealing

People spend so much money on items to make their homes prettier—beautiful curtains, fancy candleholders, new furniture. Sometimes, the best beauty makeover a house could ever receive is a good cleaning and organizing (and it's a lot cheaper, too). Think of how heavy your spirit feels when your floor is so full of clutter that you can't even see the carpet. And think of how light your spirit feels when everything is put away and organized. If there was one step you could take to make your home more beautiful and inviting, it would be organizing. When your home is organized, dust doesn't look nearly as dusty and the curtains don't look nearly as dated. When we toss out the junk and neatly organize our finest things in coordinated containers—now that's a turn-on! If my husband had

Your home can be the perfect marriage of beauty and function.

any idea what organization does for me, he would be moonlighting at the Container Store.

Organizing has also come a lot further than when I was first setting up house. Back then (when dinosaurs roamed the earth), the lines were very defined between organizing and beautifying. Some products helped make your home more organized and other products helped make your home more beautiful. But they were rarely one in the same. Today, we have an entire industry that has blurred the lines between organization and beauty. Closets are frequently just as beautiful as the bedroom. Items that help organize your kitchen or office are designed to match your decor. Beautiful wooden and paper boxes are perfectly sized to match the items you are storing. Yes, beauty and function can fall in love and live happily ever after.

Organization Keeps You Prepared

We all know that the only thing about life that stays the same is its ability to change. No matter how well we plan and schedule, the unexpected will always spring up on us. Your dishwasher leaks all over the kitchen floor, an ice storm sweeps through your town, your flight is canceled. By being organized, you are ready to roll with the punches. You have the plumber's number ready and waiting, you have emergency supplies tucked away in the closet, you brought along projects to work on while you wait for your next flight. Sure, we all know that it pays to be organized to handle life's little emergencies, but what about making the best of them?

Too many people are content to stay on the receiving end of life. They just take what they are thrown and expect nothing more. Being organized puts you in the director's seat. You are able to set the stage for your performance, and if the scene happens to change, you are fully prepared to call the shots. Some of the best scenes in movies are completely ad-lib. Perhaps someone missed a cue, the lighting was off, or the script was misquoted. Instead of cutting the scene and filming it over according to the screenplay, the director saw that the unexpected was actually an opportunity for improvement. If the director had not been fully prepared, knowing the scene inside and out, and being able to read into the script, he would have completely missed the opportunity.

> *When you live life in the driver's seat, the view is spectacular!*

By being organized, we are not only prepared for life's unexpected turns and twists, but we are also able to take full advantage of them. A good plan allows for the unplanned. For example, a friend from out of town called me once when she was nearby to see if we could get together. I hated to turn her down. It was a school day and I had some projects planned. However, it was beautiful outside and my kindergartener at the time was working on the letter C. I decided to meet her at a local park. The kids could play and we could visit together. I changed learning about "corn" to learning about "clouds." I threw some watercolor pencils and some cotton swabs in my bag as well as a bunch of paper. I also grabbed a box of outgrown girl clothes that I knew her daughter could wear. We then met at the park, I gave her the clothes, the kids sat at a picnic table and painted the clouds with their pencils and a cup of water, we got to visit with one another, and our family dined on corn that night instead of painting with it. All of it happened out of organization. Being organized prepares you for the unexpected, and increases your options when it occurs.

Organization Opens Your Life

A disorganized home has the tendency to crowd in on us. It starts with a closet or two, and then creeps over the entire house. Pretty soon, we find ourselves turning down visitors, staying away from our home, and spending less time doing family activities. Your home closes in on you, and, before you know it, your life is doing the same thing. When someone's life is disorganized, she spends time hiding from the world. She turns down visits from friends. She doesn't host any parties. She disappoints people by running late or not being prepared. Her world becomes smaller and smaller. What a waste! If this sounds at all like the kind of life you have created for yourself, then let me tell you now that you are too valuable and too vibrant to close yourself off from the world. You have the ability to be a gift to people around you. You are not doing anyone a favor (especially yourself) by living in a chaotic hole.

*Spread your arms open wide,
and take in the glory
of a full and vibrant life.*

Once you start organizing your life, you don't just open up shelf space and floor space. You begin to open up space within your spirit as well. The simple act of organizing a closet can begin a wonderful chain reaction. Once you see the fruits of your labor and experience the ease with which you use the space, you begin to extend it to other rooms in your home. Friends come over and you don't have to make up excuses for the house or, worse, play hide-and-seek and pretend you're not home. You are able to open up your home and your life to those around you. And the greatest part of it all is not the new satin padded hangers you put in your bedroom closet or the shelf paper you just used to line your cabinets. The best part of it all is that you are giving your spirit room to soar. God designed you to be a blessing to others, and now you are beginning to open up your life to all that He has in store for you. And the blessings are just beginning.

Too often, we use our messy home as an excuse to limit our abilities. We carry the badge of disorganization that exempts us from jumping into life head-first. We can't take those night classes because our home keeps us so busy. We can't have the mommy club over because we could never get the house ready in time. When we begin organizing our spaces, we find the time and the space to invest in our own lives. Don't wait until your home is at a certain point to get involved. Start getting involved today and use that activity as an impetus to get your home in order. Once you begin organizing your home, you will be amazed at the space you open up for yourself. You deserve the room to breathe, grow, and explore.

Organization Creates Family Harmony

Did you ever wonder why people tend to marry people with personalities that are completely opposite? Subconsciously, we all have a tendency to gravitate toward that which balances us. It's kind of like the city mouse and the country mouse. They're the best of friends, but the things that inspire them are in complete opposition. They live torn between their love for each other and their love for their perfect world. But enough about my torrid relationship. Let's talk about family harmony. Very rarely will everyone in the family have similar personalities, but we all are required to live together.

My two sisters always had to share a room growing up, and it was torture for both of them. They were the odd couple of the century! One of my sisters, Christina, is a clean freak. When she makes the bed, it looks as if it had never been slept in. As a matter of fact, even when she is sleeping in it, it looks as if it had never been slept in. All of her clothes are folded and put away neatly (even when she's wearing them). Now my other sister, Joanna, is on the opposite end of the spectrum. When it comes to homemaking, we'll just say she is . . . uh . . . "relaxed." When she was younger, she decided to save time grooming herself and so she washed her hair while it was still in a ponytail. I heard of her doing laundry once. It was a frightening tale. Now she figures it's easier to just go out and buy new underwear. My mother was finally forced to separate the room with freestanding bookshelves. She put Christina's side facing the doorway just in case visitors ever toured the house. Finally, Joanna got her own room. When people visited, my mother would just shrug and remark, "This is the room that we rent out to a college student."

> *When your home is in order, all the different notes in your family can create beautiful music together.*

But many of you probably know this story line all too well. Very rarely are two like personalities attracted to one another. It simply goes against the laws of nature. Perhaps you are a clean freak, constantly picking up your husband's clothes off the bathroom floor or vacuuming under his feet while he lounges on the sofa. Or perhaps you are more . . . uh . . . "relaxed." You know what it feels like to be nagged about the junk that is threatening to take over the garage or chided about the laundry being backed up for weeks. Don't file for divorce or send your kids away to military academy. Well, not right away. Let's talk organization first.

Proper organization allows for happy, healthy cohabitation. If organizing is done effectively, it allows for the clean to have room to roam and the mess to be properly contained. For example, let's just say that your twelve-year-old daughter constantly makes a mess whenever she gets ready in the morning. If you are a clean freak then you are applying your own logic to the situation: "Why can't she just open a drawer and put the brush and comb back? Why does she have to leave hair doodads, lip gloss, and lotion all over the counter?" But her mind does not think in this manner. She is not as concerned with the end result as much as she is concerned with getting from point A to B. To help both of you live together happily, perhaps you can organize to prevent mess. Instead of demanding belongings to go in separate drawers or cabinets, perhaps you could put a pretty basket to catch all of the mess right there on the counter. Not your ideal, and probably not hers either. But it works, and that's what you're after.

Organization Allows Blessings to Flow

A disorganized home is like a really bad sinus congestion (but without the green gunk in the morning—or maybe it depends on how disorganized it is). Fresh air cannot flow in and out. That freshly baked apple pie can't even be tasted, much less smelled. Your nose cannot do what it is designed to do. It can't smell, it can't breathe, it can't even help you taste. When your home is cluttered and disorganized, it also cannot do what it is designed to do. A home is supposed to nurture the family. It cannot do that when it is congested. Blessings can't flow in and out. You can't smell and taste life at its finest.

Too often we hold on to items hoping to get a "repeat blessing." We got a feeling of happiness when we opened that birthday card, so we store it away, hoping for that good feeling again. We had a great time in college when we collected all of those beanbag animals, so we keep them around us, longing for those happy

An organized home is a channel of blessing—stand back and watch it flow!

times. Blessings don't repeat themselves. Opening the card—that was the blessing. Collecting the animals—that was the blessing. Now, let that go and make room for more blessings to enter your life. They will. Let go, trusting more will pour in.

Think for a minute about the blessings that can flow in your home when it is organized. You have more time to spend with your family. Healthy meals are savored together. Books get read instead of buried on the shelves. Clothes get worn instead of stuffed in baskets. Children's schoolwork and artwork gets appreciated instead of stuck in piles in the corner. Now think for a minute about the blessings that can flow out of your home when it is organized. Those clothes your child outgrows can be passed on to another family. The extra tools you bought because you could not locate the other ones can be given to a neighbor. You have more time and money on your hands to donate to your church, a needy family, or your favorite charity. If you are sick of your home resembling a sinus infection, get rid of the green gunk and get into organizing.

Organization Saves You Money

When your home is disorganized, it begins to create a "black hole" effect, sucking everything into its gravitational field. The minute you bring items through the front door, they get sucked up into the accumulating horde. I remember once when all of the kids began complaining about not having any scissors whenever we would begin a craft project. It was so frustrating. It would be time to begin our art project, and they would spend ten minutes just trying to locate their scissors, even attempting to sneak my kitchen shears into the classroom. Finally, I went to the store and bought more scissors and stored them away. The next day, I decided we would clean out our art closet as a class project. After everything was picked up, sorted, and put away, we had six pairs of scissors (and that's not counting the ones that I bought). Disorganization always seems to hide the things that we always need. We can access that ugly sweater Aunt Edna gave us any time the need arises (as if), but our favorite pair of blue jeans are lost in the laundry somewhere.

We also seem to buy the same things over and over. My husband is in charge of most of the repair work around the house (and if you know my husband, that in itself is a frightening thought). He is the tool keeper, but not the

> Spend money on the things
> you need, not on what
> you already have.

most organized man in the world. He also seems to have a hammer fetish, bringing home a new one every time I turn around. Freud would have a field day with that one! One day, I cleaned out our tool closet and found five good hammers! How many hammers does one household need? My husband alone could hammer out danger, warning, love between his brothers and his sisters, and still have time to take in a round of golf before going to bed!

Unless you just enjoy throwing money away, organizing your home will save you a lot of money. By paring down your home to only the items that you really use and love, you will be able to get rid of the excess and get a nice tax deduction or sell it for some cash in your pocket. You will also not find yourself running to the store to buy items that you already possess but cannot locate. Being organized will also save on those last-minute convenience purchases because you did not plan ahead or were too unorganized to execute your plans. Save the money and keep the sanity!

Organization Makes You Confront Emotional Issues

Perhaps of all the reasons to get organized, this one is the most important. When you truly begin to assess your behavior patterns, it forces you to face some issues that perhaps have remained dormant for some time. There's nothing like some good spring cleaning to make us deal with some things that we have pushed back into the nooks and crannies of our closets. If you analyze it closely enough, the behavior pattern that underlies the function of the home is usually dictated by the thought pattern of the person who primarily manages the home. The look and feel of your home is a result of many variables, such as the size of your family, your time commitments, and the involvement of your family members. But, by and large, your environment is a reflection of you (the person running it). And if you are dealing with some emotional issues, then your home is dealing with them as well. If you see yourself reflected in any of these conditions, then go easy. If you must beat yourself up, then use a feather. Battling a negative with a negative never works. It just makes the condition worse.

My suggestion to you is to begin organizing your home but go very, very slowly. Take tiny baby steps because too much at one time can begin a negative spiraling effect that buries you deeper than you were before. And when you do begin the organizing process, do it with a joyful spirit. This time you are not doing it to get your husband off your back, to host that party, or so that your kids have clean clothes to wear to school. This time you are doing it for yourself. You deserve to have a nurturing home that is helping you in life instead of hindering you. Begin working through the emotional issues that may be holding you back from being all that you can be. If you are tired of living in a prison cell, then it's time to break the bars! Stake your claim, and start today to create the home of your dreams.

Putting order into your home will put order into your life.

Scarcity Mentality

This is common among those of us who know the sting of not having enough. It wasn't just by chance that the period of my life when I had the most inclination to hoard items occurred at the same time that we were at our lowest income level. Saying that we didn't have a pot to pee in was putting it lightly—we were even too poor to pee. When you live with the worry of not having enough, you constantly feel as if you are walking under a deep gray cloud. We subconsciously subscribe to the philosophy that there is not enough to go around, so we try desperately to pull as much as we can into our possession. The best things in life cannot be possessed, but that's hard to remember when you are afraid your electricity is going to get turned off or you are worried that you are going to overdraw your account. Financial worries are very real fears, and very valid ones. But when those fears begin to direct our lives, we are in need of some serious reassessment.

You are enough just as you are, with nothing else attached.

Hording items in every closet of your home is often a sign of fear—fear that your needs may not get met. This fear also shows a lack of trust. We so often fall into the trap of believing that our lives are in our own hands, but ultimately, everything that enters our lives passes through the hands of God. We are commanding our ships. But God is in charge of the sea. Every time I have been flat-on-my-face broke, there has been a good reason, as well as a good lesson. We could all spend our lives playing the blame game, or start manning the wheel. Fear and lack of trust will not provide for your needs. God will provide for your needs through your hard work and good choices. So unless you are feeding a huge family or running a daycare center, there's really no reason to line every shelf in your home with bulk groceries. And unless you are a fashion stylist, there is really no reason to cram your closet with enough clothes to outfit the Rockettes. It's all difficult to store and a pain to organize.

If you just prefer abundance, and have the room and don't mind the effort, then go for it. An elderly friend of mine, Evie, works at a fabric store. She has a guest room in her house filled to the brim with nothing but fabric. But she is an avid quilter, lives by herself, and can access the fabric because it is grouped by color and stored in clear bins. It works for her. But we are talking about abundance that has its roots in fear. And that is not abundant living at all. Start organizing your life and watch the clutter run out and blessings pour in. Let go, all the time trusting that more will fall from God's hands into yours.

Low Self-Esteem

My theory on self-esteem is the same as looking a gift horse in the mouth. God created you, and He did it in a marvelous way. When you criticize and complain, you are knocking the gift that He has given you. What you believe about yourself will be what everyone around you believes as well. And, all too often, we are content to see ourselves in the worst possible light. If you are keeping a disorganized home, it may be because deep down inside you may believe that is all you deserve. It could be esteem issues that have held over from your childhood, or maybe recent events that have thrown you into a negative slump.

Keeping things around you to affirm sensitive areas of your life is also tied in to your self-esteem. There are other ways to resolve the inadequacy you feel as a mother besides keeping the crib, changing table, and all the baby blankets in the attic (especially when your son is in high school). If you feel that you may be struggling in this area, you need to realize one thing—no one (and especially no thing) is going to change this perception except you. And no one *should* be able to change this perception. If you are waiting for someone to step in to your life and make you feel better about yourself, then pop a bowl of popcorn and watch *Pretty Woman,* because reality just doesn't work that way. You are the one behind the wheel, so you better like what you're driving. No, you better love it! Start appreciating the gift that God gave you, and let the world know how you feel.

A friend of mine, Lois, had always kept a nice home until she began to work full-time. Her home began to get more and more disorganized, and no matter what she tried, she could not conquer the clutter and confusion. She would constantly blame her disorganization on her lack of time at home. But it went a little deeper than a time investment. After some heart-to-hearts and a lot of soul searching, she realized how completely dissatisfied she was with her life. She did not want to work, she regretted leaving home, and despised having to put her daughter in day care. Her home was a mess because her spirit was a mess. After

You are a beautiful woman; let it show throughout your home!

making some financial sacrifices, she decided to work part-time in the evenings so that she could stay home with her daughter during the day. She began taking a correspondence course in natural medicine, a field that she had always been passionate about. She also began affirming herself daily with her own private mantra, "I am an amazing woman!" Pretty soon, her self-esteem began picking up. She was proud of her choices and stood by them. It wasn't long before the fresh breeze of organization began flowing through her home.

Fear of Risk

Fear of success, fear of failure, you can call it what you want. But it all boils down to a fear of the risk that it takes to step out of your comfort zone. All too often, we allow our homes to sink into disorganization because it keeps us distracted. You can't start that business because your home keeps you too busy. You can't audition for that play because you would get too behind in your housework. Your home demands so much of your time that you have little, if any, left over for other aspects of your life. A girlfriend of mine, Charlene, is an awesome writer, who could easily author the next great American novel. She loves to write, but never does so on a professional level because she is too busy trying to get control of her messy home (or so she lets herself believe). Deep inside, Charlene is afraid. She is afraid that she may actually succeed. More would be expected of her and the reality that she has created may not be able to expand to encompass her new life. She is also afraid that she may fail. She would have to face the fact that her skill was not up to the level that she perceived it to be. The disorganization in her home was an excuse to waste her time and energy. It was her "hall pass" to just putter along through life.

The housework is the maintenance part of our home life. It is what sets the stage for our performance, not the performance itself. The new and the fresh are what keep us vibrant and alive. We could spend our entire existence on this planet doing just that—existing. Your boat is meant to sail in much deeper waters. Once

Nothing is gained where nothing is attempted. Every success takes risk.

you start organizing your home, you will begin to make room for more. You will have more time, more energy, more creativity to be used in amazing ways. Don't let this scare you away. Sure, deep waters are a bit frightening. But look at it this way. No boat sails forever. Are you going to waste this one excursion through life just idling away by the dock? Or do you ache to feel the salty waves lift you in their swell and the gale winds fill your sails? The storms at sea are inevitable, and they are risks worth taking. Sure, Charlene could succeed, and she could fail too. But the saddest thing of all is that she will never know. The one thing I have learned is this: real success occurs when you know full well that you could fail, but you do it anyway. The only real success is in the attempt. And the only real failure is refusing to try.

The Cushion of Chaos

it is so much easier to blame than to take responsibility. We seem to live in a culture that enjoys playing the blame game as much as it enjoys eating fried food and wearing blue jeans. Almost all of us, at one time or another, develop cushions in our lives to accept blame where it may otherwise fall. Your subconscious is an amazing thing. It will take whatever steps necessary to provide you with primary needs of comfort and security, even when those steps eventually lead you to a very uncomfortable and dangerous place. Behaviors that are self-destructive are frequently attempts to create an object of fault, because the actual fault may be too upsetting for our minds to accept. Take the woman who gains a lot of weight during marital problems. Often, it is a subconscious attempt to create something to blame for it, thereby skirting the deeper issues at hand. "Our marriage failed because I am fat" is a lot easier to accept than a harsher truth. In similar ways, your disorganized home is frequently used as a cushion to accept blame and protect you from reality.

The worst part of it all is that the cushions you create only blind you from the truth, doing nothing to help you change your situation. When you finally

A disorganized home makes us live life with blinders on when there is so much to see.

118

come around to facing the real issues at hand, they will have gotten much worse because now you have a disorganized and cluttered home to deal with as well. Does your husband get frustrated with you because of a disorganized home, or is there another situation festering underneath the clutter? Is it your housekeeping obligations that are keeping you home all of the time, or is it an excuse for the loneliness that may be closing in on you? Reality is harsh, but the sooner we take positive, productive measures to alter it, the sooner we will reap the rewards. Look inside yourself and start taking positive steps to create a new environment. Writing in your dream journal will help tremendously. Take tiny steps to organize your home, and as you do, record how you feel along with the issues that are stirring in that beautiful head of yours. The problem with cushions is that they eventually suffocate you. Perhaps it's time to quit burying your head underneath the clutter and come up for some fresh air.

Repeat Performance

An inheritance is a great thing, unless, of course, you happen to get a windfall of counterproductive behaviors. Humans are funny creatures; we will continue behaviors over and over even if they have never worked. Too many times we just replicate in our own lives whatever we experienced growing up, no matter how unhealthy it may have been. We rarely stop and analyze before we do anything. We just act and react. Just because you may have grown up in clutter and confusion, does not mean you need to set up your home in the same fashion. Changing behaviors that you have experienced your entire life is a difficult thing, but nothing worthwhile ever comes easy. When you find yourself in a rut, you just have to dig yourself out.

Now is not the time for any "poor me's." You are not at all poor. As a matter of fact, you are far richer than you may believe. Leave the past where it belongs—in the past. The self-pity will just dig your rut deeper. You have a life and a home and a family to build right now. Start today to see yourself as worthy.

You can be whatever you want to be, so make your life your own.

119

You are worth the effort, the education, the experience, whatever it takes to change any behaviors that you may have inherited. Just because your mom was . . . uh . . . "relaxed" doesn't mean that you have to live by the same standards. And if you do decide to change your behaviors and organize your home, please be kind to yourself. Understand that it will take time. What took a lifetime to establish is not going to dismantle overnight, or even over a long weekend. Step by step you will begin to see changes as you begin to analyze your behaviors. You can still be your mama's little girl without being her mini-me. And just because you choose to live your life differently, does not mean you have chosen to live it better (so no silent guilt about surpassing your mother's skill—you need to use your kitchen for cooking instead of stepping from the frying pan into the fire).

Cold Feet

Sometimes, we are just scared to move on. We have no idea what the future holds, so it's more comfortable to just stay in the past. Surrounding yourself with lifeless junk that is left over from another chapter in your life is like living in a graveyard. You are loving stuff that cannot love you back. The beautiful memories and the happy times are the only items you need to carry with you through life. These you pack away in your heart, and you can access them anytime you want. Perhaps you really shined as a mother. It was your moment of glory. Now the kids are all in school or have left home, and you are still clinging to that period of time by hoarding items that you associate with it. Because you shined in one chapter of life, does not mean you cannot shine in another. As a matter of fact, it is more likely that you will.

Past successes are the best predictors of future successes. Let go of the past to make room for the present. God has so much in store for you. Spread your wings so that He can lift you on His breath and carry you to new and vibrant places. You are not going alone. And He will never bring you to a place in life where His grace and mercy cannot sustain you. If you could only see the bless-

You will never get where you want to be if you don't take that first step.

ings that are just waiting to enter your life and your home—you would have the Salvation Army truck there in the morning! Organizing your home will awaken you to things that you thought were well in hiding. Don't waste another day wallowing in confusion and living less of a life than you deserve. It's time to clear out, straighten up, and make room for positive energy to flow through your life.

Time for Your Prescription

When it comes to organizing, we are all completely different. We all have different behavior patterns that dictate how we live, and all organizing systems need to be designed around these patterns. It doesn't do any good to design a cute little organizing system for all of your makeup when you are accustomed to throwing it all in a vanity drawer. It will still get thrown into the drawer, while that cute little organizer gathers dust. Effective organization is demonstrated by systems that make your life easier, *not* more difficult. That is why it is imperative that any system work around your personality. It would do you little good to have a professional come in and organize your home without your involvement. She would have no idea of your behavior patterns, your personality, and what you need out of life. The old adage, "If you want something done right, then do it yourself," definitely pulls its weight when it comes to organizing. So, are you ready to begin straightening up your home? It's up to you (and your personality, of course).

Rx for MasterMinds

Your organizing strategies may be quite functional right now, but how much flair are you putting in to your function? Your home is not a means to an end, but an entire process within itself, nurturing all who live within its walls. Why not add a little sparkle and spunk? Pretend that your home is a face, and you need to put a twinkle in the eye. Find two things in your home right now that you are using to organize your belongings. It could be your napkin holder, the place you put your keys, or maybe even a laundry basket. Whatever you find, make sure it is looking tired and very ready to go to bed. Now go shopping. It could be as simple as shopping around in your own attic. Find something to replace your retired item but give it a splash of personality. For example, instead of a towel hook in my kitchen, I have little antique forks that I bent backward and drilled into the wall. Instead of a towel bar, I have an old peeling window frame that I attached a towel bar to. Don't just think in the storage and home improvement aisles. Check out the automotive or toy aisle, or even a junk shop!

Rx for Creative Spirits

Do you ever feel like you hit the ground running? With all of the things you have on your to-do list, you are constantly on the go. If you're not careful, you can easily become like the white rabbit in *Alice in Wonderland*—"I'm late! I'm late!" You scurry here and there, seeing how much you can possibly fit into a day. There are two things I want you to try to make a part of your life. The first one is to make "Be Early" your new motto. This small, but huge, step will not only help you reduce your stress level, but will also help you accomplish more. No matter where you are going this week, begin leaving fifteen minutes earlier than usual. Bring along a book or some paperwork if you like, but stick to it for a week and see how smoothly your days go. This step also shows others that you care about them, which goes pretty far in my book. The second thing I want you to do is to slow down. Whenever you do catch yourself in a rush, make this a conscious effort. Life is meant to be savored. Slow down and take the time to embrace every moment you are given, no matter how big or small it may appear, and catch its beauty in your heart.

Rx for Mother Hens

Get yourself excited about organizing your home. Check out some Web sites for organizing stores, such as The Container Store, or just take a trip down the organizing aisles of your favorite department store or home improvement store. Once you begin visualizing the organizing possibilities in your own home, you will become motivated to begin feathering your nest with them. Find the style and form of organizers that appeal to you, and narrow down the one part of your home that you would like to begin organizing. You take a lot of pride in your home, so find something that creatively strokes you the right way. Imagine it in your home—where you will put it, what you will store in it, how it will look with the colors in the room. This process will get your wheels turning so that the organizing part will be a simple process that enables you to get you to a well-defined goal. Normally, a person organizes a section of their home when the confusion hits a level that becomes intolerable. But you are more inspired by creating a nurturing home. Use that inspiration to your advantage.

Rx for Starry-Eyed Dreamers

Your emotions are so beautiful! Please don't ever try to change, because that is exactly how God created you to be. And He wants you to celebrate your emotions, not to live imprisoned by them. You may be dealing with some issues of letting go and moving on. Take it easy on yourself. If you get yourself all tied in knots about organizing, it will do you (and your home and your family) no good at all. You just need the right motivation, and a helping hand or two. The first thing you need to do is pick one room (or even part of a room, such as a closet) to tackle. Now call up one of your very best friends or a relative, someone who lives close by and knows you well enough to be brutally honest (someone who would have no trouble saying, "I don't care how long you've had this dress, it looks terrible"). Set up a time next week for her to come over and help you clean out that area, and don't back out of it. Get over the pride thing. All of us are either completely imperfect or completely deceived. It will be fun to laugh about your mess together.

Dream On!

Whip out that journal, honey, because we are going to do some dreaming. I hope you are beginning to clear out some clutter, because I want you to get excited about organizing your new space. Sometimes we women are guilty of getting so caught up in the house "work" that we lose focus and make very little real progress. We end up going nowhere fast. This time it's going to be different. Before you even begin thinking about organizing, get out your dream journal and your beautiful pen and take a tour through your home. Go in each room and write down all of the activities that you see occurring in that particular space. You are going to be answering the question, "What does this room do for me and my family?" For example, in your bedroom you may have sleeping, dressing, reading, daydreaming, and gettin' yo freak on (feel free to interpret that as you see fit).

Don't forget to think creatively. Perhaps you would like to incorporate an area that you have never had before. Do you have a favorite pastime, such as sewing or writing? Wouldn't you love to have a corner all to yourself to let your needles fly or words flow? As you tour your home, room by room, make sure you remember all family members. Where does Jill like to talk on the phone? Where does Chad always seem to be playing with his action figures? By recognizing what you desire out of the room, you can clearly establish your focus before you even lift a finger to begin organizing it. Like I said before, effective organization is about systems that work. This little exercise will help you establish the systems that you need to incorporate. This is your first step in organizing, so rev up that creative engine and get dreamin'!

Chapter 7

AS IS Organizing

By now I hope the clutter is starting to move out of your home and a positive energy is beginning to flow in. Maybe it's even beginning to feel like one of those fabric softener commercials. You just want to run through a field of wildflowers and fall back into a mountain of clean white fluffy sheets (hopefully, you won't have to share your bed with some creepy talking stuffed bear—and I'm not talking about your husband). Once you have begun de-cluttering, and you have figured out which items in your home are essential to your family's living, the next step is easy, even fun!

Setting up organizational systems within your home is something everyone can do. It doesn't require any special talent or skill, just willingness, some insight, and the determination to get it done. Yes, even that teenager who still has not learned how to replace the toilet paper can learn to be organized. The trick is to organize around a person's lifestyle as it already exists. If you live with family members who are more . . . uh . . . "relaxed," then you are probably sick of picking up after them and nagging their ears off. If you are more relaxed, then you are probably tired of the chaos and irritability. There is a better way, and it is not found in a gas-powered blower with an indoor setting. Instead of changing a relaxed person, you simply organize around a relaxed lifestyle. It can work for everyone, and that's the beauty of organization. It is not dependent upon any particular lifestyle or personality.

There are four main steps in developing and maintaining any organizational system. The method is simple, and best of all, it works! As a matter of fact, it works so well that I like to call it AS IS Organizing. The best way to organize your home is AS it already IS. Beware though, you should only attempt to organize after you have already de-cluttered. Otherwise, you are going to find yourself in a big, fat mess that only a deep tissue massage and some Prozac will be able to treat. Once you have sorted through your stuff, you should have only the things that you love and use. The rest of the stuff should be given away, thrown away, or stored away. Now, you are ready to organize it. You have cleared it out, now let's straighten it up and keep it that way! The four steps that will help you do this are:

Activity—Investigate the area and determine the activity that takes place. Ask, "What do I do here?"

Supplies —Strategize around that function to determine what supplies you need. Ask, "What do I need in order to do it?"

Implement—Determine what type of structure you need in order to contain it all. Ask, "How can I store and contain it?"

Sustain—Just what it says. Keep up your organizing strategy. Sound complicat-

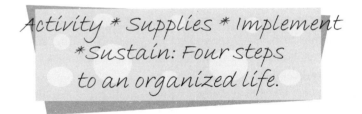

*Activity * Supplies * Implement*
*Sustain: Four steps
to an organized life.

ed? No way. Read on.

Determine the Activity

Before you come up with any strategies to organize your home, you need to investigate the area that you are organizing. Here is where you get out that dream journal you have been working on, and go through the functions of each room in your home. Think through the routines of the individuals using that particular space and their personalities as well. Your home will probably already tell you what is going on in that space. Does the laundry always pile up in one particular area? Then put a hamper there. Are the toys always played with in one particular spot? Then put some type of storage container there. Remember, it is far easier to organize around the way it already is. Think AS IS, instead of trying to force a person's style into an organized pattern. Develop the organized pattern around the person's style instead. It's easy to put a file folder here, a basket there, or some hooks on the wall. It's a lot more difficult to change a behavior. I've tried, and it just doesn't work. If you haven't already figured out by now that you can't change a person, then I hate to be the bearer of bad news. Trying to change a person fails every time, kind of like telling a six-year-old boy, "no nosepicking in mixed company (his own or anyone else's). Make it easy on yourself by organizing around the behavior (and while you're at it, you may as well blast some African Celtic music to get going).

> *You cannot make a person get organized, but you can organize around a person.*

Every evening when my husband comes home from work, he takes off his jacket and gets rid of his keys and wallet. When doing my clutter-induced detective work, I noticed that the edge of the computer desk was the closest flat surface to the front door. So, naturally, he would drop his wallet and keys right there. The reason for the clutter was because I had not provided a space that would function as a drop-off center, and it was evidently needed in our home. In order to organize around the behavior, I went out and picked up a tiny little table with a drawer in it to set beside the front door. Now, when he comes home from work, all he needs to do is open the drawer and throw his wallet in there. At a yard sale, I also found a little panel off of an old door that had peeling paint and a beautiful doorknob on it. I cut it down to a size that would hang nicely by the front door and screwed in some little black hooks at the bottom. It looks quite interesting, and it's effortless to hang your keys on it when you walk inside. Now the edge of the computer desk is clutter-free because there is a space for that drop-off function to occur right beside the front door.

Start Small

When you are first beginning to organize your home, leave the zealous attitude for sidewalk preachers and aerobic instructors. You don't want to burn yourself out before you've really even begun. Start with the little areas, such as a dresser or a closet (maybe even a drawer or a cabinet if it's particularly jumbled). Just bite off as much as you can chew and still have an appetite for more.

Putting it all in writing is a good idea as well. There's just something about putting pen to paper that helps organize your thoughts as well as your home. As you go through the AS IS method, you may want to make a chart with Activity, Supplies, and Implement as headings. Look through each space in your home, and ask yourself what activity goes on in this area. Stemming from this activity, you can then decide what supplies you need and how you're going to contain them all. Finally, it is as simple as putting it all together and sustaining it. This AS IS process can apply to every area of your home—from a single drawer or cabinet to an entire room. For example, if you are organizing a reading corner in your daughter's room, your chart may look like this:

ACTIVITY	SUPPLIES	IMPLEMENT
reading corner	good lighting	lamp (at least 15 in. tall)
	place for cups	small table (24 in. high)
	seating	cozy chair with ottoman
	books	basket (for 10–12 books)

The sustaining part is the time and effort it takes to keep order in the area. After you get this reading corner established, the sustaining process is easy. The books are contained in the basket when they are not in use, and the table takes seconds to clear. Any troubleshooting would be collecting cups on the table, too many books in the basket, and junk placed on the chair. If collecting cups in her room becomes a problem, then you can give her one single reading-corner cup that matches her decor. When it's dirty, she takes it to the kitchen and washes it out. Books can easily be weeded out once a week because only a dozen or so can fit in there at a time (that's the beauty of containers—they keep your belongings in check). And as for junk on the chair? We would probably need to go back to our Activity stage and figure out what the junk is, why it is accumulating there, and provide another space for it. Or if it is just laziness clutter you can just do what I do—either throw it in a trash bag and tell her she can have it back as soon as she can tell you what it is (if it is clutter you want to give away) or tell her that the phone only operates when the room is clean. But, try not to clean it up for her. You are her mother, not her housekeeper. Our kids may as well learn as early as possible to take responsibility for their surroundings. We don't want them growing up like the Brady kids, waiting on Alice to come in and wipe their faces for them. But, enough about child rearing. That's a whole other book (or trilogy).

Strategize to Organize

After you establish the functions of a certain space, make sure that when you move on to the Supplies part, you are thinking of everything possible you would need in order to accomplish the Activity. For example, if you are organizing a medicine/emergency-kit cabinet, you need to consider every possible item needed. The activities of the emergency kit would probably be lighting, energy, and communicate. Now think of all the supplies you would need for these functions to occur. For lighting, you would need flashlights, candles, matches, and lighters. For energy, you would need batteries in the correct sizes and perhaps a small generator to hook to your car. For communication, you would need a small radio and a list of phone numbers. Think through every little item that is used for that function and work it into the process. If you have room, you can always squeeze in a water purifier, fifty pounds of dried beans, a flare gun, and a fallout shelter.

What about the medicine kit? What activity will this perform? You will probably use it to doctor up external ouchies, such as scraped knees, splinters, and general boo-boos. You will also use it for the internal yuckies, such as colds, fevers, and the like. Also, think through any particular medical needs that a family member would have. After you have established the Activities of the medicine kit, you can move on to the Supplies part. Write down everything you will need for these activities. For example, for the external ouchies, you will probably need antibiotic ointment, various sizes of bandages, cortisone ointment, and such. Your family's needs will differ from others. In our family's medicine kit, I have three separate bins, one for external meds, one for internal meds, and another for herbal and homeopathic remedies. This has always worked well for us, but your needs may be different. The most important part of the Supplies segment is to think through every little item needed to completely perform the Activity, and begin sorting the items accordingly.

Develop your list of supplies around the items you already have and the items you need to complete the activity.

Implement the Structure

This is the fun part, because you get to let your personality speak through your organization. Perhaps you like to keep things simple, so you like the beauty of clean lines and clear labels. Or perhaps you want things more elaborate. You think along the lines of beautiful baskets with color-matched ribbon. No matter what you use to contain your stuff, it is important that it is contained. This is the part of organizing where you adopt the old saying, "a place for everything and everything in its place." Containing items in something not only makes the area appear neater, but it is a lot easier to clean (just pick up the basket and wipe the surface area, instead of picking up and wiping under a lot of little items). This is the last step in organizing the area, because you can't structure the area if you have no idea what you are putting in there to begin with. For example, take the medicine kit we did earlier. If I need it to perform the activities of external medicine, internal medicine, and herbal/homeopathic remedies, I will gather up all of the supplies that I need for those activities *before* I ever get anything to contain it.

Don't get containers before you collect what you're putting in them.

The biggest mistake a lot of people make is to decide they want to organize something and then run to the store to pick up a pile of bins and baskets. That's like running to the grocery store to pick up a bunch of ingredients before you ever read the recipe to find out what you need. For my medicine kit, I sorted through all of the supplies, and grouped them according to their activity. I ended up with one pile of tubes and bandages, another pile of bottles and dispensers, and another pile of my herbal and homeopathic potions and lotions (the eye of newt and toe of frog). After judging how many things I had in the separate piles (and figuring out if I needed to add anything), I then decided how many containers I needed to use, how big they needed to be, and got the measurements of the area where they were going to be contained.

The available space for my medicine kit is a shelf that is twelve inches deep and thirty-five inches wide, so I headed to the store with these dimensions in mind (and on paper) and measuring tape in hand. I knew I needed three plastic boxes (plastic, just in case syrup spills and I need to wipe it out—which, for some reason, always happens when my husband dispenses medicine). And they needed to be able to hold a little more than a shoebox and fit on this shelf. I came home with exactly what I needed, three plastic boxes that are ten inches wide, twelve inches deep, and eight inches high. I put easy-to-read labels on the front, threw everything into the boxes, and put them on the shelf. There! My area performs its activity, it is well organized, effectively contained, and all it takes to sustain it is simply putting items back after they are used. I applied the AS IS model, and now I get to go eat a brownie (I will never be beyond using chocolate as a reward)!

My chart for the medicine kit, looked something like this:

ACTIVITY	SUPPLIES	IMPLEMENT
external medicine	ointments, bandages, etc.	10 in. x 12 in. x 8 in. plastic box
internal medicine	syrups, pills, dispensers, etc.	10 in. x 12 in. x 8 in. plastic box
herbal medicine	weird, smelly stuff	10 in. x 12 in. x 8 in. plastic box

AS IS Is Easy

When you are first reading this, it may sound a bit complicated. All that thinking just to organize something? This is one of those things where a few minutes of thought and planning pay for itself in saving hours of confusion and clean up later, kind of like birth control. And the more you apply this model, the easier it gets. As you organize more and more areas throughout your home, you will begin to do it automatically. You can even make it part of your de-cluttering routine. For example, you may want to attack a toy closet. The first thing you would do is pull everything out and begin to sort it into your two boxes or bags and two laundry baskets—giveaway and throwaway for the bags or boxes and put away for

131

the laundry baskets. Everything that does not belong in the closet should be in one of these four places. After you have tossed the giveaway box in the car, thrown the throwaway bag in the trash, dumped everything to store in a plastic box, and put away the other items, you are ready to set up an organized system.

The first step to organizing a space is always to de-clutter.

To assess the function of the closet, it would depend upon your children's ages, lifestyles, likes, and dislikes. Do your investigation, and figure out your family's needs. For example, you may find that your family's toy needs are board games, building blocks, action figures or dolls, cars, dress-up clothes, and miscellaneous small and midsize toys. Sort the supplies, so that you have separate piles. Now you can figure out how to contain them. Find containers that will keep the toys separated and organized, such as plastic boxes or baskets. And if you choose baskets for toys, make sure that the ones containing the tiny toys, such as little Legos or tiny Barbie doll items, are lined with fabric to prevent the little toys from getting lodged in the weave. But whatever you choose to contain the toys make sure they are easily accessible. That way, when children want to play with something, it's easy for them to grab the entire box or basket out of the closet and put it back in its spot when they are done.

Make sure that you organize the closet around your family. You may want the board games at the top, so that an adult can get them down. You may want the building blocks on a higher shelf so that the older kids can get to them, but your toddler won't run around the house sticking Legos up his nose (note: no matter how efficiently you organize this closet, your toddler will still find ways to stick legos up his nose). And you may want more of the toddler toys in a box on the lower shelf, but don't believe that this will cause him to play with them. He'll still go for the Legos every time—either that, or the bread knife.

Not only is the organizing easy, but sustaining it is also a piece of cake. Kids don't have to pull out every toy in the world to get to what they want, and when it is time to pick up, they know just where everything goes. Clutter is gone and housework is reduced. Clean up takes place in a fraction of the time, and everything is there, accessible and enjoyable. And as I said before, if you continue to apply the AS IS model to other areas of your home, it becomes easier and easier with each new challenge.

Your chart for the toy closet may look something like this:

ACTIVITY	SUPPLIES	IMPLEMENT
games	8 boxed games 5 sets of playing cards	top shelf for boxes baby shoe box (covered)
building blocks	small Legos K'Nex	plastic shoe box plastic shoe box
doll stuff	9 Barbie dolls, Barbie clothes and misc.	large fabric-lined basket
toddler toys	12–15 plastic toys	medium basket
cars	35–40 cars	large plastic box
dress-up clothes	10–12 outfits	plastic laundry basket

Family Function

When you are managing a family, not everyone will have the same living patterns. Don't fight the person. Change the environment instead. Analyze how an individual functions, and organize around that behavior. It does little good to demand that he live his life the way you live yours. It will never happen. For example, you can scream and holler at your daughter until you're blue in the face for dumping her dirty laundry in a heap in the corner of her room. This will do nothing except build up walls between you and your daughter and give you a throbbing headache. Instead, do your detective work. Where does the clutter accumulate? Why does it land in that particular place? Perhaps your daughter gets undressed in her room and doesn't think to go into the bathroom to dump her clothes. Wouldn't it be easier to just put a pretty laundry basket in the corner of her room where all the dirty clothes seem to gather? You're not after perfection here. You want harmony. Think of ways that will work, and then make these as aesthetically appealing as possible. You will have your whole life to make your home fit for the pages of *House Beautiful* magazine. But during those years when the children are small, make your home accommodate their lifestyles and yours. You may not have a pristine house, but you will have a happy home, and that is far more important.

> *Organization will allow family members of all different personalities to live together more harmoniously.*

You Creative Spirits and Starry-Eyed Dreamers usually don't have much of a problem with the happy home part, but remember that it's all about balance. How happy can your children be if they can't find their shin guards before they leave for soccer practice or their permission slip to go on the fourth grade picnic? One reason to organize is to prevent frustration and create a peaceful home where your family can blossom and grow. And you MasterMinds and Mother Hens need to remember the same thing. It's about balance. You may pride yourself on your organized home, but does your organizational technique encourage enough mess and play? Do your kids feel free to dump out toys in the living room? Are the paints and brushes accessible enough for them to get them out when the creative instinct hits? Remember as you organize that you need to build the family first, the house later.

Rest Stops

Every home has got them, so be on the lookout for them when you investigate the functions of a space. And these are not the rest stops where you can get a cheap cup of coffee and a pine-scented air freshener. These are the rest stops that exist all through your home, and I am praying that you won't find a "honk if you're horny" bumper sticker in any of them. These rest stops are the places where everyone feels compelled to put things before reaching the final destination. Some popular places for rest stops are at the bottom of the stairs, your kitchen counter, or any piece of furniture that happens to be near an entrance to your home. They just sit there so innocently, drawing in more and more clutter until they become hot spots all through your home—ready at any moment to set your house on fire. These rest stops are the strategic places in your home where clutter just naturally accumulates, so it is imperative to develop an organizational system around them.

You MasterMinds and Mother Hens may not have a big problem with these. As for the Creative Spirits, you are constantly on to the next big project, and often have a tendency to put things down en route to your next goal. It's no fault of yours that the clutter accumulates in these spots. Your mind is miles ahead of the action you are taking. For you Starry-Eyed Dreamers out there, your mind isn't on the action either. You are caught up in your daydreams (which, by the way, is a beautiful place to be). Sometimes you may feel like your entire home is one big hot spot. Even though you notice the details, you are much more verbally and visually oriented rather than physically oriented. You don't often focus much on your actions. Instead of fighting your personalities, it is imperative to develop organizational techniques that do not require thought. Instead, they are simply incorporated into the action you are already taking.

> *Put your hot stops through a fire drill before they ignite your entire home.*

Do your detective work. Find out where the action is and organize around it. Behaviors are difficult to change, so don't try. Let the actions that already exist in your home dictate where and how you organize your surroundings. For example, my kids always kick off their shoes when they come inside the house. Even though the coat closet is four feet away, shoes never make it inside. I gently reminded, I cajoled, I pleaded, I screeched like a demonic shrew. Finally I decided that instead of battling the behavior, I may as well organize around it. I simply placed a big metal washtub by the door where the shoes usually land. Okay, it's not the prettiest thing in the world, but it works. I don't nag at the kids and I'm not faced with a pile of dirty shoes all over the floor. As you all know, we need to choose our battles wisely. This battle was not one worth fighting. World hunger, yes. Dirty shoes, no. In our homes, we are after as few battles and messes as possible. Organization allows that to happen.

The AS IS chart looked like this:

ACTIVITY	SUPPLIES	IMPLEMENT
shoes by the door	5 kids x 2 feet	metal washtub

Where are the rest stops in your home? Most likely, they are where you exit and enter, near any stairways, where you do your paperwork, and where the family hangs out. It is the place where one piece of clutter is placed, then that welcomes another, and on and on it goes until you are faced with a pile of homeless junk. As long as we are alive and breathing we will have clutter hot spots, so instead of trying to get rid of them, apply the AS IS model and develop a system around them.

Perhaps you could incorporate a pretty basket to collect the children's paperwork from school, a hook for their backpacks, and a bucket for their shoes. Or maybe you get tired of seeing the mess collect right beside the bed. Instead of yelling about it, put a magazine stand there and a little table to collect the cups (one at a time, preferably). What about your kitchen counter? They are infamous for being used as rest stops. If mail gets dumped there, you may want to put a pretty tray to collect it until you have the opportunity to go through it all. Or you may want to develop a strategy that prevents the mail from accumulating. We have a cute little rusted toolbox to collect all of our bills. The business mail goes in one side and the home bills go in the other. The reading material is placed in the living room, and a trash can sits right under the kitchen counter for all of the junk mail. This system of organizing is easy and it makes us go through each day's mail immediately as it enters the house. Rethink those rest stops and organize a system around the activity that is already taking place.

Love That Logic

As you figure out the living patterns in your home, it will be fun and easy to organize around them. But in order for these strategies to work on a daily basis, you need to think carefully as you set them up. Many of our actions are learned techniques that may not be efficient or effective. We just do them because we have always done them, even though we waste enormous amounts of time and energy. For example, when I first started setting up house, I would always fill up the empty ice cream container and leave it in the kitchen sink. The next day I would dump out the water and throw it away. Pretty soon, I realized that it was a waste of my effort (filling it up with warm water and dumping it out the next day) and it was also a waste of space (where do the dirty dishes go when there is an ice cream container in the sink?). When I finally asked myself why in the world I did this, I realized that it was simply because my mother had always done this. Then I found out that the reason she did this was to clean it out so that melted ice cream wouldn't drip in her (unlined) trash can. Wow, talk about history repeating itself!

Make a habit of asking yourself, "Is there a better way?"

You are striving for both efficiency and effectiveness, so it helps to think before you act. For example, putting all of the baby doll items in plastic boxes with snap-on lids that stack on top of each other is efficient. You have grouped like items and contained them in something. However, it is not effective. As your child plays with her baby dolls, she is not going to put them back in the same place. She will pull out the totes and then leave them on the floor because she is not as adept as you are at putting on the lids and it takes too much effort to stack up the boxes. As quick as you can get it organized and put away, you're going to walk in and see bottles with pretend bubbly milk (that always fascinated me) and satin baby doll bloomers all over the place.

A better option that would be both efficient and effective would be to put a small set of drawers in the same spot. There are no lids to snap on and no boxes to stack up. All she has to do is pull open the drawers and push them closed. She will also be able to access all of the baby doll items because they are all within her reach. In the case of the stackable totes, she will most likely only play with the items that are available in the top box. And if she did want something in one of the bottom boxes, the others would crash down on top of her (not a good choice). Think through the function that is occurring in that space, as well as the individual performing it.

Your chart may look something like this:

ACTIVITY	SUPPLIES	IMPLEMENT
playing with dolls	3 baby dolls	cart with 3 compartments (bunkbeds)
	doll clothes, bottles, and misc.	set of 2 drawers

Efficient versus Effective

Efficient organization means that like items are grouped, they are contained, and they are out of your way. Effective organization means that it actually works. A lot of times, we confuse efficiency with effectiveness and wonder why the clutter accumulates all over again. Put on your thinking cap and apply some logic to the situation. For example, you can efficiently store items underneath the bed in long, flat boxes. But it is ineffective if you store items there that are used often because they will never get put away. If you put enough thought and effort into your organizing, then it basically maintains itself.

While you are developing a strategy around an activity, ask yourself if it is stored as effectively as possible. Is it close to where you use it? Can you get to it without any hassle? If something is an effort to access, you will be tempted not to put it back in its appropriate place when you are finished with it. For example, I have a huge bookshelf outside of my children's rooms. At nighttime, when they were finished reading books, it was a hassle for them to get up out of bed and return the books to the bookshelf. Instead of yelling at them for books all over the floor (which I did on several occasions), I decided instead to place a basket to hold the books where they were most likely to drop them—beside their beds. Now all they need to do at night is summon up enough energy to roll over and toss the book over the side of the bed. Since they seem to have enough energy to do cheerleading jumps on their bed after lights out, this simple action should not pose a problem.

The chart looked something like this:

ACTIVITY	SUPPLIES	IMPLEMENT
Reading books in bed	a dozen books	midsize basket with color-matched ribbon
	adequate light	2 side lamps mounted on wall

Location, Location, Location

One key to logical organizing is to make sure you store together all the items that you use at the same time. For example, if you are making a pot of coffee, it is ineffective to have to run to the cabinet for a filter, go to the pantry for the grinder, and drag the coffeepot all the way over to the sink to fill it up with water. Think logically. Put the socks near the shoes, the toothpaste near the toothbrushes, the black lace negligee near the eggbeater and the chocolate sauce (okay, I'm digressing). The important thing to remember is that if you are going to use all of the items at the same time, then it saves time and effort to just store them all together.

This is important to remember in the kitchen, where saving time and effort is extremely important if the family is going to eat anything other than delivered pizza or bowls of cereal. When you eat together as a family, it nourishes the body as well as the soul. Make it easy to accomplish by setting up your kitchen as efficiently and effectively as possible. Whenever I make bread, I cook it from scratch (including milling the grain). By storing the grain next to the mill next to the mixer and containing it all in one area, it is a breeze to get it all done quickly and easily. I also store the ingredients together so that I can collect all of the items in one swoop. And swooping is definitely a skill worth developing.

Another important thing to remember is to store items as closely as possible to where you use them. This prevents you from running around the house looking like Harriet the Harried Housewife (for those of you who actually want to look like Harriet the Harried Housewife, I strongly recommend a superb pair of leather boots, some self-tanner, and a strong Cosmopolitan to snap you out of it). Storing items where you use them saves a lot of time and effort when it comes to gathering them. When you are paying bills, do it near the file cabinet with the stamps and staples. That way you can get it all done at the same time without getting up

Group items and put them where you use them.

for anything. Write out the checks, stamp the envelopes, staple information together, file it away, and, if need be, store pain reliever close by for those recurring tension headaches. Now all you have to do is stick the envelopes in the mail. Again, think through all of your organizing techniques. Are you storing the craft supplies close to where you use them? Are the children's toys in neat compartments in the playroom? Are the movies close to the television? Make it less effort on yourself and your entire family by keeping items close to where you use them.

Make It Easy

A final thing to remember is to make frequently used items as accessible as possible. Storing out-of-season clothes in boxes in the top of your closet is fine, but storing your underwear there is not, unless of course, you never wear underwear. If you don't make it as easy as possible to get items out and put them back, then the clutter will accumulate quicker than you can say, "Sister Susie sitting on a Thistle, sans panties."

I cannot remember how many times I have hollered at the kids for leaving their towels all over the floor of the bathroom and their rooms. I finally decided to do my detective work. I realized that the towel bar I had in their bathroom was difficult to reach for the little ones, and it was a pain to stuff a towel between the bar and the wall. Evidently, I had placed appearance over function, and made the system of organization too difficult for my children to access (that sounds a lot better than saying they're lazy, right?). I then investigated to see where the mess was accumulating. The girls always left their towels on the floor of their room. So obviously, they prefer to leave the bathroom in their towels and then get dressed in their room. My boys, on the other hand, always leave their towels on the bathroom floor. Obviously, they bring their clothes into the bathroom with them (or at least, I hope so. Running naked from the bathroom is not something we encourage in our family, at least not for the kids anyway.) The boys enjoy a quick wipe off with a towel and then toss it on the bathroom floor when they get dressed. In order to organize around their behavior patterns, I put two easy-to-reach hooks in the bathroom for the boys, and then two hooks for the girls on the back of their bedroom door. What do you know—no more towels on the floor! Unless they forget. In that case, they are not allowed a towel for a month and are required to air-dry (kidding!).

When you are organizing, think KISS (Keep It Simple, Sweetie).

The trick in strategic organizing is to make it easy. If you are organizing toys make it a cinch for your kids to get them out and put them back. Otherwise, you're the one who is going to be cleaning it up. I remember for the longest time I had all of our board games stuck in a trunk in the living room. Whenever we wanted to play one, we had to clear off the trunk to open it and then drag out all of the games just to get to the one we wanted (which, of course, was always at the bottom). Needless to say, our time spent playing board games as a family dramatically reduced. I finally got a clue (get it? Clue?) and stored our collection of Middle Eastern textiles in the trunk and moved the board games to shallow shelves in our living room closet. Now we actually get to play all of those games that we have collected over the years (we just no longer lounge on our Kuwaiti blankets when we do so).

Time for Your Prescription

If you have some problems organizing your home, relax! Every one of us will attack our organizing projects in different ways. Some of us will get fired up about it while others would rather cram toothpicks underneath our fingernails (if only we could find the darn toothpicks. They were in the junk drawer last time I looked, or perhaps in the pantry.) Begin organizing your life, and feel it begin to take form and shape. No longer are you just floating in a mass of chaos. This is your ship, and you are going to command it! Your potential amazes me. I hope it amazes you as well. You can do so much, and be so much. You can build and structure your home so that it nurtures every member of your family—beginning with you.

Rx for MasterMinds

You enjoy structure in your home, but you may frequently get frustrated with other family members because they don't seem to share your same lifestyle. As you do your investigation work throughout your home, make sure you are organizing around the person performing the function instead of you. Putting the children's books on the top shelf may work well for you when it's story time, but putting them on the bottom shelf will allow them to enjoy them more. It does not prevent clutter, but it is a happy clutter, and it is important that you know the difference. Happy clutter is stuff that is always being used, but the user does not always have the ability to put it back (baby toys, bikes hanging from the ceiling, etc.). You should have a lot of it in your home. Yeah, it's a pain, but it lasts so briefly. Keep in mind the functions of all people in your home when you are organizing. Investigate your living room. Do you have a selection of toys and games available or age-appropriate reading material? What about enough blankets and pillows to snuggle in for a movie? Don't relegate these activities to a certain room, such as the playroom or the bedroom. Remember that it is living you want to do, and you want to live as a family, not as separate individuals.

Rx for Creative Spirits

It's time to express your creativity through your organization, and reorganize one entire room in your home. But make sure that it is a room that you see and use often. Do not do a child's bedroom or a closet, because the visual reward for you will not be as permanent. Perhaps you could do your bedroom or the laundry room (my kids stay as far away from the laundry room as possible for fear that they may have to match up socks, so I pretty much consider it my domain). Start from the very beginning (the sort-into-four-piles method). Once you are left with the things you love and use, you can begin organizing the space with the AS IS method. Pick out the containers that you want, but do not purchase them until you have sorted your items and know how many to get and how big they need to be. Plan to go out and get those containers as soon as you have everything grouped and the strategy set. If you keep this reward waiting for you, it will be much easier to accomplish this goal and get back on task if you get distracted. You love visual stimulation. Make your containers attractive so that it will be easy to sustain your organized system. If the new containers are not enough of a reward for you, throw in a splash of something new as well, perhaps some curtains, new dishes, or a pretty spread. You decide what it takes to get you going, but whatever you do, get going!

Rx for Mother Hens

When you are beginning any organization project, you may be likely to jump ahead of yourself and bypass the chart every time and just pick out a bunch of cute little bins and baskets that match your home. But that is a sure way to wind up frustrated, overwhelmed, and making return trips to the store. In the case of organizing, doing it right the first time is so much more efficient and gratifying. Pick one area in a room, or if it is not too confusing, the entire room. After you have de-cluttered and thrown away, given away, put away, or stored away, you are left with the items that you use and love. Now you need to get out that paper and pen and start making your AS IS blueprint. And when you are organizing, remember to do so around all of the family members. You often get a picture in your head of how you want your home to look, and overlook the convenience factor. If it is a room that the whole family uses, then make sure that you make it simple for all family members to use it (even those three feet and under).

Rx for Starry-Eyed Dreamers

Grab your purse or your diaper bag because it's time to dump it out. For me, my purse and diaper bag are one in the same. I can't imagine a day when I won't be lugging around travel wipes and some diapers. By the time that day comes, I'll probably be carrying around adult diapers for myself! Anyway, turn the entire thing upside down on a flat surface, such as your dining room table, and drag over a trash can. Set your timer to five minutes, and see how much you can sort through in that amount of time. Remember that the first step is to sort it into give away, throw away, put away, and store away. You will probably just have one pile of junk to throw away, another pile of things to put away somewhere else in the house, and another pile of stuff that belongs back in the bag. After you throw away and put away, don't just dump everything back in. Apply the AS IS method and find the best way to sort it into groups. My family calls me the bag lady, because I have a series of bags inside a bag. In my diaper bag, I have a small purse that holds miscellaneous items such as lotion, pens, pocketknife, et cetera. Within this small purse is another smaller bag that holds all of my makeup. Inside a separate compartment in my bag are the wipes and diapers. It's the nesting doll philosophy behind diaper bags. But, hey, it works! And that's what organization is all about. Find out what works best for you.

Chapter 8

Keeping It Up

Wouldn't it be cool to have a marathon weekend? Just the two of us? We could whip that house into shape and get it all organized and straightened up in a mad fury of charts, junk piles, trash bags, and caffeine. But, there are just two problems with that. First of all, by the time my six kids and I had been there for a day, it would probably be in far worse condition than when we had started. And second of all, no matter how strategically it had been organized, it would never stay that way unless you have the skills to sustain it. It's like AS IS without that last S. And then it's just AS I, and I have no idea at all what that means, although it does sound like it could pass for the title of some ballad by Sheryl Crow or a poem by Robert Frost. I do know, however, that no system operates alone. If you don't keep up with the organized system that you establish, you will soon find yourself surrounded with clutter and confusion. It is going to take regular maintenance and input from you and working with your personality to keep the system going strong.

Everything Has a Home

As you are organizing your home, you will find that you are creating a place for every little thing. Your goal is to not have any homeless items in your house. The number one reason clutter accumulates is because items do not have final destinations. Junk just gets shuffled around, about, in, and under. We duck under it, step around it, and trip over it because it doesn't have a home. Before you can put items away, you have to know where to put them. There is nothing more frustrating for a child (or adult, for that matter) to be told to clean up an area without having a clue as to where it all goes. As you apply the AS IS model to areas throughout your home, you will find that you are creating homes for all of your stuff. The sustaining part is easy because it is simply a matter of returning items to their final destinations, which, if you have applied logic, is close to where you use it and easy to access.

You Get It Out, You Put It Up

In an ideal universe, whenever people take things out, they would put them back. We would also have naturally blond hair and kids that never embarrassed us in public. But, here we are on planet Earth with dirty socks on the floor, books scattered over the furniture, and a bathroom counter full of barrettes and clips (not to mention highlights every four to six weeks and kids who say, "Mama, you better put that ice cream back so that you can button your pants" while you're standing in line at the grocery store). The thing with an ideal universe is that everyone's ideal is different. Ideal is not something that you find in the glossy pages of a magazine or on the Home and Garden Channel. The ideal home is what brings you pleasure and contentment. And it's different for everyone. But no matter what your ideal, it is important that your home have a sense of order so that the beauty of it can shine through. And the primary way to sustain order in your organized home is to make a rule of putting up what you get out. But, don't get me wrong. Just because you make that rule doesn't mean that everyone in your home is going to live by it. Now we're back to that ideal universe we were talking about. Find a level that satisfies everyone in the family, and stick with it. And if you're having trouble buttoning your pants, do not, under any circumstances, let your child know about it. It will come back to haunt you, I promise.

If you have difficulty with the whole "get it out, put it up" philosophy,

Consider putting back as a necessary step of the entire process—it is not optional.

think about it this way. It's going to have to be done sometime, so you may as well do it now. You can either enjoy life today or spend it playing catchup from yesterday. It's your choice. But I can tell you now that spending your life catching up is no fun at all. It's frustrating, time consuming, dangerous, and expensive. The people at the front of the pack get the best views, enjoy the best things, save more money, and have more time on their hands than the rest of the crowd. For example, you need to do dishes. You can either do them immediately while the cleaning is easy or wait while the food gets stuck on and spend more time scrubbing plates. You need to rotate your tires. You can either do them now or wait until the treads wear out. Then you're stuck buying new tires, or worse, caught with a blowout on the highway. You and the kids need to pick up the toys in the playroom. You can either do it now while you can still tell where things belong, or wait until you are knee-deep in clutter, little toys are lost in the crevices, and someone steps on a Ninja Turtle. But either way, it is going to be done at some time. Doing it immediately saves time, money, and your sanity.

I would like to say that I am always on top of things, but life has a way of sneaking up on me when I least expect it. We're out of wipes at the precise moment that my daughter has a sudden case of diarrhea, or I realize I forgot my travel sewing kit just when I decide to bend over and split my pants. I was the girl in high school who passed a note from girl to girl in history class that read, "Does anyone have a tampon?" I would never be prepared because my mind was always scattered in a million directions (kind of like the Fruity Pebbles theory of thought pattern development). To compensate for this, I had to get pretty darn serious about organizing. But, I am still left with the occasional mouthful of Fruity Pebbles that I need to swallow along with my pride. Be easy on yourself and know that no one in this beautiful world is perfect by a long shot. Be on top of your game to the best of your ability, and never be satisfied with good enough. Always try for better and better. If we are constantly improving ourselves, then the occasional sports injury won't bench us forever.

When you finally get your home de-cluttered and organized, the little bit of effort to sustain it will be the difference between night and day. Make it a habit to put things up immediately after you use them. Consider it part of the entire process. You take it out, you use it, you put it up—it's that simple. The tiny steps add up into saving you enormous amounts of work later on down the road. And you have too many wonderful things to do with your life to waste time playing catchup. An important thing to remember is that if you are not accustomed to putting items away after you use them, it will take some time and effort to develop this habit. But it is definitely a habit worth developing. And you may have your work cut out for you with the rest of the family. We all know that children who naturally clean up after themselves are either desperately trying to earn Brownie points, make their siblings look bad, or are running a low-grade fever. So, you may have to keep after them.

Establishing the condition of "when you put away toy A, then you can get out toy B" will help tremendously. Children, like everyone else, need incentive. They have to put away the Barbie dolls if they want to play with the makeup. So, how about you? What is your incentive? Just think about clear spaces, neat bedrooms, raindrops on roses, and whiskers on kittens. Putting things away after you use them will be the most important step to take to sustain the organization in your home, but it's only the first step. Maintaining your dream home is going to require developing some more great habits.

Staying on top of it all gives you the best views.

PM Routine

The best time to begin your day is the night before. It may sound a bit strange, but every great work requires a certain measure of preparation. Your day should be viewed as an opportunity, a masterpiece waiting to be accomplished, a symphony waiting to be composed. Opening night would never be spectacular without all of the hard work that takes place the night before. So many wonderful things can happen in a single day, but it's up to you to set the stage for it to happen. And it all starts the night before. By preparing for your day, you will be able to handle the day's activities with a wink and a smile. You won't be playing catchup. Instead, you will be operating ahead of the game.

Make a pact with yourself to prepare the home for the day ahead before you go to bed. It will make all of the difference in the world. Leave the rooms clear from all clutter so you don't have a task waiting for you the second you walk in the room. Leave the kitchen clean and nothing in the sink. Waking up to a clean house will not only set your mood into a positive gear, but it will also jump-start your activity level. When you are greeted with mess and clutter, you immediately shift into low gear. Lethargy takes hold because of all of the negative energy in the room. You don't need that. The mess has got to be picked up sometime, so do it before you go to bed and don't wait until it makes you cranky and tired. Create a positive energy by clearing the floor and surface areas and getting the room in order before your head hits the pillow. Some days, by the time bedtime rolls around, it is all I can do to slouch around the house picking up messes here and there. But as much as I want to go to bed, I want to start my day refreshed and positive even more. A great beginning to the day is worth spending those last minutes of the evening hauling myself around the house at night finishing those few remaining chores with my tongue hanging out, my eyes half closed, leaving a trail of drool as I go. Preparation sets the entire tone for the day, not only for me but for everyone else in the family as well. Believe me, I know straightening up the house when you're totally exhausted is one bitter pill to swallow. There are nights when I am so tired that the stairway leading to my bedroom looks more like the steps of a Mayan temple.

This little step will save loads of time as well. Ten minutes of preparation at night can easily save one hour of effort in the morning. In the morning you are working against the elements. You know what I mean, elements such as, "I can't find my good pair of khakis" or "Me go pee pee on sofa!" From the moment that first set of eyes are open (not including yours), you have got to be focused on the task at hand, and not worried about the dishes from last night or those playing cards the kids left all over the living room rug. You've got to be in the game and not on the sidelines filling up water bottles (those water bottles should have been taken care of the night before—now it's time to play). You got game, lady, so get it going!

One of the kindest things you can do for yourself is to prepare in the evening for the day ahead. Make a habit of straightening up and getting everything ready before you go to bed. Go through a mental checklist of everything that is required to begin your day, and don't let your head hit the pillow until you get to the end. Make sure the house is straightened up, your clothes are picked out and ready, and everything you need for errands is by the door or in the car ready to go. Imagine how sweet it will be to drift off to sleep knowing what waits for you in the morning. Try this for at least three weeks, and see if it doesn't completely change your life. By incorporating this habit, you are setting the stage for miracles to happen. And they will.

> *The very best days begin the night before.*

AM Routine

Sleep tight, honey, because your day is going to begin before you know it. As a matter of fact, it should begin early enough for you to spend a few moments alone. Everyone needs a tiny sliver of time to call her own. Before the morning mayhem lies a special world where imagination thrives, daydreams flourish, and creativity flows like breast milk following a baby's cry. This is your world, and it is there every morning just waiting for you to join in the magic. In the quiet moments of the early morning, while a black licorice sky turns into a ripe slice of cantaloupe and the birds begin tuning their instruments for the morning symphony, there is an entire realm of opportunity. This is the time when you can feed your spirit and explore your dreams. It is your morning Dreamtime.

Just as those last minutes of the night will set the stage for the day ahead, those first minutes in the morning will set the stage for your dreams to take shape. More goals have been reached, businesses launched, prayers answered, and dreams fulfilled in these early morning minutes than in any other time of the day. You need this time because there lies within you an infinite ability to accomplish more than you can imagine. If you started today to get those creative juices flowing, there is no limit to where your imagination can take you. What problems do you face during the day? What have you always dreamed of doing someday? What are your goals in life? What issues are you dealing with that stand in the way of reaching those goals? This is the time when you set your mind free to conjure solutions, work through problems, create plans of action, imagine the impossible, and dream. Most likely, there is no other time of day when the world will just leave you alone. Either the phone is ringing, people are knocking at the door, little ones are awake and needing attendance, or deadlines and appointments are looming. This is the time when the world sleeps, and you can explore all those beautiful nooks and crannies of your imagination. And here's how you do it.

A world of opportunity waits for you each morning.

Dress for Success

Your first step to getting your Dreamtime going is to completely prepare yourself for the day ahead and get fully dressed from head to toe. Yes, I said head. That means you are going are going to do your hair. I don't care if it's a braid wrapped around your head or a blowout touched up with styling wax. But do your hair. God gave it to you so work it, baby! And, yes, I also said toe. You are going to put on shoes. If you're worried about messing up the floor, then get some with a soft sole, but wear something. I usually wear moccasins or laced-up tennies around the house. They're comfortable, but still adequate to run outside or go on a short errand. Find what suits your style and wear them. Putting on shoes just does something for our mentality. When we have on our shoes, we are ready for anything. We can scrub a bathroom, run out to play a game of catch, change the baby, and then dump the diaper in the trash can outside without even pausing to catch our breath. If you are used to running around the house barefoot, or in a pair of slouchy socks, then please just trust me in this and try it for three weeks. I guarantee it will improve your efficiency around the house, and increase your effectiveness as a home manager.

With almost any other career, you are required to arrive at work fully dressed—hair done, shoes on, et cetera. As a home manager, however, you have an option. But just because you are allowed to arrive at work with bare feet and a bed head does not mean that you should. This demonstrates how well you respect your career. And, as with anything else in life, you eventually become what you believe yourself to be. If you happen to have a negative attitude about your abilities at home, just go through the physical motions of getting yourself completely ready for the day, and see if that attitude doesn't make a remarkable transformation. Action and thought go hand in hand. Sometimes, if the thought isn't there, then the action can be the impetus to develop it. And if the action isn't there, creating the belief within will result in a physical demonstration. It's

> *Get yourself completely ready for the day and watch miracles unfold.*

amazing, isn't it? Little things like styling your hair and tying your shoes can make enormous differences.

When you get dressed, make it something sharp—something that makes you feel and look incredible. Save the sweatpants for the workout videos, and put on some comfortable pants or jeans (they come in all colors) and a cute little top. You are beautiful, so don't hide your body behind shapeless garments that would look better covering a bed. No matter what your body shape or size, rectangle dresses (It looks like a rectangle on a hanger.) and dull, boring sweatsuits belong nowhere but in the trash can. Even if you're working out or doing chores around the house, you can look good. Replace the T-shirt with something that has a shape to it (they cost about the same) and replace the sweatpants with some pants that have a good line for your body. Stains come out just as easy, and the cost isn't that much of a difference.

And put some frosting on the cupcake with a few pieces of jewelry. I try to wear different earrings every day and slip on a necklace. And a little makeup never hurt anyone. Even if I see no one else but my own children, I believe it teaches them that I respect my career and love staying home with them. Whether we realize it or not, the majority of what we say about our children, our husband, and our career is unspoken. Beautify yourself every morning before you start the day and you will experience dramatic results. Dressing for success applies just as much to the home as it does to the boardroom.

Your Dreamtime

After you have gotten yourself ready for the day, you can sit down in a cozy corner of your home with your dream book, a pen, and a book that will feed your spirit. (Remember, you cleaned up the night before so you don't have to worry about that. Just pick a nice clean spot and let it be your own private corner.) And, whatever you do, don't be tempted to flip on the television to check out the morning news. The world will be able to spin for a while without your knowledge. This time is for you, and you only. So, find a cozy spot that is far away from the TV. Personally, I feel that I can't really begin the day with a load of emotional baggage, so the first thing I need to do is pray and let my cares and worries go to God. He knows how to deal with things much better than I do. After emptying my spirit, I then feed it. I usually read a passage out of the Bible or another inspirational book. This is my spiritual tune-up, checking in with God to get my oil changed, tires rotated, and sometimes even a rusty part replaced. I highly recommend this part of your Dreamtime. It's not always comfortable, but then again, God has bigger things to do with your life than to provide comfort.

Now that your spirit is emptied and fed, it's time to let it go exploring. This is your time to spend alone with your dream journal, just to daydream and imagine. Think of anything and everything and jot down all of your ideas. What business would you like to begin? What activities would you like to do with your family? How would you like to design the family room? Imagine it, and create it on paper. Write a plan, draw a picture, color the sunrise, list everything you love about your husband and slip it into his coat pocket. It doesn't matter what you do, as long as you give those creative juices room to flow. This time is not trivial, so don't downplay its importance. You need this time as much as you need the very air you breathe. You can only live a full life when you allow every side of your personality to prosper. Without allowing your creative spirit to grow, you are merely living a half life, and that's no life at all.

> *Your Dreamtime is a romantic date between you and your imagination.*

Be patient with your Dreamtime. This is the time when you are letting that creative child within you come out and play. And, if you are like most women today, and especially if your personality gravitates more toward the MasterMind side, your lifestyle and obligations have pushed that little girl deeper and deeper inside of you. It will take time and a bit of coaxing to convince her that it is safe to come out and play. Pick out books and passages that are colorful and exciting.

Whip out those colored pencils and doodle until the sunlight paints its portrait over the horizon. Close your eyes, and think, think, think. We don't give ourselves enough room to daydream, and daydreaming is where all great creations are born. Imagine the impossible, and you just may attain it! In the immortal words of Dr. Seuss, "Oh, the thinks you can think of if only you try!"

Those Off Hours

As far as sustaining the order and organization of your home, more will take place during those off hours in the late night and early morning than in any other time of the day. As the primary manager of your home, you set the thermostat of your home's level of functioning. As goes the captain, so goes the ship. When your needs are met, then it is far easier to meet the needs of the family and keep order in the home. You can't get too far running on fumes. Feed your spirit and watch it take flight throughout your home. If you are having difficulty in various areas of home management, this one step will make a tremendous difference. Take advantage of those minutes when the rest of the world clocks out. Use it to your advantage, and you will find yourself strides ahead of the rest of the pack. Your PM Routine will prepare your home, and your AM Routine will prepare yourself. Without this necessary prep time, then the rest of the methods to keep order are futile. If you disregard this time, then you may as well disregard the rest because you will be spending your day playing catchup. These off hours will yield the biggest return on your time investment. Try it and see. When the prep work is done, the rest of the work is a piece of cake. But the piece of cake still needs quite a bit of maintenance (we all know what happens when a cake is left alone—the frosting is swiped off quicker than a person can say, "How did you decorate that mermaid cake so perfectly?") So, now let's talk about all of those tricks we can pull during the day in order to sustain some sense of organization in the home.

Fire Drills

Remember those rest stops all through your house? You know, those places where people just naturally have a tendency to throw things and run off? The table by the back door, the dresser by the stairs, that one spot on the kitchen counter—you know what I'm talking about. Well, no matter how well you have organized it, people will still toss anything and everything there, and you will have to regularly sort through it all and put it away. Make sure you attack these hot spots before they turn into a full-blown fire. You need to regularly put them through a fire drill. While you are talking on the phone, waiting for the oven to warm up, or engaging in some other activity that frees up at least one hand, grab some items and put them away. This takes just seconds, but those few seconds add up to a lot of saved time in the long run. Don't keep glancing at that basket that is about to spill over or that dresser that no longer has any visible surface area. Do something about it. You don't have to do everything at one time. Just bite off little chunks when it is convenient. Grab a handful and put it away. Make a habit out of clearing out these rest stops every chance you get, and then the mess won't accumulate on you. We have a little table by our front door where everyone feels compelled to drop items on their way outside. At least once a day I have to grab the closest kid (they all try to stay out of arm's reach) and give her something to put away. You've got to stay in control of the mess, or the mess will get control over you!

> *Little nibbles every day will save you from having to tackle the whole enchilada.*

Ten-Minute Tidy

There used to be a children's show that my kids would occasionally watch about a clown. The clown would make a mess while she played, and before she would take a nap, she would have to do a ten-second tidy. She would run around in a mad fury, putting away all of the toys that she had played with. I figured if it worked for a clown, maybe it would work for my kids (but we would definitely require more than ten seconds—it takes them that long to scratch their heads and say, "Huh?"). We started doing a ten-minute tidy, where we had ten minutes to speed through the house and put everything away. If we finished one room, and still had some minutes left on the clock, then we would rush into another room and attack that area. It worked splendidly! We all knew it was a short (and finite) period of time, and we also saw it as a type of contest to see how much we could get accomplished. If it is only you cleaning up, it works just as well. For some reason, the tick of the clock helps us get ourselves in gear.

Commercial Cleanup

By and large, television is a waste of time and it is completely overused. However, there is a great method of cleaning that I incorporate whenever I allow the kids to watch television. I figure TV is a privilege, so they may as well earn it while they watch it. Some may consider this torture. I figure that I am just giving them good material to use later in life (especially at cocktail parties or therapy sessions). The commercial clean-up also works well when you really want to just take a time-out but there are still chores left to do. For example, that cool home show is on, but you still haven't washed the dishes. Television commercials are the perfect window of time to rush around the house putting away stray items and straightening up. Believe me, if you really needed that miraculous hair remover for your upper lip, you would have known about it by now (or at least I hope you would have known about it by now). Take this opportunity to get things done around the house, because it's the perfect length of time. Just when you are getting tired of folding the laundry, ta-da! Your show is back on.

Take advantage of little pockets of time throughout the day.

The Number Game

There is a reason I was never a math major—I hate numbers. Well, not all the time. I happen to be very fond of them when it comes to picking up and putting away. Setting a certain number of items to put away helps because you are working toward a specific goal. You can even be a bit sneaky. We have a basket at the bottom of our stairs that holds items that belong upstairs. You can just imagine how many things accumulate at this rest stop. One day, it was so full you could not even see the basket. The contents were spilling out everywhere. I told the four oldest kids to each get four items and put them upstairs where they belong, then do three items, two items, then one item. Everyone jumped right on it, except the oldest, of course. She rolled her eyes, filled her arms with stuff from the basket, and said, "I'll just go ahead and do ten right now."

May I Have This Dance?

Keeping up your home's level of organization is really just a dance that takes place all over the house. And the dance takes place between people and stuff. You dance with a cup out of the kitchen, and you dance it right back in. You dance that laundry into the washer, from the washer to the dryer, and then do a little merengue with the fitted sheet as you try to shape it into a neat little rectangle. Your son dances that spaceship all over the house, and then you cut in and dance it right back into the toy basket. Every time you leave a room, you should have a dance partner. If you are walking into the kitchen, look around for something you can dance back in there. If you are going upstairs, what item can you sashay with?

Don't gear it down to the slow dance either. Put some wiggle in it, baby! Grab that dance partner on your way out of the room and shake what your mama gave you! If you don't have something to dance with, then feel free to do a little victory dance all by yourself because your house is in perfect condition. As a matter of fact, it's probably too perfect. Relax a little bit and dump the flatware drawer out on the floor just for the sheer heck of it. It makes a great crashing sound that works as an excellent catharsis! But if your home is anything like mine, there are not nearly enough dances to go around. So, grab a partner and get that boogie down. What is that you've got in your hands? It must be jelly, 'cause jam don't shake like that!

Dance your way to a well maintained home.

Around the Room in Eighty Days

Or at least in eight minutes. Another good way to structure your pick-up routine is to start at one end of the room and go all the way around, picking up and putting away as you go. By the way, when I talk about your pick-up routine, that does not refer to slipping on some fishnets and going clubbing, although I do

157

know women who have been able to do this in eight minutes or less. When you pick up and put away, you are going to put things exactly where they go. I have to be specific with my kids. If I don't instruct them to put items *exactly* where they go, they will usually walk within three yards of where they belong, and toss them in the general vicinity. Not that there's anything wrong with that, mind you. It's no fault of theirs that they are lazier than a pack of mutated slugs. I hear it's just a natural side effect of childhood and adolescence. But getting back to the round-the-room method, it works well because you can track your progress and know how much further you have to go. You also have a clearly defined path of direction, and you're not just floundering in the middle of a pile of junk.

Pit of Despair

When you are not sure where to begin, just start tossing everything into the center of the room. Or if it is the bedroom, then make up the bed and toss everything on top of it. This is your pit of despair. But at least it's all piled into the center instead of strewn about all over the room. This method works great with kids, especially when their version of "neat" is dramatically different from yours. For example, after they clean up their bedroom, then you can go in and throw all of the dirty underwear, used towels, toys, brushes, and dress-up clothes on top of their bed. That way, they know exactly what they need to put away, and it is much more manageable than you peering over their heads, barking orders. It works for children as well as adults because it consolidates the mess. We can see at a glance what we're dealing with. It may be a pit of despair, but we can usually work through it in no time at all if we apply ourselves.

Life is not meant to be lived in the pits! So, get out of them!

Guess Who's Coming to Dinner?

This is a last-resort method to get the house straightened up. It's an act out of sheer desperation, but it works every time. Invite someone over. Take a good look at all of the junk strewn across the floor, the mess in the playroom, and the counter full of filthy dishes, and pick up the phone and ask someone over. There's nothing like a visit from someone to give you the kick in the pants that you need to restore order in your home. You always want to put your best foot forward, and when you know someone is going to show up at your front door, you want the house looking good (or if not good, then at least decent). The effort to straighten up won't feel like work at all because you are anticipating a visit from a friend. You don't need a formal meal, or really any reason at all. Just invite a friend over for a short visit—maybe just a jar of nuts, iced tea, and some delicious conversation. Or if you feel that you need an excuse, ask her to come over and help you make a double batch of something yummy and she can take half of it home. You will have a good time together, get something accomplished, and straighten up your house as well. You can't beat that for results!

Time for Your Prescription

Remember all that hard work you did to get your home de-cluttered and organized? Don't let all of that effort slip through your fingers by neglecting to sustain it. If you are not accustomed to the little habits of keeping order in your home, then start developing them today. Some women may find this more difficult than others, but there are all different ways to work with your personality to get things accomplished around the house. So forget about the one way to do things. Your way is the right way, and that's all there is to it. And also remember that the maintenance level of your home is no reflection on who you are as a person. You want to find the level that works for you and your family.

I am convinced that there is no more difficult task than running a family. The president has nothing on us. We not only have to manage all of the tasks of running a household, but we also have to work with a myriad of different personalities to build a family as well. So give it time, and don't get frustrated if everyone under your roof isn't on board the organization train when it takes off from the station. It will take a while for everyone to come around. Try to understand that they may just not share your personality or your perspective. Be patient and keep up the good work. They will eventually come around when they see your dedication and joyful spirit. We set the tone for everything that goes on under our roofs. So, let your husband believe what he may, you know who is really wearing the pants in the family (and they better be a pair that is flattering).

Rx for MasterMinds

It's time to close your eyes and dream. You probably spend a great deal of time looking around your home figuring out what you need to do here and there. Now it's time to look inside yourself. Make it a point to get up before anyone else so that you can spend some beautiful minutes in your Dreamtime. You are a remarkably creative woman, but you may just need to pump up the juice a little bit. Don't shrug this time off. Invest in it, and watch entire dimensions open up within you. Start by putting your daydreams down on paper. Grab that miraculous pen, and write it all down in your dream journal. Invest in this time, and watch the rest of the day just fall into place. And when it comes to keeping order during the day, you respond best to very precise methods, such as the number game. But, remember not to let your standards impose on those of other family members. The purpose of setting up organized systems is so everyone in your family can live happily ever after, not so that your home fits your idea of perfection. Perfection is boring. Family harmony, now that's exciting.

Rx for Creative Spirits

At first you may resist the idea of developing routines around the house. But fret no more, darling. No one is going to try to cram that beautiful square peg into a round hole. You are perfect just the way you are. By starting your AM and PM routines, you will be opening up time and space for your creative spirit to soar. You are a wonderful work of art that is in the process of creation every day. But when the space and time in your life is crowded, your development is stifled. All artists must be disciplined to create their form of art. Let your passion motivate you to begin those morning and night routines. You have a keen sense of being able to see what is unseen, so open your eyes and see the big picture of how your life is being created and recreated. As you invest your time in these routines, you will see an amazing work of art develop. And in order to keep some sense of structure in your home during the day, have fun with those ten-minute tidys and stay on top of the fire drills.

Rx for Mother Hens

Keeping up the organization shouldn't be much of a problem for you. You love routine, so it should be a snap to fine-tune those methods that work best for you. And when you go around doing what you do best, add a little moxie to it. Blast some funky music and get your groove on while you clean the mess up. Try some of those Britney Spears moves if you don't think anyone is looking or if you are not in danger of throwing your back out. As far as developing your morning routine, this is imperative if you are going to operate as a fully functioning woman. You love your family and your domestic life, but sometimes you expend so much of your physical and emotional energy in this line of work, that you forget to maintain the pacesetter—*you*! You have a duty to your home and your family, but you also have a duty to yourself. Take some time in the morning and spoil your-self a little bit. You deserve it. Pull a chair up to the table, grab a latte, and chill for a while. Set the scene with a delicious-smelling candle and the prettiest col-ored pencils you can get your hands on. Instead of planning or organizing, spend this time just pausing and looking within. Take in the glorious sunrise, listen to the sound of your breathing, color a beautiful rainbow in your dream journal. Grab the moments as they present themselves and hold them in your heart because that is where the true treasure lies.

Rx for Starry-Eyed Dreamers

You can do this! When that alarm goes off in the morning, you're going to have to kick yourself out of bed. By incorporating this one single step of getting up before everyone else, you will save yourself tons of effort and time during the day, not to mention your sanity. You have so much to bring to the world, and you are full of blessings to pour out to those you love most. For too long, you may have been hiding that beauty underneath confusion and chaos. Life is not meant to be lived from the sidelines. It's time to take a deep breath, close your eyes, and jump in the pool. It's adult swim time (but that doesn't mean you have to wear a little rubber daisy cap)—so jump on in and splash like crazy. You have the poten-tial to create the world you want to live in, but it's up to you to take matters into your hands. When you are tempted to push the snooze button and stay in bed, ask yourself if those few minutes of extra sleep are worth spending the rest of the day lagging behind. On the coldest day with the warmest flannel sheets, it's still worth it to get up early. And when you are having difficulty getting motivated to straighten up the house, you respond best to people situations, so pick up the phone and invite someone over. This will motivate you to clean up, or you can even solicit some help in the process. If she's a good friend, then the two of you could turn it into a party!

Dream On!

Time to get out that dream journal and make a fan page to yourself. Remember those teen magazines with a picture of your favorite rock star in the middle and around it all of his amazing accomplishments? Okay, so maybe driving around in a Porsche isn't that amazing. Anyway, find a picture of yourself, glue it in the middle of a blank page, and with all different colors, write your amazing accomplishments all over the paper around your picture. It could be as simple as, "makes the meanest pralines this side of the Mississippi" or "looks fantastic in purple." It doesn't matter. Just fill up the page with glorious praises for you. And if you feel a bit neurotic about putting your picture on the page then just fill it up with applause for yourself. The way I figure it, if I'm not neurotic by now, then at least I'm close. So put your neuroses aside and take a lesson in admiring yourself. We can all do with a little more self-love here and there.

After you finish your fan page, glance back through your journal until you come to the page where you made your list of buggers. Now find two that you can cross off your list, either by dealing with it or just letting it go and forgetting about it. If you decide to deal with it, then start taking action right now. Set a time or date to gather up any supplies that you need, and give yourself a clear date to finish it. Now start working on that goal. Enough planning and postponing, take action! And it's okay if you find the two easiest ones to accomplish. The most important thing is that you set a clearly defined task and you succeed at it. The positive energy that results from reaching a goal will propel you forward to do more and more.

Part 4

Clean It!

Chapter 9

Make Your House Work

Every one of us loves a clean house, but there is just one problem. It never stays that way for long. I guess dust, dirt, grime, and mildew are just some of those wonderful things we get to deal with as a result of the spiritual fall of mankind. We managed to do something about painful childbirth, and good ole John Deere managed to ease our woes with working the land. So, why are we still running around with our mops and dust cloths? Well, there's good news—you have options. You can hire someone to do it for you, you can learn how to do it quickly and painlessly yourself, or you can actually enjoy cleaning and opt for doing chores as opposed to, say, eating a pan of brownies. If you are the latter, then feel free to bypass this section of the book and please let me know if you are available next Tuesday.

My Standards, Your Standards

Everyone has a different idea of clean, just as everyone has a different method to attain it. My neighbors are a wonderful retired couple. She vacuums the house every single day (no lie!) and considers fingerprints on glass surfaces as a sign of neglect. She goes through vacuum cleaner bags quicker than I go through loaves of bread. If her grandkids come over, she puts up baby gates to keep them out of certain rooms, and wipes their hands, faces, and other body parts continually. Now walk next door, and step into my house. Eight people live under one roof (seven of them are at home all day long). I probably vacuum once a week, more often in the family room when I can no longer make out the design on the rug. The kids have free reign over the entire house, and they are responsible for cleaning their own bathroom (you can just smell it right now, can't you?). If your shoes don't track through something sticky on the kitchen floor, we're having a good day.

Every one of us has different standards of clean when it comes to our own homes. What is clean to one person is not necessarily clean to another. And it is vitally important not to let your standards impose on other people (especially your kids). There is no criterion for clean when it comes to your own house except one:

> *It should be clean enough to be a house, messy enough to be a home.*

Your home should be clean enough to bring out the beauty of your house and rid the environment of potentially harmful germs and bacteria, and it should be messy enough to allow for comfortable living to occur. If it is too dirty, it detracts from your home, demonstrates a lack of respect and gratitude on the part of the inhabitants, and can also cause accidents and illness. It's disturbing, frustrating, and dangerous. A dirty home is not just unsanitary, it's just plain ugly, too. Then, on the other hand, if your house is too clean, the time and effort to maintain it is pulled out of other areas of your life and the inhabitants cannot relax enough to live comfortably. Too clean is no fun for anyone. It's just a bunch of shine and sparkle without the love and laughter. Like with anything else in life, it's all about balance. You need to find the happy medium that works with everyone in your home.

And that means everyone in your home. My standards have lowered following the birth of each of my children. If I keep on having kids, then we will eventually be dining from a feeding trough and changing our sheets on a yearly basis. I can divide my standards into BC and AD (Before Children and After Dementia). In my BC years, I would hang my clothes on matching hangers and laundry was not allowed to stay in the hamper for longer than twenty-four hours. Now here I am living happily in my AD years, hanging my sundresses on Winnie-the-Pooh hangers and battling mildew on my dishtowels that have been hibernating for a week in the bottom of the laundry basket. Standards are meant to help us live in a personally gratifying manner, not to be held over our heads, or making us feel inadequate. Adjust them to a level that will suit everyone, including the kids. A home is meant for living and loving, not showing and telling. What good are those pillows, if the kids are never allowed to throw them on the floor and pretend as if they are stepping-stones? What good is that sparkling glass door, if the kids are never allowed to paint on it with watercolors? Build memories first, the house later. But, enough talk about standards, let's start talking dirty!

An Ounce of Prevention

Everyone always wants to know what product best cleans your bathtub or how to get out carpet stains. Well, the best way to keep your house clean is not to do any work at all. Make your house do the work instead. Preventing a mess is a hundred times easier than cleaning it up. The hotel and restaurant industry has known about this for quite some time, but they have been keeping it a secret from homemakers. People are paid good salaries for designing interiors that reduce the cost of labor and maintenance. Have you ever wondered why it takes a woman less than ten minutes to clean an entire hotel room (including the bathroom), and it takes you thirty minutes just to do your bedroom?

The next time you step into a restaurant, check out how the interior differs from yours. The lighting probably does not collect dust easily, and can be wiped off in seconds. The carpet probably has a design that can easily camouflage stains and spills. The furniture probably has very few points of contact with the floor (tables probably have one large point of contact in the center instead of four legs). Fabrics are those that can be wiped off easily or bleached for whiteness. Surface areas have a smooth finish for easy clean up. And walls are often warm colors or covered in wallpaper that can be sponged off. This industry has been designing out the housework for years. Homemakers have only recently begun to incorporate more low-maintenance design elements in their homes. By incorporating some of these design elements in your home, you can dramatically reduce the amount of time you spend cleaning. I mean, honestly, don't we have better things to do than to scrub out the grout between the tiles all day long? The number one way to get rid of dirt and scum is to prevent it.

Preventing the mess is a whole lot easier than cleaning it up.

Keep the Dirt Out

The best trick in the book when it comes to getting the dirt out of your house is to keep it outside where it belongs. If you walk into a major department store, you probably don't even realize that you step over yards of matting before you even enter. They have better things to do than sweep up all of that dirt that you carry in their store. And you have better things to do than sweep up all of that dirt that your family carries into the home. Keep the dirt out by putting mats at the outside and inside of all entrances to your home (that includes the garage, as well). And I'm not talking about these piddly little do-nothing mats that are one-fourth inch thick. No one really cares if your mat is welcoming them or not. As a matter of fact, if you get a mat that says "Welcome," then in less than three weeks, it's probably just going to say "We" if your door opens from the right side. And then people may think that it really says, "We . . . don't want you to come visit us" or "We . . . really don't take to your kind around here." On the other hand, if your door opens from the left, it will eventually say "me." Then people who come to your door may just think that it says, "I don't want you to visit . . . me" or "If you think I don't have anything better to do than to wait around the house for you to visit, then you obviously don't know . . . me." Something to think about, isn't it?

Pass over on the wimpy mats, and go for something that can earn its keep. Industrial mats are not necessarily the prettiest things on the market, but neither is that dirt that accumulates in your foyer. You can find industrial mats at janitorial supplies stores or shopping warehouses. They are much larger than your standard mats, and work extremely well at pulling the dirt off the bottom of shoes. Put one outside and inside of each door. Personally, they are not pretty enough for me to put one inside the front entrance to my house, so I have an industrial quality mat outside and on the inside I have a large rug that matches my decor.

You also need to make sure that your mats are large enough to perform. Leave those little tiny ones on the top shelf of the department store. They do not belong on the inside or outside of your home because they won't do a bit of good. You may as well put a paper towel there. They need to be big and roomy in order to get the dirt off of shoes. Make sure the inside and outside mats together cover at least six steps. And in order to keep your mats looking good and performing well, vacuum or sweep them off regularly. When they get really nasty, give them a good scrubbing with your outdoor broom and a couple drops of dish detergent, rinse them with a power washer or trigger hose, and hang them over a railing to dry. Make sure they are completely dry before you use them again, or else you are just asking to have mud tracked through your house.

> *Keep the dirt outside where it belongs!*

Another way to keep the dirt out is to have a shoes-off rule when you step inside. I am the only one who runs around the house with shoes on. I told my kids that when they begin working as hard as I do to keep the house clean, they can wear shoes, too. So far, I have not had any takers. The kids drop their shoes into a washtub by the door, and I am constantly amazed at the mountain of shoes that can accumulate. And since our front yard usually contains more bats and gloves than blades of grass, the opportunity to track in dirt is endless. Mats will get a lot of the dirt off of shoes, but my kids don't just have a problem with dirt on the bottom of their shoes. With three wooded acres and a creek in the back, the dirt usually stops about mid-thigh. Sometimes it's not just the shoes they have to take off. When I can no longer discriminate between the kids and the mud, they usually end up running inside in their underwear (fortunately, our home remains pretty hidden).

Pick Easy-to-Clean Surfaces

The smoother the surface, the easier it is to clean. Just visualize the difference between changing the poopy diaper of a girl versus a boy (for those mothers out there who have only girls, a boy's crotch region does not provide optimal smoothness—we're talking one major aggregate surface). If you don't have a hand in designing your own house, then you're pretty much stuck with what you've got. But, everything wears out eventually. When it does, replace it with something that cuts down on your housework.

When we moved into our last house, I spent two and one-half years with tile countertops that I despised. I could never rationalize replacing them because they were in good condition, but every day I would scrub those suckers like a crazed woman, trying to clean the grout. I make bread two to three times a week, and every time I did, I would have to take a scraper and clean the dough off the counters—talk about a pain! Finally, when the grout started to chip off (the hammer and chisel helped), I saw it as an excuse to replace the tiles with a smooth surface in a yummy shade that complemented my home. Instantly, cleaning the kitchen took a fraction of the time it had previously, and kneading bread dough was no longer a chore. Looking back, I should have done it when we first moved in. If I had, it would have probably added a week to my life with all the time I spent cleaning that tile!

Smooth surfaces hold true for painted surfaces, as well. The more reflective the paint surface, the easier it is to clean. And when a company advertises their flat paint as "scrubbable," it actually means that compared to that shag carpet or that big fat unshorn sheep grazing in your backyard, the painted surface is much more scrubbable. I once painted a nursery with flat paint. By seven months in, the area above the changing table looked like a page out of *Diapers I Have Known and Loved.*

As far as furniture goes, leather surfaces beat fabric hands down when it comes to clean-up. No Scotchgard protection in the world can beat the ease of wiping off the surface with a little bit of diluted oil soap. Vinyl also repels dirt and stains, but it attracts a little too much skin on my fleshy thighs, and it also causes little farty noises to erupt from sweaty legs, which is not appealing in the least (or at least I'm hoping they come from sweaty legs). Find the furniture that both creates comfort and provides easy cleanup. If you still have questions about the whole "smooth surface" thing, then come over and check out the woven seats of the ladderback chairs that surround my kitchen table. I could fill up a casserole dish with all of the dried food stuck in the cracks and creases.

If you can't prevent the mess, at least make it easy to clean.

And the same theory of "easy to clean" holds true with fabrics in your home. Whenever I am picking out anything fabric for my home, whether curtains, tablecloth, slipcovers, or duvet covers, there are three words I want to avoid like the plague—dry clean only. You don't want to have fabrics around your kids that you can't just toss into the washing machine. Once, I was searching for the perfect fabric to cover a loveseat in our living room. I came across several that I liked but, alas, those three words—dry clean only. Finally, I found it—a corduroy in a beautiful shade of purple that was completely washable (yes, I have a purple loveseat). It took me an entire day (and deep into the night) to finish the project, and two of my kids managed to catch a cold that same week. After the slipcover had been on the loveseat for a whole ten days, I was walking through the room and caught a glimpse of it in the bright afternoon sun. It was a sight to behold— my beautiful purple loveseat, shimmering all over with gleaming trails of mucus. It looked as if it had been attacked during the night by an army of slugs. Fortunately, I was able to throw it in the wash, and it was as good as new. I then went out and bought twelve boxes of Kleenex.

If you ever get a chance to design your interiors or to replace surfaces in your home, go for smooth, seamless, and washable surfaces. Remember that the more cracks and crevices you have, the more dirt, grime, and bacteria can accumulate. Unless you just have this thing for cleaning and polishing furniture, then pick out the furniture with woodwork that does not resemble a study in Baroque architecture. Forget tile in the bathroom, unless you just enjoy spending an extra twenty minutes in the shower with a toothbrush and some cleaner. But, if you're already naked in the shower with the toothbrush, I can think of a lot better things to do than scrubbing tile, especially if you're not showering alone. So, keep the toothbrush, and replace the cleaner with caramel ice cream topping.

The Art of Camouflage

This little secret is not to be kept strictly within the armed forces. Messes, spills, fingerprints, and other mishaps are inevitable (especially if you have little ones around). Figure out which areas in your home get the dirtiest, and design around them. I wouldn't go so far as to paint a faux-finished rug on the floor underneath the dining room table that looks like Cheetos. That may be taking it one step too far. But, the busier the design, the better it disguises. I have a friend who put up a chair rail in her foyer and living room just so that she could put wallpaper on the bottom portion of the walls. She picked out a pretty pattern of flowers and ribbon that had all of the colors she used throughout the first floor of her home. The finished effect look great, but what looked even better were all of the fingerprints and crayon marks that you could not see. The entire reason she wallpapered was to disguise all the marks her toddler (the blossoming Picasso) left all over the walls.

If you can't clean the mess, go ahead and hide it!

If wallpaper is not your thing, you could always do a faux finish on your walls, such as a leather, suede, or fresco finish. This is also a great way to disguise less-than-perfect walls. These techniques are quite easy and there are excellent books describing how to do them. Also, every tool you could imagine is in the paint aisle. The only things I've ever used are a paintbrush and a rag, and it always has turned out great. Besides looking fantastic, these finishes also do a great job hiding the dirt and smudges that build up over time.

Floors are also places that attract dirt like crazy (I hear it has something to do with gravity). If you get the opportunity to choose carpeting, I would highly recommend picking out a shade that resembles something your son would track in off the football field. If you are choosing a rug, get one with a pattern that fills up the entire thing, not just a border. That way, you have the entire square footage of the rug working in your favor by hiding juice spills, bits of popcorn, and the occasional episode of potty training gone awry. And I don't even need to mention white carpet, do I? Anyone who chooses white carpet for their home either (a) does not have children or (b) does not want children or (c) has children and asks herself every day, "What in Sam Hill have I done?" I once had a friend with white carpet—until the day I tracked dog poop through her living room. Our friendship was washed away with an entire bottle of Resolve carpet cleaner.

As far as hard floors go, avoid very light shades in tile and laminate. I once had a bathroom with a floor covered in white tile, and I never will again. Tile that has a natural mixture of different shades of the same color hides dirt much better than tile that is one precise shade. Wood floors are an excellent choice, and the more natural shades will do a better job hiding wear and tear. However, all wood floors will need to be properly maintained to keep them in good condition. Before you invest in new flooring, get the lowdown on how well it hides dirt. If you have to, go in the home improvement store with a chocolate bar, smear it over all of the samples, and see which one still looks good—that's the keeper!

Camouflage also works very well when it comes to fabric surfaces in your home, such as furniture, curtains, bedspreads, and such. When you are choosing any type of fabric for your home, plan ahead about its ability to hide stains. We have a deep red easy chair in our living room. I don't even want to think about the stains that lie hidden on its surfaces, but they're hidden and I'm happy. Our curtains are in a rich shade of wheat (or should I say peanut butter?). And I didn't make a quilt for my daughters' bed just to create an heirloom. I sewed it in a myriad of different shades because I knew how much they enjoyed playing with makeup! A house is to live in, not live for, so go ahead and make a mess. Just remember to design around it, so cleanup is easier on everyone involved.

Knickknack, Break My Back

I have read that 70 percent of housework is caused by clutter, and I completely believe it. If this figure is correct, then we could cut the amount of time we spend cleaning our homes by two-thirds simply by getting rid of all of the stuff that we clean between, around, and underneath. By and large, people have way too much stuff displayed on the surface areas within their homes. A few nice things are fine, but too much of a good thing is a bad thing. The few nice things get lost amid all of the clutter. And then you are left cleaning every last little bit of it. Cut down on the time you spend cleaning by getting rid of the stuff you need to clean.

> *Don't spend time cleaning stuff you don't even need or want—toss it!*

Consider replacing a lot of the little things you have with one big one. For example, instead of having six different picture frames for each of my kids, I got a picture of each of the kids, matted it in black, and put one in each pane of a large six-pane window. Now I just have one big thing to dust and keep straight instead of six little ones. This idea can work for anything. Instead of a bunch of little plants, what about one beautiful tree? Instead of a shelf full of memorabilia, what about one large shadowbox that can hold and display everything?

If you do have lots of little things, remember to contain them somehow. The time it takes to pick up a basket of action figures and wipe the surface underneath sure beats the time it takes to clean underneath every last little one. This method of containing items should have already been accomplished as part of your AS IS organizing. You may be awfully proud of that shot glass collection, but do you love those little pieces of glass enough to dedicate a portion of your life to its care and upkeep? Forget it about, baby, you've got bigger fish to fry. If you can't part with it, pack it away. And if you can't pack it away, then at least contain it somehow. By simply clearing away the surface areas in your home, you will dramatically cut down on the time you spend cleaning. Now you can take those belly dancing lessons you've always wanted.

Cover-up Scheme

Remember to protect the surfaces that you have within your home. A great way to do this is to cover them up! If you don't have the luxury of picking out new carpet with stain protection, then protect the carpet that you currently have. As far as stain protection goes, a can of Scotchgard is worth its weight in gold, and you can apply it to your upholstered surfaces as well. If you purchase a new rug, always spray it heavily with Scotchgard and allow it to dry completely before using it. This will make clean up easier and will greatly extend the life of your rug. Make sure you read the directions completely before using, because it requires a liberal amount, and you want to make sure that you purchase enough to cover the entire area.

You can also protect hard surfaces with contact paper. Lining your shelves is a good way to protect them from damage, and it is also a nice incentive to get you to clean out your cabinets. If you prefer not to cover the shelves with paper, but still want to protect them, then go for clear contact paper. I use this on almost all of my shelves, especially the ones that hold messy things such as plants or laundry detergent. You can't even tell it's there. Don't put it on a painted surface unless you are willing to repaint it or if you are content with it remaining there forever. When you pull off the paper, you will take some paint with you. In other words, get it right the first time.

Think about all of the other surfaces in your home that you should cover up to prevent damage and mess. Mattresses are a must. Whenever you purchase a new mattress, or even if you are just trying to extend the life of one that you currently have, it should be covered in a waterproof mattress cover. These don't cost much at all, and you can always disguise the slickness of the waterproof mattress cover with a soft, thick, and washable mattress cover underneath the fitted sheet. If you don't purchase these, I guarantee you will live to regret it. Once your mattress is baptized with urine in the middle of the night, it's as good as written in the lamb's book of life. Forget about cleaning it all up. You can scrub until the apocalypse, but you will never get out that golden halo.

Off the Floor

As far as furniture goes, the fewer points of contact with the floor, the easier the maintenance. When objects rest on the floor, you will have to figure out some way to vacuum, sweep, or mop around them. You could be struck with sudden ingenuity, such as my son when he pushed his younger brother headfirst under the bed, grabbed him by his ankles, and used his body to sweep out the hardwood floors underneath. For the rest of the day the poor kid looked like Pigpen from the Peanuts cartoon with a cloud of dust following him. But if you don't want to resort to such drastic measures, then figure out a way to suspend it. Bar stools that are attached to the wall have no point of contact with the floor at all, so there is minimal effort required to clean the floor underneath. Pedestal tables are much easier to clean under than tables with four legs. Built-in benches beat single chairs any day. But, let's face it. We don't live at Denny's. Find the happy medium that provides beauty and comfort but also provides low maintenance.

How much stuff can you get off the floor and on the walls?

There are many ideas to reduce floor contact that you may be able to incorporate into your home. Built-in beds and cabinets are easier to clean around than free-standing ones. Built-in drawers are easier to clean around than a dresser. Built-ins are great because they have no points of contact with the floor, and little surface area. That way, you don't have anything to collect dust and no temptation to pile it full of all your collectibles. There may be several little nooks around your home that are just begging for some built-in drawers or cabinets.

Be a Design Detective

Whenever you are choosing items for your home, think maintenance. Sure, that lamp with all of the feathers looks cute, but stop and consider for a moment how you're going to clean the darn thing. The ivory chenille furniture is lovely, but do you really want the pressure of maintaining it? Go for something that will work with your home and your lifestyle. Remember that the purpose of your home is to nurture, not impress. Sometimes the happiest home is the one with the little fingerprints all over the place and the mud tracked in through the back door. Embrace this beautiful part of family life. Instead of struggling against the beautiful messiness of life, design around it. Keep one question burned into your brain whenever you go shopping:

Do I love it enough to spend part of my life maintaining it?

This one question alone has caused me to put more silk plants and throw rugs back on the shelf than I can count. Investigate everything you pick up before you throw it into your shopping buggy. Does it have a smooth surface to provide easy cleanup? Do the patterns coordinate with my family's lifestyle? Will it increase or decrease my workload? Is it washable? Replacing high-maintenance items with low-maintenance items will create time for you to do other things. You have more exciting things to do with your life than to clean around those knick-knacks all over your kitchen counter. Cut down on the workload and increase the excitement. Give your home a quick wipe down and sweep out and then go on a canoe ride, a nature hike, or a walk in the rain. Take up a new sport such as yoga or fencing. Stomp in puddles, fly a kite, or simply close your eyes and dream. But cleaning? Puh-leeze!

Time for Your Prescription

We are all different women, and we all have different standards when it comes to cleaning. But, no matter what your personality, you have to strive for balance in your home. There is a fine line that exists somewhere between Felix Unger and Oscar Madison. By being an extremist, you are going to be chasing out the very people your home is meant to shelter. And you're either going to chase them out in a spray of disinfectant or a cloud of dust. Find the place where everyone's needs are met, and train yourself to be content remaining there. It's worth it, because you love your family. If you need to, just bite your lip when you hear that box of cereal spill out all over the floor and stay in the sidelines, waiting until you're needed. And if you need to, kick yourself in the fanny to get up and mop up the floor before the entire surface is covered in apple juice. Cleanliness is not next to godliness no matter what they may say, and in all of our toils and efforts, we can never mop our way to heaven. But cleanliness is a wonderful way to show gratitude for God's providence, and I think if He were raising a family today, He would go for solid surfacing over tile any old day.

Rx for MasterMinds

When it comes to home design, you have the tendency to go for function over form. Let's face it, you've got your act together and can get your home running so streamlined that it makes the rest of us look as if we're running an obstacle course. But sometimes, when you're rounding third, it's fun to wave your cap or do a little power punch to the grandstands. The whole point of getting your home in a condition of easy maintenance is so you have more time and energy to enjoy other parts of your life. Make it a point to go for a little bit of fluff to round out the tones of your home. Glance through your home and check out the functionality of all of the furnishings, and find one thing to add that is strictly for a decorative purpose. Sure, it goes against making your house do the work for you, but you probably have no problem with that. You are all about strategically solving dilemmas, so go for something with more pizzazz than performance, maybe a scrumptious throw pillow or some nice new curtains. Exercise that creative side of your brain, and see where it takes you.

Rx for Creative Spirits

And when it comes to form and function, you run to form as if it were a long-lost lover. You definitely focus more on aesthetics than you do on performance. Remember to put items through your checklist. It's your life that you are devoting to its care and upkeep. Function can be beautiful, but try to find the happy marriage. If you don't love it enough to serve it with care and upkeep, then bypass the purchase (or toss it out). This doesn't mean you have to run your home like a Super 8 Motel. Personally, I tend to go for pictures that can actually change position on the wall or a bed that can house a lost sock underneath it for a month or more. Housework doesn't have to be one extreme or the other. Just make sure that those items you choose to clean are worth the effort you put into it.

179

Rx for Mother Hens

You don't mind the work that you put into your home, but make sure that you are not neglecting to invest some effort in yourself. Instead of spending the time maintaining your home, try spending a little bit of time figuring out how you can lower the maintenance. Find one thing that you have always wanted to do, but have refused yourself because of the demands that home management has placed upon you. Have you always wanted to learn how to play the guitar? What about taking some cake decorating classes or learning a foreign language? The choices are endless. Cut out some of the unnecessary chores around the house, and use the time and energy that it frees up to invest in yourself for a change.

Rx for Starry-Eyed Dreamers

Incorporating more cleaner-friendly designs around your home is your best bet to keeping a cleaner and less cluttered home. You have much higher pursuits than dusting furniture or folding laundry. Your heart is constantly pulled in other directions, and your mind quickly follows. Don't be hard on yourself because you don't keep your home in pristine condition. Dirt can always be swept up later, so feel free to chase your dreams right now. But a cluttered and messy home will soon begin pulling that sweet spirit of yours down to the ground. Take five minutes every day and find one thing in your home that you can design in a way that cuts down on some of the cleanup time and effort. Can that silk plant be packed away? Could you consolidate all of those separate framed pictures into one big collage? Can you use that towel a couple more times before tossing it into the laundry? Be kind to yourself and create a home that is designed for you to follow your heart. Once you start making your home easier to maintain, then you will be able to whip out those crayons and color yourself impressed!

Dream On!

Designing your home to minimize maintenance is a great way to enjoy your home more and free up time and energy to be invested in other areas. Perhaps you want to invest in creating some new dimension of yourself. Doing a little exploratory work in your dream journal is an excellent way to figure out just what dimensions you would like to develop. So grab your journal and spend some time thinking of people you really, really like and admire. Think of at least five people—past, present, famous or not, it doesn't matter. Just think of five people and write their names down in your journal.

Now consider for a moment why you admire these people. What qualities do they exhibit in their lives that ignite that fire of passion within you? Okay, so maybe "fire of passion" is a bit too strong. We'll save that one for the bedroom, or at least a nicely carpeted stairway. But what do you see in these people? What do you respect about them? For each of the five people you listed, write down the qualities that you admire about them. And spend some time thinking about this, because it sheds a lot of light on our value system. For example, my son really admires Bugs Bunny. Obviously, he values the important things in life, such as eating carrots, executing perfect practical jokes, and running around naked. So put some thought into this activity. It will tell you a great deal about what things are important to you in your life at this moment in time.

After you know what you really value about these people, you can then ask yourself what is preventing you from exhibiting these same qualities in your own life. You don't need to be a slave to your home. Spend time in your home caring for it and loving it because that is what you love to do. But don't forget to give yourself a little TLC also. Invest in yourself and fuel your engine by developing the same skills in yourself that you admire in others. Nothing stands between who you are right now and who you want to be but determination and effort.

Chapter 10

Tools of the Trade

Where would we be without our wonderful cleaning tools? They help us dissolve stains, reach corners, and extract dirt like nobody's business. But it seems as if there is a new product invented every other day. There's a new broom that will gather up microscopic pieces of dust or a new cleaner that is guaranteed to remove every stain your family could possibly produce. The right ones can easily cut your cleaning time and effort in half. The wrong ones make your job twice as hard, and twice as long. How in the world do you choose your tools?

Schedules? We Don't Need No Stinkin' Schedules!

Probably the most important tools that we employ when cleaning our homes are our schedules, and it is one of the biggest hang-ups as well. We get too caught up in the "shoulds" of life. How much should we weigh? What clothes should we wear? What food should I eat? And the world of cleaning is no exception. How often should we clean our windows? How often should I vacuum? How often should I clean the bathroom? Well, here's a clue. If it's dirty, then you clean it. If it's not dirty, then you don't clean it. Cleaning for the sake of cleaning is a waste of time and effort. Instead of asking, "When should I clean it?" ask yourself, "When does it get dirty?"

Figuring out where your standards lie is a much more effective way to structure your cleaning. What things are important to you and your family? For me, I can let the laundry go for a few days and fingerprints don't bother me a bit. For others, clean clothes and sparkling walls and doors are a must. I have to have spotless countertops. For others, some cup rings and breadcrumbs here and there are no biggie. Find out what you and your family need to keep clean in order to keep happy, and set your schedules accordingly.

I strongly suggest having a family meeting. We women have a tendency to impose our own standards on other members of the family. Perhaps if you can find out what areas of housekeeping are important to them, you can incorporate them into certain areas of housekeeping. Are you reading me? It may go something like this,

"Yes, Susie, you are absolutely right when you say that it's frustrating not to have matched-up socks to put on every day. You can start folding laundry twice a week!"

"What was that, honey? You don't like coming home from work to find bikes and skateboards all over the driveway? Maybe you can come up with an organized system to store all of it in the garage."

Family meetings equals family involvement. That's what I'm talking about!

When it comes to setting up your schedules and charts, use your standards to help develop yours. Is clean laundry imperative? Then you may need to schedule laundering every day. Does dirt or dust on the floor bother you? Then you may need to schedule vacuuming more than once every week, or just do the high traffic areas more frequently. What about clean windows? I have never cleaned the outside of windows except when I'm hosing off the house every now and then. But I know some people who clean their windows immaculately every six months—to each his own. But, as far as scheduling chores around the house, there is no right or wrong, only what suits the needs of your family, and no one can do it better than you.

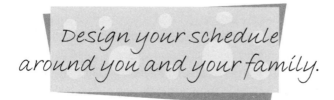

Design your schedule around you and your family.

Personally, I have tried everything in the book. I have scheduled days of the week to do various chores around the house. I have scheduled zones for different weeks in the month. I have even done the knock-yourself-out-in-one-day cleaning. What I finally found that works for me is all of the above. I regularly clean as I go. I vacuum when popcorn gets all over the floor, mop when mud gets tracked in, and clean the bathroom when it becomes less than fragrant. I also have regularly scheduled days during the week for my regular chores. Some weeks I focus more on one area of the house than others, such as when I'm reorganizing a room or cleaning out a closet. And then there are those days when I feel the urge to tackle the entire house (which usually strikes right before a visit from the in-laws). My normal week usually goes something like the following (but then again, normal for my family may seem more like a trip into Willy Wonka's Chocolate Factory for others—Oompa Loompas everywhere!):

Monday: Collect the trash, dust or polish furniture,
    change bed linens, vacuum

Tuesday: Clean bathrooms, water plants, clean mirrors, windows,
    and glass doors

Wednesday: Sweep (or run the floor vacuum) and mop

Thursday: Collect trash, clean kitchen

Friday: Vacuum, outdoor chores

Saturday: Write or scrapbook

Sunday: Church and chill

A lot of the chores are not scheduled because they are simply a part of my everyday maintenance. For example, I have to give the children's bathroom a quick once-over every other day because it is used so often. However, I only clean mine once a week. I should probably do laundry every single day, but only do it about three times during the week, and then several loads on the weekend. I suggest that you try everything, and find out what works best for your style. But whatever you do, just don't quit trying. If one method doesn't seem to click, then try something else. Ruts are easy to get into when it comes to housekeeping, so continually try to add some life to it by switching things around.

After you design your weekly schedule, keep in mind that the purpose of it is to help you structure your tasks around the home. Don't invent a schedule that is going to make you a slave to the house. Develop your schedule so that the tasks are spaced out evenly, and they are easy to accomplish. The purpose of your schedule is not to nag you into getting your chores done. If a day goes by and you didn't get to finish your work, don't let it hang over your head. Just let it go until the task rears its head again the next week. It will wait for you. Some dust accumulating on the bookshelves or the entertainment center isn't going to kill anyone. So, forget the guilt. Move on to the next day and face it with a clean slate. If you get around to it, great. If not, let it go. Those dust bunnies under the sofa aren't going anywhere.

Your cleaning schedule is meant to assist you, not imprison you.

What About Supplies?

I never cease to be amazed at the plethora of products created to clean a house. Instead of having every bottle and canister in the world crammed under your sink, I'm going to give you an entirely new perspective on cleaning products. There are only two things you should keep in mind—simple and friendly. Forget strolling down the cleaning aisle tossing this and that into your buggy. This method will save your wallet as well as your health.

Simple Cleaners

No, sister, every surface in your home does not require a separate cleaner. Instead of trying to stuff twelve different cleaners into one caddy, and grabbing blindly at whatever is available, let's take a short course in chemistry. If you remember from high school (or from soil tests in your garden), there is this thing called the pH scale that runs from one to fourteen, and measures how acidic or alkaline something is. The lower the number the more acidic, the higher the number the more alkaline. Because the majority of cleaning is a process of neutralizing soil, all cleaners rest somewhere on this scale, depending on what they are supposed to clean. Most soil, such as dirt, oil, and grease, is acidic and is best removed with

185

alkaline cleaners. On the other hand, there is soil, such as lime deposit and rust, that is best eliminated with acidic cleaners.

The majority of surfaces in your home can be safely cleaned with an all-purpose cleaner that is neutral on the pH scale. This is a safe cleaner that is gentle on your skin and lungs, and can get rid of most of the soil in your home. For tougher soil, such as grease buildup, you will need a heavy-duty cleaner that is more alkaline. To make it simple, they are labeled as all-purpose or heavy duty. And for the reflective surfaces in your home, you will need an alcohol-based glass cleaner that does not leave any smears or smudges. If you are worried about cooties in your home, you can also get a disinfecting cleaner or get an all-purpose cleaner that also disinfects. However, the majority of germs are not bad at all, and most surfaces will remain relatively germ-free with regular cleaning. For your wood furniture or floors, you will also need a safe oil-based soap that you can dilute with water (this also does a great job on leather furniture) or an oil-based furniture polish.

So, there you have it—the four cleaners you will use to clean 99 percent of your house (and maybe 100 percent if you're not a stickler). You need an all-purpose cleaner, a heavy-duty cleaner, a glass cleaner, and a wood cleaner. And if you prefer to use abrasive cleaners on some areas in your home, try using plain old baking soda instead. It works just as well, it is extremely alkaline (to cut down on that acidic dirt and grime), and it doesn't leave dangerous air-born molecules floating around in the air. Many companies are also combining cleaning properties in one bottle. For example, you can get an all-purpose cleaner that also cleans glass, or a heavy duty cleaner that also disinfects. Think as simple as possible, and don't make life more complicated than it already is. You can also purchase these cleaners in bulk concentrates at a warehouse store or janitorial supplies store. You can make your own cleaners for pennies a bottle! And they clean just as well (usually better) than those slick bottles at the store for dollars a pop. If you are purchasing cleaners for the nice smell, I can completely understand. But remember that the scent only lasts for a few minutes. Use that money you saved to buy some nice candles or air fresheners that will scent the room for hours instead.

Cleaning does not have to be complicated— keep it simple.

If you do buy your cleaners as concentrates, remember to dilute them properly. If a little bit works well, that does not mean that a lot will work even better. Follow the directions on the bottle meticulously. These companies run test after test to find what levels of ingredients will yield the very best results, and there is little, if any, that the consumer can do to improve on their products. Using a cleaner that is too concentrated will only leave residue on the surface, causing dust and dirt to accumulate. You will actually be creating more work for yourself.

Homemade Cleaners

You may have some of the simplest and friendliest cleaners right there in your kitchen, and not even know it. You can make most common cleaners at home following these simple recipes:

- Child-safe all-purpose cleaner: $1/8$ cup baking soda and 2 cups water
- All-purpose cleaner: $1/4$ teaspoon liquid dish detergent and 2 cups water
- Abrasive powder: baking soda
- Acidic cleaner (for soap scum and mineral deposits): 1 part vinegar and 1 part water
- Disinfecting cleaner: $1/4$ teaspoon liquid dish detergent, 2 cups water, 4 tablespoons bleach
- Glass cleaner: $1/2$ cup isopropyl alcohol, $1/2$ cup water, 4 tablespoons ammonia
- Furniture polish: $1/2$ cup vinegar, $1/2$ cup mineral oil, 2 tablespoons lemon oil (or scent with essential oil)—spray, then buff thoroughly with a dry cloth.

Friendly Cleaners

Harsh chemicals do nothing but burn our eyes and skin and infect our lungs with potentially dangerous molecules. You don't need that, and neither does this beautiful earth we all share. Save your health and the planet by using ecologically friendly cleaners. A spoonful of baking soda or a little squirt of dish soap in a bottle of water can serve as an all-purpose cleaner in a pinch. And most oil soaps are safe for the environment. White vinegar mixed with water does a great job on tile or floors. As the watchdog for the health of your family members, don't allow anything to touch the surfaces in your home, or leave molecules in the air that could be potentially dangerous, especially if you have little ones running around.

Their systems are much more sensitive to chemicals in the environment. You don't need a hose to put out a match, so go for the gentlest, mildest cleaner first before resorting to anything harsher.

Remember when you're cleaning to do spot tests. We all read this little warning on the back of the bottles, but does anyone really heed it? I didn't until I tried to clean some dry-erase marker off of the wallpaper. I used my all-purpose cleaner, and it didn't do anything. Instead of going for the next step up and trying a dry sponge or eraser, I went for something harsher and did not test the surface first. One strip of wallpaper later, I can tell you that spot testing is a good idea.

By using the simple and friendly method to clean your home, you can march through that aisle at the store with confidence. You don't need to be a label collector, and there is almost never a "new and improved" anything. The only thing you need to worry about is developing a new way of looking at things and improving your strategy for cleaning house. Clean smarter, not harder!

> *A cleaner doesn't have to be brutal to be powerful.*

Choose Your Weapon

Now that you have picked out your ammunition, it's time to choose your weapon. So, what will it be? The soft cloth or the scouring pad? The string mop or the sponge head? Well, it all depends on which battle you're going to fight. But the most important thing to remember when choosing your cleaning tools, is to get good quality items. It will be worth the extra money. They last longer, work better, and save you time and effort. Pass on that wimpy mop that spans all of eight inches or that sorry excuse for a broom that leaves an entire cornfield of straw behind. Get something with some umph! to it.

Your Caddy

Whether you play golf or not, you need a caddy. You can either choose a nice, roomy plastic one that is easy to carry from room to room or you can choose a young high school student who is trying to earn some money during summer vacation. I would go for the first one. It's much more affordable. When you do get your caddy, it's important to keep it with you. You waste time and effort running back and forth with different cleaners and scrubbers. Just keep it right by your side, so that you are ready for the task. And a good idea would be to have several located strategically throughout the house. You should have a loaded caddy conveniently located on each floor of your home, and a toilet scrubber by each toilet. I read somewhere, that it is convenient to store all-purpose cleaner in the holder for the toilet scrubber. Nice idea, unless you have little ones around the house. I just put a squirt of hand soap into the toilet (out of the dispenser that I keep by the sink) and swish it around with the toilet brush every other day or so. It takes just seconds, and prevents a stubborn mess later. Now that you have your caddies, make sure you keep them loaded at all times with everything you need to tackle messes around the house.

- window/glass cleaner
- all-purpose cleaner
- furniture cleaner/polish
- baking soda (for toilet or bathtub rings)
- toothbrush or grout brush (gets in the tight spots that a scrubbing brush can't reach)
- scrubbing brush
- plastic scraper
- pumice stone (perfect for toilet rings)
- cleaning cloths

Cleaning Cloths

How much can you say about a rag? Well, a lot! First of all, quit using little do-nothings unless you just like wiping and wiping and wiping. Buy some good, roomy white towels that look like nothing you currently use (you wouldn't want to get them confused). I use white hand towels that are cut in half because it's the perfect size for me to work with. If you like them thicker, than get hand towels, fold them in half, and sew them to create a tube. This will provide a cloth that is twice as thick. By using only white cloths, you can bleach the load to get rid of germs and discoloration. And after you launder them, you can throw them all in a drawer or bin. At one time, I was anal-retentive and folded all of my cleaning cloths. Now, I'm just more anal than retentive and throw them all in the bottom of my 1920s file cabinet.

The canisters of ready-to-go cleaning wipes are a nice idea if you are just doing surface treatment, such as cleaning mirrors, doing quick wipes, or disinfecting fixtures and doorknobs. And they are also a lot more convenient because you just toss them in the trash. But, forget about it when it comes to real cleaning. They can't clean like your thick cleaning cloths because they don't have a lot of fibers to trap dirt and grime. The purist would consider these an abomination to the art of cleaning. I grew out of purism in the mid-90s. For the real cleaning, stick with your cloths. But if you are going for the daily wipe up or trying to find some method other than arm-twisting to get your kids to clean, these handy wipes are excellent.

> *The right tools make the job a lot easier.*

Brooms

You are going to be using your broom a lot, so get a good one. Save the straw brooms for sweeping off the back porch or for your daughter's witch costume, and get a nice angled broom with nylon bristles that won't fray and fall out, or one with rubber bristles to pick up every little speck. And if you have more than one floor that uses a broom, then buy one for each floor. Don't be tempted to use that nice broom you bought to do any of the work outdoors because it will ruin it. Get a separate broom for outdoor purposes, and make sure you store it where you use it. For large outdoor areas, such as your driveway, you may want to use a push broom. And if you have an enormous area to sweep indoors, such as that indoor basketball court in your basement, you may want to purchase a push broom to do some of the indoor work as well. As far as the little areas that need sweeping, such as bathrooms, buy a little hand broom with an attached dustpan to store with your caddy. It's a lifesaver (or at least a backsaver). When you do sweep, remember that no broom is going to help you while there is junk all over the floor. You need to pick up the junk first. I still am perplexed as to how my kids can sweep the entire dining room and leave half a sandwich and a toy police car on the floor.

You should also have plenty of hand brooms with attached dustpans in your home for the little spills. And a good idea is to keep a tiny one in one of your kitchen drawers designated specifically for counters and tabletops. By sweeping off the high areas before you wipe them off, you are skipping that lovely step of wiping junk into your hand or wiping all of the mess onto the floor and sweeping it up later. And if you ever roll out dough on your kitchen counter, it's a tool you will grow to love.

> *Sweep all that junk away with the right brooms.*

Mops

The type of mop you buy really depends on the area that you're mopping. If you have a huge area that requires mopping, then purchasing a large string mop with a rolling bucket is going to best serve your purpose. If you prefer not to look like the janitor at your kid's elementary school or if you have a smaller area to clean, than stick with a good sponge mop, and two buckets (one for your cleaning water, and the other for the gunky water that you squeeze out of the mop. For just doing spot mopping, a mop with cleaner attached and a disposable pad at the end fits the bill just fine. This is the best little invention in the world, next to disposable diapers. When you don't have enough time (or energy) to really mop, you can at least give the impression that you did. I believe some genius of a woman came up with the idea for those disposable mop pads when the hospital sent her home with those enormous sanitary napkins that they use following a delivery (and those lovely fishnet undies that can make the skinniest woman look like a netted porpoise). She probably just had too many of them, so decided to mop the floor with them instead! Mopping is a favorite pastime for me, second only to shoving a hot dog up my nose and chasing it with sweet pickle relish. I do a quick once-over every couple of weeks, and only really cover the high traffic areas. I figure the broom or floor vacuum gets the rest. I may not be meticulous, but at least I'm honest.

191

You may also want to get a dust mop with a head that you can treat with furniture polish and stick in the washing machine to clean. When I was little, this was my job around the house—dust mopping. I loved it only for the playtime that would follow. I could put my socks on afterward and slide all over the floor. It was also the perfect surface to slide my pet cat, Max. He would just lie there while I slid him across the floor. He either loved it immensely, or he figured there was no escape for him so he might as well just sink into a self-induced catatonic state. Dust mopping also leaves a great surface to pull people on blankets. As a matter of fact, in my home we don't even have a dust mop. I just let the kids take turns pulling each other all around the first floor on top of a bedspread. Every now and then, I will spray some polish on the floor to keep the game afoot. We stop when the floor is shiny or when we see blood.

> *Add a little fun to the cleaning,*
> *and it quits being such a chore.*

Vacuums

This will be your most valuable cleaning tool, so get one that really sucks (I'm sorry, but I just could not let that one go). You need a good vacuum, and if you have an enormous house, I would suggest one for each floor. The two most common types of vacuums are uprights and canister vacuums. Uprights are more convenient and easy to maneuver, and canister vacuums usually provide a bit more power. I have a canister vacuum that I love. It was one of the most expensive ones on the market, but is has paid for itself over and over. It gets rid of airborne allergens and also stands up to the constant abuse offered up by disgruntled children who have to do chores, such as attempting to suck up dirty underwear so they don't have to go to all the effort of bending over and picking it up with their hands. Whatever vacuum you get, do not skimp on this purchase. It can clean your floors as well as the air, and also extract the dirt and dust out of furniture and aggregate wall surfaces, such as brick. You can also use a vacuum with a hard surface head to vacuum your hard floors, such as tile or wood. This is a hundred times better than sweeping and watching the little dust storms as they brew into squalls in the shafts of sunlight. If you get an upright vacuum, pass over on all of the fancy models, and go for one that is designed to be used commercially. They work better, are more durable, and easily repaired. Many vacuums on the market today are manufactured with obsolescence in mind. They will eventually tear up and force you to replace them—bad for the environment and your wallet.

You may also want to purchase a wet/dry vacuum. This is a miracle worker when it comes to huge spills and busted pipes. If you purchase one with a floor squeegee, it's even better because you can give the floor a good scrubbing, and then suck it all up. You may not think purchasing one of these is worth your money, but when the toilet overflows after your son ate bright blue and neon pink fruit wigglies at Grandma's house, you will be cursing the day you passed on the purchase.

> *You need a vacuum that doesn't mess around when it comes to cleaning.*

Dusters

You will also need something to dust off those places that are difficult to get with your cleaning cloth. Don't get a cheap feather duster, because that just stirs the mess up. You may as well use a leaf blower. Instead, get a wool-head duster, an ostrich feather duster, or a synthetic duster that is polarized to pull dust off of surfaces (there are some amazing things on the market). Use this on your furniture between cleanings, in high places where spider webs and dust like to cohabitate, and on surfaces that are difficult to clean, such as rows of books, plants, keyboards, and that entire collection of miniature football helmets that your son has mistaken for valuable assets.

Sponges, Scrubbers, and Scrapers

You may want to get some soft sponges to use for cleaning purposes. I don't have any because I figure a cleaning cloth does just as well, and I can toss it in the wash to remove the dirt and bacteria that it collects. Sponges with tough scrubbing surfaces are excellent for stubborn grime such as the ring in the bathtub or that dried-up toothpaste spit in the sink. If the scrubbing side of the sponge doesn't seem to do the trick, then try the scrubbing brush or the toothbrush. Remember to go for the gentlest method first. Surfaces can easily be damaged by too much scrubbing or by a tool that is too abrasive. And if you do need to use a brush with bristles, try not to bear down. By pushing hard against the bristles, you are actually bending them and preventing them from working effectively. Use a light stroke so that the bristles can get into the cracks and do their thing.

You should also acquire a tool that will allow you to clean with zen-level satisfaction. This is a dry sponge or eraser, you can usually find these in the cleaning aisle or at janitorial supply stores. It feels somewhat rubbery, and works wonders at removing stubborn marks on hard-to-clean surfaces such as painted surfaces and wallpaper. If you start using one of these, make sure you set a timer to stop you, because you will get carried away with the results and start searching all over your home trying to find marks to remove. If you have a hard time finding any, just hop on over to my house.

And no cleaning closet is complete without a plastic scraper. You should have one of these in every caddy, and one close by your kitchen sink. In a pinch, you can use some old credit cards (Just don't expect Macy's to accept it with crusty scrambled egg residue all over it). Nothing works better at dried-up lumps of indistinguishable material than a sweet little scraper. You can use it on everything from that baked-on food that is covering your dishes to the lumps of odd things stuck to the wall beside your child's bed that you would really rather not

Scrub away all of that junk that invades your home.

194

know anything about. These are also handy to keep around when you're washing windows and come across a stuck-on blob. We can live without these unknowns—just scrape them off.

Spray Bottles

If you do choose to make your own cleaners from concentrate, you will need spray bottles to put them in. Get good quality bottles that aren't going to shoot cleaning fluid in your eye (unless you're in to that sort of thing). You can get great bottles at janitorial supplies stores or shopping warehouses. These are good quality bottles that will perform for you, but let's face it—they're ugly. If I have to spend my time cleaning, I'm going to make it as enjoyable as possible. This is a fun part of getting your arsenal ready to win the war against dirt and grime forever. You can choose pretty spray bottles that match the room or coordinate with your caddy. I know, it's pathetic, but every little bit of motivation helps when it comes to cleaning.

The bottle I chose for the kitchen cleaner matches the room, so I just leave it on the counter. And anyway, it seems pointless to go to the effort of putting it under the sink when I seem to need it every fifteen minutes. You can usually find a lot of cute bottles for sale in late spring or early summer when all of the pool toys start appearing. You can also find some nice ones in the hair care aisle or at beauty supply stores. Make sure you buy a size that is convenient, and can easily fit into your caddy. And remember to label them clearly. One "hair spray incident" is enough to keep guests away forever. If you don't have laminated labels, then cover the paper label with clear packing tape.

Squeegee

If you've been cleaning those big picture windows in your home with a rag and a few squirts of glass cleaner, it's time to squeegee your way to happiness. This is one of those personally gratifying jobs like pulling huge strips of wallpaper off the wall in a single pull or popping the little air pocket dots that are used as padding in packages. Try it and see if it does not become addictive. You'll soon be trying to squeegee every flat surface in sight (just please leave my chest alone, and stick to the glass surfaces). To squeegee like the pros, you will need a professional squeegee with a replaceable rubber blade. You can usually find these at home improvement warehouses or janitorial supplies stores. When you have secured your squeegee, it's time to apprehend the bucket. Get a big wide rectangular one that can easily fit your squeegee (there's nothing like trying to force a squeegee into an inadequate bucket; there's just something about it that goes against the laws of nature).

When you are armed with both bucket and squeegee, fill the bucket with water and put a few drops of dish detergent in there. Please remember to only use just a few drops. If you put more than five or six drops, you will leave a film on the glass that will make it look worse than ever. Now scrub the window with a cloth and the water in your bucket, or you can use the scrubber side of your squeegee if it has one. Now, squeegee away, starting at the top and working your way down. Ah, the sweet satisfaction! Now you know why those thrill seekers risk life and limb dangling on the sides of skyscrapers—all for the love of a squeegee!

Cultivate a love of clean, and bring sparkle and shine into your world.

Cleaning Station

Cleaning is an extremely important part of home maintenance, so give it the credit it's due. Your cleaning supplies should have a central location, such as a closet or the corner of a large pantry. Don't just try to stuff everything under the kitchen sink or balance all of your tools against a wall. Instead, try to find a spot where you can keep everything up off the floor. Put holders or hooks on the wall to hold your brooms, mops, and hand tools, and install some type of shelving, if you don't have it there already, to store your cleaners, cloths, and other tools. Remember to use the AS IS model, and keep things contained so that it's easier for you to clean and keep organized. Having your own cleaning closet makes the task easier, more efficient, and even pleasant (as difficult as that may seem). I have a rack mounted to the wall in my pantry where I hang all of my tools. And when I'm buying a tool that belongs there, I always make sure that it has a hole in the end just for this purpose. Now once you have collected all of your cleaning tools and stored them all in your cleaning closet, there's no stopping you!

Time for Your Prescription

No matter who you are or what your personality, cleaning is something that we are all going to eventually have to face. Some of us enjoy nothing more than scrubbing away those hard-water stains in a bathtub. And then there are those of us who would choose a pap smear over a sponge mop any day. But, like it or lump it, most of us need to do it. The trick is to make our efforts as easy, effective, and enjoyable as possible. And it all begins with the right tools for the job.

Rx for MasterMinds

Of all people, you know what works and what doesn't. As a matter of fact, you make it your job to always be improving at the tasks you assume. But with your continual analyzing you may often lose sight of the forest for all the trees. The point is to get your home clean, not to be the professional efficiency consultant of your primary residence. Sometimes, with the time and effort it takes to figure out which one would be better—the string mop or the sponge mop, you could have already dropped to your knees and cleaned the entire floor with a rag. Find the best tool for the job; don't fret over it. And when you must, just use what you've got even if you know something else would work better. The science of efficiency needs to take a backseat to performance. If not, you're going to have the best-looking cleaning closet in the world—and dirt in every corner. Put feet to your methods and take action on deep cleaning one room in your house today (even if it's a tiny room). This will give your mind a break, your hands a workout, and your face a smile.

Rx for Creative Spirits

When those commercials come on television that show the woman wiping off twenty years of scum with a single spray of a brand new miracle cleaner, you are the woman they are advertising to. You will do anything for a shortcut. And with so much going on in your life, it's easy to see why. Buying the latest and greatest tools for the task isn't always the easiest way to get from point A to point B. Sometimes, it can even complicate matters. Like the time I bought the groovy flaming red flexible duster. It worked okay, but then my son used it as a sword in the backyard, followed by the dogs using it as a chew toy as soon as he dropped it. I glanced outside an hour later and it looked as if it had rained red electrostatic fire from heaven. But the dogs didn't have a speck of dust on them! Feel free to try out some new toys, but don't hold on to them if they don't work. Find what works and stick with it. Take a few minutes before the next time you clean up and weed through your cleaning supplies so that you can toss out the tools and cleaners that aren't worth their weight. Just don't toss them outside, especially if you have dogs.

Rx for Mother Hens

You love the tried and true! If you run out of a certain cleaner, then you want a refill of the same thing. If your broom gets worn out, you replace it with the same thing. It's great that you stick with what works. But (Surprise! Surprise!) there may be something on the market that works even better. Talk to your friends—the ones in the same cleaning boat as you, not the ones who are afraid to scratch paint off the floor because it may mess up their acrylic nails. Find out what they think of that new mop or that cleaner that just hit the market. You may find a brand new star that you can hitch your wagon to and whip that house into shape in no time flat! There are a ton of new items that are hitting the stores every other month. In the mass you are sure to find a winner. Try out something new this week. If you like it, then add it to your arsenal. If not, then throw it out and pat yourself on the back for breaking out of the same-old, same-old.

Rx for Starry-Eyed Dreamers

It's not always the tools that are the problem, but just the incentive to use them. Putting a bit of something new in your cleaning agenda may be just what you need to motivate you to put in some of that hard labor. Take a trip to the store and check out all of the groovy new cleaning tools. Take your time and shop the aisles as you would the cosmetics department in Niemen Marcus. Read labels, hold tools and feel them in your hand, check out the colors and styles of all the different items. If you don't already have a caddy, then now is the time to purchase one. Pick out a nice, roomy one that will hold some pretty bottles and a few cleaning cloths. Now assemble the caddy at home and make it impressive enough to wow the pants off the Tidy Bowl Man (could you imagine a worse job?). Use your weapons to thoroughly clean your kitchen, every last little bit—cabinet doors, behind the coffee pot, the works. Then top it off by plugging in an air freshener. This positive energy may be enough to propel you to keep up the good work.

Dream On!

I said earlier that we get way too caught up in the shoulds of life. So many of us wake up every morning with a big fat cloud of shoulds hanging over our head, and we carry it around all day long. If the should is important enough, then take action on it. If the should is something you have just chosen to stick in your backpack and carry through life, then pull it out and toss it away. It's time to break up that cloud of shoulds just like a fresh spring rain.

Take out that dream journal and prepare to play in some mud puddles. Make a list of all the shoulds that you carry around through the day. Here are some common ones, so let them spark your thought process:

I should lose weight.

I should spend less money.

I should exercise more.

I should clean the house.

I should be a better mom.

And the list goes on and on! So many of us choose to carry around a ton of unnecessary baggage packed full of inadequacy. Open up that baggage and start pulling out all of the reasons you find for kicking yourself at the end of the day. Write down all of the shoulds that you impose on yourself. Now prepare yourself for a hefty dose of honesty.

Go through your list one by one and ask yourself truthfully if that should is important enough to take action on immediately. If it is, then find a constructive way to do something proactive about it today. Make one small daily action that can replace the should. For example, if you believe you should lose weight, then find one small way to eat healthier, such as replacing processed starches with whole grains. Live out this one small positive action instead of carrying around a bunch of negative pressure.

And some of the shoulds just need to be tossed out of the window. If you are a size twelve, and you have been a size twelve for four years, and you keep telling yourself every morning that you should be a size eight, then maybe you need to just empty that baggage once and for all. Let it go until you are in a spot where you are ready and willing to take action on it. It will come. And if not, you are not going to waste any of your emotional energy fretting about it. Enjoy every day of your life—without a self-imposed cloud over your head. At the end of this activity, make sure that every should on your list is either scratched off and left behind or replaced with a positive action.

Chapter 11

Top Techniques

Basic housekeeping can be efficient and effective by applying some basic principles. Why spend an entire day cleaning when you can get everything done in less than two hours or in bits and pieces as you go along throughout your day? Some of these principles may seem obvious, but we fall into a lot of behavior patterns that are inefficient or ineffective without even realizing it. If we applied the same principles to housekeeping that are applied to production facilities or service industries, we could easily get our work done in one-fourth of the time that it usually takes. It is important that we view our housekeeping as a profession that deserves all of the thought and analysis we can devote to it. Efficiency experts devote hours of scientific analysis to the cheapest, easiest, and fastest way to make a cheeseburger. Isn't your living room just as important as a cheeseburger? Well, I guess that all depends on how hungry you are.

Clean from Top to Bottom

As we become older, we become frightfully aware of gravity, especially on two occasions—when we are cleaning our houses and when we step our naked bodies out of the shower. Gravity is the reason, when it comes to cleaning our homes, that it is imperative that we clean from top to bottom. As for our naked bodies, that is another book at another time. But for now, just look for words such as "lift" and "support" whenever you're buying undergarments, and learn to appreciate the beauty of low lighting when you're making love. As far as your home is concerned, always start cleaning up high so you can shake all of that dust and dirt down to the bottom. When you start in one room, get your duster and attack the lighting fixture or ceiling fan hanging in the center of the room, and then get the periphery. Dust off all of the hanging plants, the curtains, the spider webs in the corner, and all of that mysterious stuff that enjoys resting in those high-up hard-to-reach places. It takes seconds, and if you do this every time you clean, then the junk doesn't have a chance to accumulate. There's nothing like flipping on the fan in the middle of the first warm day of the year and creating a miniature dust storm in your bedroom. But unless you're a camel or a willing candidate for a bronchial infection, I wouldn't recommend it.

> *When it comes to cleaning, make gravity work in your favor.*

After you get everything up high, then you can start attacking the walls and everything displayed on them—the windows, the mirrors, the ancient goat-hair and ox-blood fertility mask, and all of the other stuff that we hang up there. Then comes the surface areas of all of the furniture. Hopefully, these aren't covered with a bunch of clutter to make your task more difficult and time consuming. After you finish there, continue working down until you are left with a floor to sweep, mop, or vacuum. There you are—top to bottom cleaning. You have used the force of gravity to your advantage. Now if only they sold a bra that worked that well.

Spray and Sit

Most people never use chemicals to their advantage. Chemical is not a dirty word, so say it loud and say it proud. Just because it is a chemical does not mean that it is hazardous. We would never be able to make sourdough pancakes if we did not take advantage of the chemical reaction that occurs between an acid (the sourdough starter) and an alkaline (baking soda). We also could never enjoy those endless volcano experiments that our kids do. By the way, even safe chemicals can be potentially dangerous in the company of children who are left unattended, like the time my parents left my oldest sister in charge of all of us (their first mistake). In their absence, another one of my sisters had ingested an entire cup of vinegar and pickle juice. Her stomach, of course, did not feel too well after that. So following the advice of my brother, the chemistry major, she drank baking soda mixed in water. By the time my parents returned, two sisters were on one side of the room and my brother and I were on the other side, rolling my other sister back in forth, while a white foam was literally coming out of her mouth and nose. In our collective wisdom, we decided that the "rolling" procedure was the most effective way to reduce her belly that had swollen to resemble that of a woman in her seventh month of pregnancy. But, enough about my childhood. We could be here all day, and it just keeps getting stranger. I can spend time on the couch later. For now, let's clean.

Cleaners are great inventions—so use them to your advantage.

As I was saying about chemicals, the majority of people never take advantage of them. Women stay in the aisle forever reading labels, trying to find the miracle solution that will work wonders in their kitchens and bathrooms. Then as soon as they spray it, they wipe it right off and never give it a chance to work. In order to cut down on the time you spend cleaning your home, try using the "spray and sit" method. It's the same principle as allowing dirty dishes to soak in the sink with a few drops of dish detergent. Cleaners are amazing things. They have the ability to neutralize and dissolve dirt and grime, so let them do their stuff. If we use them to our advantage, we don't need to apply nearly as much elbow grease.

When you are cleaning a room or surface area, spray the entire area with your all-purpose cleaner first. Then go back to your starting point and begin wiping. You will be surprised at how quickly you can clean the entire area when you don't have to stop and scrub. This applies to floors, walls, and furniture as well. Cover as large an area as you are able, and then go back to your starting point and wipe it off. We live in an advanced civilization; and there are better ways to clean house than scrubbing, scraping, sweating, squatting, and swearing. Let those wonder cleaners work wonders.

Use the Correct Tool

There is a tool for every job out there. It's just a matter of finding the right marriage. I am notorious for pairing up mismatches. For example, duct tape is used for minor repairs around the house, right? But I was certain it could also serve as a pore strip for my nose. After two minutes of an excruciating "Band-Aid pull," and an entire afternoon with a red nose, I realized that it could not. Fingernail files are perfect for filing nails, right? But could it not also perform microdermabrasion on my face? For nine freaky days I was walking around with huge scabs on the sides of my mouth and between my brows. But on the good side, the mild case of leprosy did serve to hide my wrinkles. So, speaking from a little too much experience, always match the correct tool to the task at hand.

Don't spend your precious time (and it is precious) fooling around with inadequate or inappropriate tools. Get the right tool, and make sure it is good quality. Using good brooms, mops, scrubbers, and scrapers make all the difference in the world when it comes to cleaning house. You can sweep a driveway in half the time if you have a large, industrial-quality push broom. If you try to do it with a distorted corn broom that looks as if it belongs in the hands of Marilyn Manson, then you're going to be struggling with that driveway all morning long. Make it a habit of asking yourself if there is a better tool. If there is, then get it and use it.

But don't fall into the trap of trying to buy convenience. There are very few shortcuts when it comes to cleaning. Scrubbing the toilet is the only way to get it clean, so don't fall into the trap of buying that swirl-o-matic for $19.99 that not only cleans the toilet, but also chops julienne carrots. However, there are tools that make your job quicker and easier. You will find some of the best tools at janitorial supplies stores, home improvement stores, shopping warehouses, and cleaning supplies Web sites. Shop where the pros go. They don't have time to mess around with gimmicky diddly-squat, and neither do you. Get what works, and use it. Go for quality tools and then take good care of them so that they will last.

> *Great tools make your work easier, faster, and much more pleasant.*

Finish One Room at a Time

This technique is a great way to check your progress and motivate you to keep going. If you save your major cleaning to do on one day, try setting a goal of completing one room entirely before moving on to something else. This way, you will feel more like you are chewing on bite-size pieces instead of tackling the entire pizza. The knock-down-drag-out cleaning is easier if you do it one room at a time because you are focused in a single area and you can keep all of your supplies right there with you. And remember to work your way out of the room. The last step should be the floor, and when you do this step just mop or vacuum your way out of the door.

Now look back and take in the beauty of your work, because it won't stay that way, no matter how badly you want it to. With five children, my mother could never keep a clean kitchen for long. She would clean it, turn out the lights, and declare, "the kitchen is now closed." That did not, however, prevent us from going in and making batches of popcorn and platters of nachos after she went to bed. I guess you could put up those velvet ropes that they have at the movie theater or maybe even police barricade ribbon. But since you don't live in a museum, and your home is not a crime scene (even though there are those days when it feels like one), I wouldn't suggest it. Just enjoy a longing glance at the fleeting beauty of cleanliness, and then get on with real life.

Magic Rituals

When you do finish a room it will help to find some signal that you can use as closure. It will be the cherry on top for cleaning your room. I like to call them my magic rituals, for they do indeed have a supernatural way of getting you to finish your work and they can magically transform a room. For example, I have a friend who turns off all of the lights after she completes a room. My daughter sprays the bathroom rug with a fragrant linen spray when she finishes cleaning the bathroom. Every morning, when I go through the house preparing it for the day's activities, I have my little rituals that I do to finish off the rooms. I flip on the little decorative lamp in the living room. I turn on a little trickling water fountain in the study. I light a candle in the kitchen to burn throughout the day. The pretty glow serves as a reminder to keep the kitchen neat and clean. These little rituals not only provide the incentive you need to clean up a room, but they also provide the incentive to keep it that way. I'm not saying you need to vacuum a room and then light incense and do a salutation to the sun. Just incorporate little symbols to set the stage for wonderful things to happen. When you establish these little rituals, it helps to set the tone for everything else that goes on in your home for the remainder of the day.

Never underestimate the power behind a good ritual! Here are some ideas you may want to try out in your home:

- Place a beautiful candle somewhere conspicuously. After you get the room shiny, then give yourself permission to light it and enjoy its scent and beauty.
- Put strings of tiny white lights and drape them over a silk tree or string them along a shelf. Plug them in after you get the room straight.
- Throw open the curtains to bathe that newly cleaned room with light and energy.

- Place a couple of perfect throw pillows on your bed so that you will be motivated to make it up every morning.
- Purchase some scented oils to place in lamp rings. These work wonders to get you to clean the room so that you can enjoy the aroma.
- Prepare a perfect cup of cappuccino after you have finished cleaning house.
- Get a beautiful tablecloth to place on the table after it is all cleared and wiped off.

Use your imagination, and put some little magic rituals into practice. Now I do hereby declare you Priestess of the Ancient Housekeeping Sect and Order. Go forth, sister, and practice your rituals of divine magnificence!

Clean As You Go

You know by now the disadvantages of playing catchup. The same principle holds true when it comes to cleaning your home. Inch by inch, cleaning is a cinch. Yard by yard, cleaning is a royal pain. If we take measures every day to keep our home clean and sparkling, we won't have such a huge chore waiting for us at the end of the week (or whenever you decide to get around to it). Cleaning a bathroom can take just a few minutes if we develop a habit of doing it every day or every few days, depending on how frequently it is used. It is a simple procedure of spraying cleaner everywhere and follow that with wiping off mirrors and fixtures, counters, and lastly, the tub and toilet. And the toilet can be cleaned with a squirt of hand soap and a quick scrub with the toilet brush. The final step is to spray cleaner all over the floor, and then wipe it (yes, with your hand). If you are opposed to this, you can always drop the rag, step on it, and using your leg as the mop handle, "mop" the bathroom floor (I do this one a lot). Depending upon the size of the bathroom, this can usually be done in less than five minutes, while your little one is in the bath.

Treating your home to daily cleaning blesses everyone who lives there.

The cleaning as you go applies to everything else around the house as well. Clean dishes immediately after you eat. Vacuum as soon as you see dirt accumulate so you don't grind it down into the carpet. Squeegee off the walls after you take a shower so that you're not left scrubbing hard water deposits. Little steps here and there will save you loads of effort in the long run. Get into the "maintaining mind-set." Instead of letting the chores culminate into one enormous monster that you have to beat down with two quarts of grease cutter and a long-handled scrub brush, just do a little wiping and sweeping here and there. You wouldn't completely ignore your hair in between going to your stylist to get it cut or colored (or at least, I hope you wouldn't), so treat your home with the same daily care and upkeep. Cleaning your home in this manner also shows that you love and respect your home while teaching little ones around you to adopt this same attitude.

Clean with Convenience

When you are cleaning your home, it is important to live by the Boy Scout motto—Be Prepared! In order to consolidate your efforts, you can't run here and there collecting the items that you need to accomplish your task. Be prepared for your work, and have everything you need right there with you so that you can get your work done quickly and effectively. Anticipate what you need to do and arm yourself with all of the tools you need to get it done. This is the reason for having your essential cleaning supplies located in a caddy close by. You need to minimize your efforts and maximize your results.

Go for Good, Not Perfect

Don't let good be the enemy of perfect. So many of us women want perfection so badly that we never reach a level that is good. Perfection is not only impossible, it's boring! Sometimes our lifestyles and our standards seem to butt heads. We want a sparkling kitchen floor, but with our lifestyle we are constantly getting juice spills or food crumbs all over it. Many of us see that we cannot obtain perfection, so we give up trying to maintain a functional level. We either want it all, or nothing. Well, unless you plan on putting your lifestyle on hold (and I would highly discourage you from trying to do that), we have to find that sweet spot where are standards and our lifestyles can exist together in harmony. That sweet spot is called good.

Mopping your entire floor is perfect. Spot mopping where the dog shook the water off his coat is good. Scrubbing the entire kitchen counter is perfect. Wiping off those dollops of mustard is good. Cleaning your bathroom from top to bottom is perfect. Giving it a four-minute wipe down is good. If you only settle for perfect, then you are going to wind up going nowhere at all. However, it you continually strive to maintain a good level of housekeeping, then you will improve on your abilities and be able to reach a level that is closer to perfection. When you clean your bathroom, don't kill yourself trying to attack the mineral deposits, just go for a level that is good and gives the appearance of clean. Keep telling yourself that you can always go back later and get the stubborn spots. With this mind-set, you can clean your entire home in record time. Okay, there may be some dust bunnies that you missed here and there or some toys that were kicked under the bed, but at a glance, it rocks!

> *Kick perfect out the back door so that you can make room for good.*

I have read that you should approach cleaning as if you were hired to do it. You should get dressed in your coveralls, do all the de-cluttering before you begin, and set aside an entire morning to clean the entire home. Personally, with caring for a baby and a toddler, homeschooling four others, managing a baby products corporation, and writing books and articles, I never have two uninter-rupted hours at my disposal. Our cleaning has to be incorporated in our daily living. It is part of the beautiful process of living instead of a separate endeavor. We all share in the chores. We live together, mess up together, and clean together. And in the road that I have chosen, I had to leave perfection on a highway exit about two counties back.

Put cleaning in perspective. The purpose of cleaning is to improve your way of life. Once you reach the level where your home functions in a happy and healthy way, anything beyond that is purely for the enjoyment and satisfaction you receive from the process of cleaning. No one is coming in to your home with a white glove to test your skills at homemaking. And if they do, feel free to show them the back door. You can be good at a lot, perfect at little. Go for good, and leave the guilt or feelings of inadequacy at being the less-than-perfect housewife back in the dark ages where they belong.

Beat the Clock

I already told you about the beauty of timers. Try employing one when it comes to housekeeping. Before you start in a room, set the timer for fifteen minutes, and see if you cannot complete it in that amount of time. This will jump-start your engine to tear through the task. When you get proficient at this, try beating your own record. It's amazing what a little competition can do.

Adding variety to your cleaning routine is usually enough to start the momentum.

Dress the Part

I know I already told you about setting your AM Routine and getting completely dressed before you start the day. This is vitally important when it comes to doing your cleaning because it puts you into the mind-set of arriving at work and getting your game on. You wouldn't go to work in a slouchy pair of pajamas and slippers, so get dressed, look sharp, and get going. Wear good, comfortable, functional clothes that will serve your purpose well. And if you have to dress for a job outside of the house, you can still give the house the once-over before you leave in the morning. Very little housework is done on your hands and knees. So don't even bother with the "I don't want to get my clothes dirty" routine. I have only ruined my clothes once when I was cleaning, and that was because I foolishly splashed bleach on them. And I am well known for ruining clothes, like the time I was painting in a khaki miniskirt. I'm not sure why I do these things. At the time, they made sense to me. Looking back, it's all a fog of confusion. And I don't even drink.

Dive In

If you wait for the perfect time to begin cleaning, you will never clean. Just dive right in where you are. Where you start when you begin cleaning does not matter nearly as much as when you start, so start now. There's no doing it wrong. Even if you only do a little, or do it inefficiently, you are still doing it. And every little bit helps immensely. If the kitchen is a mess, just begin somewhere. I usually try to clear the area completely before I begin cleaning, but sometimes that is just not an option. I have pushed toys to the side of the room so that I could vacuum the main traffic area. I have left mountains of dirty dishes in the sink just so that I could wipe off the counters. I have thrown bath toys into the tub so that I could do a quick mopping of the floor. When you see that a task needs to be done, don't try to go to point A so that you can work your way to point C. Sometimes you just need to jump right in and get to C. The A and B can always come later.

Apply the "Within Arm's Reach" Rule

Sometimes when we see a little task that needs to be done, we skip over it in order to wait until we can do the entire thing. If we see a coffee ring on the counter, we just wait until we can clean off the entire thing. If we see a toy misplaced in the corner of the room, we just wait until we can pick up the entire room. One of the best ways to conquer cleaning is to establish this rule for yourself: if something is within arm's reach, take care of it. That includes that glop of toothpaste that you can just wipe off with some wet toilet paper (moistened with water, please), that magazine that needs to be placed back in the basket, or that baseball cap that you can pick up off the floor as you're walking down the hall (for those Cro-Magnon women whose arms extend to the ground). The other day I went into the bathroom and there were three kernels of popcorn on the floor. I ask you, what manner of evil is this that eats popcorn in the bathroom? I was tempted to just leave it, but it was within arm's reach, so I took care of it. Don't gloss over this rule. Make it a habit. Cleaning isn't difficult at all if you take care of the daily upkeep.

> *Little steps here and there will prevent the break-your-back cleaning sessions.*

Pump Up the Volume

Sometimes if you just can't seem to get in the mood to clean house, then you need to take any means necessary to get you there. This includes blasting the stereo. Put on some music that will get you dancing around with your duster and singing into your broom handle. I don't know about you, but I can clean house a lot better to Aerosmith than Air Supply, so put on something that will get you moving. If you really get into the motions of good cleaning, then you will have that heart pumping in no time. You will get a good workout and have a sparkling clean home to show for it (instead of a bill from the local gym). Fifteen minutes of aerobic activity is a good amount for an average woman, and you can get that by raking the yard and scrubbing the cabinets. And you don't need to get in your spandex or stick any weird devices between your legs to do it. You will be surprised at how many calories you burn from just a moderate rate of activity. So, blast the music and get going. And make sure it's not music that encourages you to pour a nice steamy cup of tea and lounge on the sofa. Put on something that will put some hop in your step and some swing in your hips.

Strike a Balance

Being a good homemaker and a good mother can coexist, no matter what you have heard in the past. You can have it all. It just depends on what you want, and if you are willing to do what it takes to get it. You can have both by incorporating caring for the home as part of the daily activities. My children are encouraged to get messy because I believe that in the messes, mistakes, and chances of life is where all real learning takes place. They also are aware that they are required to clean it up, because I also believe that knowledge is useless without responsibility. My two boys were playing with bubbles all over the bathroom the other day.

That's fine with me because they also know how to use cleaner and cloths (this mess required towels, though). My daughters spilled body glitter all over their blanket. That's fine with me because they both know how to do laundry. My toddler spilled crackers all over the floor, and then decided to dance in it. That's fine with me because dancing in our spills is exactly what we should be doing. And anyway, a few minutes with a hand-held vacuum was a small price to pay for his enjoyment.

Mess is the shadow of creativity.

Don't try to be an extremist. If you feel your personality pulling you to one extreme, then make a conscious effort to draw yourself back into balance. You will know if you are out of balance. Comments such as, "Don't make a mess" or "Keep your clothes clean," may demonstrate a bit of unbalance. Just as, "Kids will be kids" or "They have more fun in a messy house" could also be signs of being unbalanced. You can have a clean house and happy kids. It just means being on your toes, teaching responsibility, and adjusting your standards.

Initially, it is easier to just clean up after family members because you can do it in a way that reaches your standards (and also because making them get off their tushes to lift a finger is about as easy as training your two pet dogs to dance the final number from Chicago). But you are not helping them at all by doing the work for them. You are only helping yourself. Take the time and effort to teach them skills that they will need throughout their lives. Then bite your lip and turn the other way. When I was teaching my six-year-old to sweep, it was all I could do not to go after him and get all of the crumbs and dirt that he left behind. If I had done that, it would just show him that his performance did not meet my standards. Instead, I just beamed at the amazing job he did, and made sure that I wore socks and shoes every day. Although this messy little chapter of your life may seem as if it's going to last forever, it does not. As a matter of fact, it's gone before you can even turn around and take it all in.

Cultivate the Art of Deception

Have you ever received that phone call? You know the one I'm talking about. A girlfriend is calling from her cell phone, and she says, "I'm in your neighborhood, and thought I would drop by for a bit." You feel your stomach do a flip-flop as you say, "Wonderful! See you in ten!" You may as well begin now to cultivate the art of deception because you will probably have good use for it your entire life. When you have limited time to make an impression, you want to get the most bang for your buck. So, here's what you need to do:

- Check outside first. Most people think that a person's impression of a home is formed after they walk through the front door—not so. It is formed immediately after they pull into the driveway. Remove toys (especially the ones that are strategically placed on the sidewalk). Give it a quick sweeping, straighten the mat, and if you have time, clean any glass on the door (by the way, I just went outside and two of the front windows are covered in blue silly string—that's what I'm talking about).
- Check the entrance. Pick up any clutter that has been left around the door and put it away. Straighten the mat, and move on into the main visiting area, which is probably the living room.
- Check the living room. Pick up any toys. Shut any cabinet doors. Straighten throw pillows and stuff any clutter that is on surface areas into drawers and cabinets (you can put it away later). Spray linen freshener on all upholstered furniture. Turn off the TV (hopefully, it's already off) and turn on some pleasant music.
- Check the kitchen. Shut all cabinet doors. Start filling the sink with hot water and a squirt of dish soap. As you are clearing the counter, throw any dishes that are left on the counter into the sink. This way, it looks like you were right in the middle of doing dishes. Give the counters a quick wipe (just the main areas), and light a candle.
- Check the bathroom. Make sure that the seat is down, there is adequate toilet paper, and no popcorn is on the floor. Reach under the sink and grab the spray bottle of all-purpose cleaner or a cleaning wipe and give the counter and the seat a quick wipe. Straighten up the towels.

- Shut any doors to incriminating areas, such as the playroom or laundry room. Pick up a magazine, wipe the sweat off of your forehead, and have a seat on the sofa so that you can lower your heart rate. Make sure you stay there until your friend is almost at the door, and hopefully she will get to see you put down your magazine and act as if you are pleasantly surprised to see her.

Or, if she's a good friend, just meet her at the door with that beautiful smile of yours, and say, "I was just in the middle of cleaning. Come on in and give me a hand." When friends drop in, they are not there to inspect, observe, or be entertained. They are there to share your life (your real life). Numerous times when a friend showed up at my door, I've greeted her with, "Thank God you're here. I could use an extra pair of hands." So, no matter what stew you find yourself in the middle of, if she's a good friend, you may as well dish it out and serve it up.

Being messy and real beats being clean and fake any old day.

Clean with Attitude

I have a little sign that I keep posted in my house. It says, "Attitude is Everything." The right attitude can turn a trip to the dump into a play day, or a closet clean-out into a treasure hunt. It's all a matter of perspective. I remember when I was little, I could play house for hours. Of course, instead of dressing up my baby dolls, I insisted on dressing up my cat. If you think the image of a cat sliding across a wood floor is funny, try a cat dressed in a pink romper and bonnet sliding across a wood floor. And to beat that, the cat was a he! I think I may have caused some serious identity issues for him later in life. But anyway, I loved playing house then, and I love playing house now. And I'm still sliding my babies across the wood floors.

Start developing your attitude muscles. Some of the biggest problems in homemaking exist specifically in our thought patterns. A good attitude has a way of making good things happen. And a bad attitude does just the opposite. This phenomenon doesn't just happen by chance. By and large, our lives are a product of our thoughts. By some cosmic, supernatural force, our world around us bends and changes in order to mirror the world that we create in our heads. We attract to us what we believe of ourselves. It operates just like magnetism, but in the reverse. A positive attracts a positive, just like a negative attracts a negative.

To begin creating a better life for yourself, you need to begin by creating a better perception of yourself. To create a better home, you need to start by creating a better perception of how you believe your home to be. If you drag through your day complaining about how small your home is, what a state of disrepair it is in, or how ugly your furniture is, you will never create a better environment for yourself. You have no motivation. The seeds you are planting in your heart are ones of discontent, and nothing good can ever grow out of that. It's not the home you have; it's the home that you create. If you believe you have an ugly home, you will have an ugly home. If you believe you have a beautiful home, you will have a beautiful home. It all begins with *you*.

Clean up your thoughts before you even think about cleaning up your home. Instead of seeing yourself as doing menial chores, see yourself as creating an environment that nurtures those who you love most in the world (and that includes you). Instead of just keeping house, why not start playing house for a change? Grab hold of that joy that came so easily as a child. Blow bubbles through the slotted spoon while you're washing dishes. Throw some socks in the air while you're folding laundry and watch the ceiling fan sling them across the room. Drag your kids (or your cat) on a bedspread across a polished floor. This is your life, your home, your family. Make it what you want it to be. Not all the great careers in life come with a paycheck attached.

Time for Your Prescription

There are as many different ways of keeping house as there are homemakers. Some may not be happy until they can see their reflection in their kitchen sink, and then there are those of us who are happy once we can get from the front door to the backdoor without having to step over anything. Cleaning a home and keeping house is indeed one of the most personal and nurturing art forms in the world. No matter where we go during the day, what we do, or the schedules we keep, we all come home. And we should have the comfort of knowing that our home is a place where we can fill our souls and inspire our spirits. Our home should be clean enough to allow the filling of our souls with clarity, and messy enough to inspire our spirits to feel free. Yes indeed, homemaking is an art. And when it comes to keeping house and cleaning up, don't think that one way is the right way. It all depends on your home, your family, your needs, your standards, and, of course, your personality. Begin today to develop the techniques that work with your own distinct style, and watch your house begin to shine.

Rx for MasterMinds

You know the techniques that work best for you, and you are constantly improving and innovating to make these techniques work better. When it comes to methods and procedures, you wrote the book. But as you tread that path to success, make sure that there is a song in your heart along the way. Develop those attitude muscles and work on spreading as much happiness around your home as you do disinfectant. Spreading a little sunshine here and there makes a bigger difference in your home and in your family than a bucketful of elbow grease. Whistle a tune while you wash the windows. Look at your reflection in your nicely scrubbed sink and give it a wink and a smile. A little joy goes a long way (and I'm not talking about the dishwashing detergent). Try to strike a balance in your home between cleanliness and liveliness. Mess happens, so don't stress about it. Just know that it is a side effect of living a full and abundant life, then roll up your sleeves and deal with it (smiling the entire time).

Rx for Creative Spirits

Of all the personalities that need to try on different cleaning techniques, it's you. You fall in love with the newness of things, and once this wears off, it's almost impossible for it to command your attention. You tire of things easily and are ready in a heartbeat to move on to the latest and greatest. Try on all different cleaning techniques for size, and find out what works best for you. And don't get frustrated with yourself when the technique no longer inspires you to clean after a month or two. Just move on to something new and different. You can always alternate between different procedures to keep it fresh and new. Try dressing the part. If you look sharp, then your home probably will, too. And don't be afraid to pump up the music to get your activity level switched into high gear. If the neighbors complain you can always blame it on the kids.

Rx for Mother Hens

You know what works and you stick with it come hell or high water. But what is life without a little variety now and then? You tend to be more product-oriented than other personalities. You work to get somewhere, and not just for the pleasure of working. Sometimes the process can be just as much fun as the product. See the work that you put in as part of a full and vibrant career. Every step not only gets you closer to a goal, but is also fulfilling in itself. When you go about your cleaning, try going for good, and not for perfect. You have in your mind an image of perfect, but you need to replace it with a fuller and more vibrant image of good. Let the milk spill and the dirt get tracked in every once in a while. Remember that a home is for living a life, not reaching an ideal. It is meant to house our hopes and give feet to our dreams. Add a little variety to your routine, and remember that letting go of control sometimes adds the best touch.

Rx for Starry-Eyed Dreamers

Sometimes it is so difficult for you to get motivated enough to clean your home. You love your home—that is definitely not in question. But you frequently view the cleaning process as a waste of time and energy. It's just going to get all dirty again, and you could be spending your time in much better ways. Try to think of your cleaning routine as blessing your home and your family. As you make the bed, you are blessing the marriage. As you clear off the dining room table, you are blessing the gathering of a family. As you do the laundry, you are blessing the little bodies that play so hard in their clothes. Cleaning house is never a waste of time when you understand the significance of your home. When you feel like your "get up and go" just "got up and went," then try some techniques to get you moving. You love spending time with people, so invite a friend over and let the invitation motivate you to tidy up a little. And remember that cleaning is not an all-or-nothing process. Sometimes, it's all a matter of deception. If need be, just vacuum the main traffic areas and wipe the parts of the kitchen that everyone sees. A little dirt never hurt anyone (especially if it remains undetected).

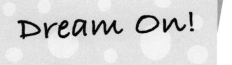 

What are your greatest chill pills? What activities do you incorporate in your life that help reduce your stress level? We all need our own private little stash of antianxiety pills that are available without a prescription. When the going gets tough, sometimes we have to resort to desperate measures, like a yoga class and a long, hot, bubble bath. I love taking long walks that clear my head or going out on a date with my husband. We all have different ways to take our blood pressure down a notch. And with the breakneck speed with which we women tend to drive our lives, all of us can use a little more chillin' here and there.

Draw a big fat fluffy bed in your journal with beautiful colors that calm your spirit. Now in a bold color, write down all over the bed all of the ways that you love to calm your mind and body. Fill up the bed and let it spill over onto the rest of the page. Turn your thoughts inward to find those activities that are deeply relaxing on a very personal level and write them all down. After you finish, look through your list and see how many of these activities you have done in the past week. If it has been a long time since you took some "me time," then it's probably long overdue. Don't wait for your life to calm down so that you can enjoy some relaxing activities. Make yourself take a break for a relaxing activity so that your life can calm down a bit. Every week, glance at this dream bed and make sure that you are easing up the pace enough. Life is short enough—don't rush it!

Part 5

Decorate It!

Chapter 12

Formula for Success

Now that you're beginning to find out how that personality works, it time to let it shine. And I can't think of a better way to express yourself than through decorating. Hopefully, you haven't grown too far away from that little girl who used to doodle in her coloring book or scribble on the walls. If so, it's time to invite her back for playtime. And her canvas has gotten a whole lot bigger. Now she can scribble on the walls—with permission.

Decorating is a fantastic way to personalize your world. For some reason, ever since I was little, I have always had this urge to make my mark on the world around me. Once, on Valentine's Day, I went in to my sister's room with a knife and carved Happy Valentine's Day onto the front of her wooden dresser. The oddest thing of it all (beside the fact that a young girl with that kind of mentality was actually wielding a knife) was that I was never punished. There are three options as to why not: (a) my mom figured it came that way and just never noticed before (highly unlikely), (b) my mom thought it was an adorable expression of my childhood love and innocence (would like to believe, but highly unlikely), or (c) it was my sister Joanna's room, and because her clothes were always hanging out of her dresser, it remained hidden. My mom probably didn't even notice until late spring, and then it was too late to do anything about it (quite likely). When I urge you to make your mark on the world around you, just give it a lot of time and consideration before going for that knife. A paintbrush would probably be a safer bet. But, if you've thought about it, and you still want to carve holiday greetings on your furniture—why not?

Start Dreaming

Before you even pick up a paintbrush (or a knife), begin a collection of design ideas that you love. Start tearing through catalogs and magazines—literally. Find the pictures of interiors and exteriors that you are drawn to and rip them out. I keep my collection (and it is ever evolving) in the binder. I glue the pictures onto paper, slide them into sheet protectors, and snap them into the binder. You don't have to be as formal with yours, but it makes it fun and easy to look through. Begin by just tearing out pictures and stuffing them into a folder.

Everything wonderful begins with a dream.

And when you do this little exercise, don't stop to think about any practical issues at all. This is merely a way of pinpointing your design style. That plan that you came across in a magazine for a six-thousand-square-foot home may not be that practical, but there are qualities that you love about it and may be able to adapt for the home you are in right now. The stained concrete floor and exposed beams of the renovated winery may not be practical with little children underfoot, but there is something you love about it. Perhaps it is the open feel, or the way the light creates a pattern on the floor. It doesn't matter why, really. It just matters that you are drawn to it. So, tear it out and stick it in that folder.

As you build your collection of ideas, don't just limit it to home magazines and catalogs. Think for a moment about your favorite places in the world, your biggest loves, your fondest memories. How about that honeymoon in Bermuda? I'm seeing walls in the palest of peachy pink with sky blue accents and crisp white trim (who says the honeymoon ever has to be over?). How about that exquisite restaurant you dined at in New York? I'm seeing butcher block and stainless steel in the kitchen, with crusty artisan bread served up in willow baskets with tall glasses of red wine. Are you a movie buff? I'm seeing handy refreshment side tables with thick, soft furniture, strings of lights along the floor, and classic movie posters framed on the wall. Decorating is just like everything else in life. If you go with what you love, you will never be wrong.

A Few of My Favorite Things

As you build your collection of images, remember to consider other things that you are drawn to, perhaps even items that you have in your possession right now. Maybe you can use that beautiful teacup collection as a starting point for designing your home, or that gorgeous platter you brought back from Tuscany. Any number of things can inspire us. There may be no rhyme or reason for the things that make our heart smile, but they do. And that's all that matters. Keep these items in mind when you are in this dream phase of decorating. I have a glazed clay cross that my sister Christina gave me for Christmas one year. I love the deep browns, reds, and oranges in the glaze and the pattern that is etched into it. After hanging it up, I realized it lost some of its luster. The cross clashed with the bright yellow paint on the wall. After some consideration, I realized that I was much more inspired by the depth of the cross than the brightness of the room, so I changed the paint color to something that more reflected where I was emotionally.

Let your home evolve along with your tastes.

Your tastes can change after some time. So, even if something you see in a magazine doesn't match anything at all you would find in your home, tear it out anyway. There is obviously some reason that it catches your eye. Perhaps the last time you painted a wall, you were in a different phase of life, experiencing emotions that you projected to your environment. We mature, we regress, we feel vibrant, we feel introspective, we grow, and we change. And it is perfectly all right for our homes to change along with us. Our style at one time does not have to remain our style forever. Give yourself complete permission to dream, and dream big. Do not allow yourself any parameters. Whatever makes you go, "oooh" and "aaah," tear it out and put it in your book. Collect all of the pictures in a notebook or binder, and don't forget to list those items already in your possession that pluck at your heartstrings.

Don't skip over this phase. When it comes to decorating, we are often tempted to just do something without even realizing what we want done. The dream phase allows for us to nail down a certain style or feel for the space that we want to decorate. It provides cohesion among all of the elements of design, as well as gives us an opportunity to discover our style. Your home should be a source of inspiration to you, but you will never get to that point until you first figure out what it is that inspires you.

What Is the Best Function of the Space?

Whether you are decorating the powder room or doing a full-scale makeover on the entire house, you need to step back and look at the space within your home in a new way. There is no need to stick with the traditional layout of your home. Just because someone wrote dining room on the blueprint, does not mean that you need to stick a table and six chairs in there. See your home as empty space to fill in a way that nurtures your family, and design it around your own personal needs. The dining room is one area that is not often used, so why not turn it into a room that can function better for your family? One girlfriend of mine, Lisa, turned hers into a playroom with cabinets and shelves lining the walls. Now it is a favorite hangout for the kids. Kristen, another girlfriend, pulled everything out of her dining room and left it completely empty, with only gorgeous wallpaper on the walls and beautiful curtains hanging in the windows. Her kids absolutely love the empty space for doing puzzles, building models, and even hosting disco parties (complete with disco ball). And Janice turned her dining room into her own personal office. With deep mahogany furniture and forest green walls, it sets a nice tone for the traditional style of her home.

What about your bedroom? Does it just have to stay a bedroom? Caroline turned her master bedroom into a suite for her three daughters. She and her husband did not need the huge space, so they used the largest of the three remaining bedrooms as their own—with two closets and an adjoining bath, it made the perfect little retreat for them. The master bedroom was converted into the teen suite.

Even with three twin beds in the room, there is still ample room for the girls to enjoy the space together and even hang out with their friends. The large bathroom is another plus, since we all know that teenage girls spend approximately two-thirds of their time in front of the mirror (and the other one-third talking on the telephone).

Think of the Possibilities

When it comes to home decorating, there is one principle I have learned—forget about what *should* be, and imagine what *could* be! Take that space you are given and turn it into whatever works best for your family. The possibilities are endless! If you never use a breakfast nook, then imagine what the best use of that space could be. Perhaps you could install shelves, cabinets, and a desktop to extend the entire wall and turn it into your home office. If you have a study but no need for it, why not turn it into a game room, a library, or even a dance studio? One of my favorite decorating ideas came out of the movie *Big*. The main character took one look at his new loft apartment with the high ceilings and immediately ordered a trampoline.

> *Your home is your creation,*
> *so let your imagination*
> *run wild.*

This is your canvas, honey! And it's time to paint up a storm. Make that space your very own. Anyone could duplicate a room from a model home, but you are not just anyone. You are a one-of-a-kind woman, so let your home advertise it. Instead of relying on the given layout, find ways to adjust it to meet the needs of your family. Do your detective work, see how your space is being used and develop your home around it.

For example, our home had a beautiful hardwood study located off of the foyer. Initially, I placed our computer in there and designed it to become our home office. However, it was inconvenient to go in there and write when the mood struck, since I was usually preoccupied in different areas of the house.

Eventually, I had the room carpeted in a lush caramel shade, pushed our computer to the edge of the room, moved the toys in, and got a laptop. The room is now being used ten times more than it was previously. The kids are in there all the time playing with toys, and you can find me writing away all through the house. Sometimes I'm at the kitchen table. Sometimes I'm lying on my bed. Sometimes I am downstairs in the schoolroom. My mobile office is just that—mobile. And it suits me perfectly.

Study Your Space

The best way to get some ideas on how to use the areas within your home is to investigate how it's already being used. Where do the kids love to play? Where do you enjoy dining? Where do people most enjoy hanging out? What rule book says that you can't move your dining room table into the family room to enjoy a meal by the fire, and move the televison and sofa into the front living room? If you entertain a lot, and the big, fat dining room table always seems to get in the way, then why not take a cue from the pubs? Move the big table out, and put a couple of tall smaller ones—the perfect height to stand at or pull up a barstool. Do the kids need more room for their friends to hang out? Why not give them the entire attic or basement? Move a couple of them in together (same gender, please) and build some mattress platforms that extend from the wall to get more floor space. You can then turn the rest of the space into their own apartment—paint every wall a different color, add some slipcovered furniture, a table and chairs, maybe even a bar with some stools surrounding it. You could even bring in a little minifridge and stock it with juice boxes and Popsicles. You better be ready for the onslaught. Because once word gets out, everyone in the neighborhood is going to want the hang out with the cool kids.

Make sure when you study the space, that you include all members of your family. Sure, you may want to create your own little Victorian tea chamber in the living room, but it may have to wait until the kids are a bit older (or maybe even out of the house). Meanwhile, perhaps you could settle for a spot of tea on a cute little upholstered chair in a back corner of your bedroom. Or if the kids are really little, you may just have to lock yourself in the bathroom and enjoy your tea on the toilet. But if it helps any, you can decorate your bathroom in a Victorian style.

> Study the space
> and design it
> with everyone in mind.

What's Your Style?

After you have collected a bunch of ideas in your file or notebook, and you have studied the best use of the space in your home, then you can sit down with all of your ideas and thoughts, and narrow down a sense of style. As long as you don't feel the pressure to conform to some type of style mode, this process is actually a lot easier than it seems. Once you know what you like, you know what you want. And you have already been brainstorming and collecting ideas of the things that you like. Don't think that you have to have a style that's set in stone. You may very well fit into a category. I have a friend who is traditional down to the banker's lamp on the office desk and the matching curtain rods at every window. But, then if you come over to my house, you see a little bit of everything. You are not required to write out a script before you open a can of paint, so let go of the pressure to fit into a style. We are all evolving, so let your style evolve with you. It will come as it comes.

Pore over your material and figure out what things you are naturally drawn to. And you can incorporate some design elements without soaking your home in them. Sometimes less is more. Just because you like exposed wood and fireplace focal points, does not mean that you have to make your entire home look like a ski lodge. And just because you are drawn to floral prints, does not mean that you have to live in a greenhouse. Variety is the spice of life. You can have a different temperament and feel to each room if you like, as long as there is an element of cohesion pulling it all together. So, leave the pigeonholes for pigeons and create your home the way you want.

When you are looking over all of your ideas, take note of exactly what you like about each one. You may already have something you can adapt right under your nose. For example, when I was doing this, I had torn out a picture of a stone house in Ireland with bright, green rolling hills surrounding it. Well, I don't know about your neck of the woods, but a stone cottage is a little difficult to

228

come by in Chester, Virginia. As I pondered the picture, I realized that what I really loved about it was the wide, open feeling that it communicated. So, I cleared out a bunch of brush, and created some walking trails through our woods. The kids love exploring in the woods, and just enlarging the space available to us gave me that wide, open feeling I was searching for. Anyway, I don't like Irish coffee.

> *Create your own little paradise here on earth.*

Look for common elements among the items in your collection. Are you drawn to deep warm colors or bright intense shades? Do you like high contrast or enjoy some variation in the same color family? What about furniture? Are you fond of decorative, painted furniture or do you prefer natural wood tones? If you don't see any rhyme or reason for anything you've collected, then don't fret. You just have a more eclectic style and enjoy bits and pieces of everything. If you ever come to visit me, I won't make you decide on dinner—we'll just go to a buffet restaurant.

Don't feel pressured to fit into one design category. It would be easy if we could say that all MasterMinds are contemporary, Creative Spirits are eclectic, Mother Hens are traditional, and Starry-Eyed Dreamers are romantic, but it doesn't always work that way. Find what you are drawn to, and splash it all over your home. If it evolves into a certain style, then go with it. But don't feel that you need to place a title on your decor. Categories become too restrictive, and then we often don't feel the freedom to venture outside the boundaries. Go ahead, go with what you like, and feel free to color outside the lines. Life would be as boring as Wonderbread if we never tried anything new or different.

That One Thing

When you're finally ready to get your hands dirty with decorating, then the starting point is to find that one thing that is going to serve as your color palette. This one thing will be as the glue to bind all of the decorating schemes in your house, and create flow from one room to another. You really only need to make sure that

229

the main areas of your home flow together. In the side rooms you can veer off your palette, and in the bedrooms you can go a bit crazy (no comment). This one thing can be absolutely anything that you love and holds all of the colors you want to incorporate in your decorating. It is your muse and your inspiration.

Once when I was decorating, the entire process began with a simple teapot that was given to me by a friend. She said, "I saw it and thought of you." She was right, because the design eventually spread throughout the entire first floor! This last time I was redecorating my home (the itch comes on every few years), I had a lot of difficulty finding that one thing for the main living areas of my home. Finally, when I was walking through a home improvement store, I saw *the* rug. It had a myriad of colors that I absolutely fell in love with. And then I especially liked one nursery that I designed (one of the many times—it's all a blur). I used a vintage Hawaiian shirt for the design and color palette. I went a little crazy in there, to the point of hot-gluing a Hawaiian girl hood ornament to the changing table. It must have rubbed off. The little baby boy from back then is quite the dude today.

As you are searching for that starting point, make sure that you keep in mind any restrictions. For example, you may have to work around a certain color of flooring or carpeting, unless you are considering replacing it. If you already have some furniture that you love, then keep the color in mind as you explore your options. Whatever you do, don't plan a decorating scheme around something you hate. I have seen people cringe at their orange carpet and then go out and buy furniture to match it. If you are stuck with a color and cannot see anyway of replacing or covering it, then at least use it as an accent color. Build your palette as far away from it as possible, while still incorporating it into your design. As you design more toward something that you enjoy, you will eventually be able to replace that eyesore, and the rest of the room will flow just as you envisioned it would.

> *Finding the starting point for your design scheme is usually love at first sight.*

Your starting point could be anything at all. If you are doing a bedroom, you may want to start out with a comforter or duvet cover. It's a whole lot easier to match paint to a finished design, than to try to find a design to match the wall paint. Fabric stores are a great place to find inspiration. You can easily pick out a bunch of fabrics, and get some swatches to take home. You could also look at some pieces of art that inspire you. Perhaps there is a painting that you especially like, or perhaps you could discover a local artist who uses color in amazing ways. Look through some prints of paintings at art stores or attend some local art exhibits. You may find your inspiration.

Color Combo

After you find that one thing, consider dragging it with you to a home improvement store. Since I'm usually dragging six kids with me when I go shopping, I consider a three-by-five rug a light load. When you do get it there, go in the paint aisle and find a corresponding color card to match every color family that is represented in your one thing. Collect these cards and hold on to them, because this is your palette that you are going to pull from as you decorate your home. You will want to bring these cards with you everywhere, just in case you run across something that may look good with your design scheme. You want to be sure that it coordinates before you dish out any money. I keep mine in a zipped compartment in my day planner. These cards are free, and you will more than likely bring one of them back to buy some gallons of paint.

Hunting and Gathering

Grab your coat and get your hat. Leave your worries on the doorstep. It's time to go hunting and gathering. With your palette in hand, it's time to go shop around. Remember as you gather samples, there is no right or wrong. Anything goes, so grab it all. And grab plenty of it because you want a wide range to choose from. Your home improvement store is going to be a great place to look at wallpaper samples and paint finishes. And remember that you don't just have to use wallpaper on walls. I've added wallpaper to yard sale furniture many times with excellent results. You should also visit your local fabric store to gather up samples of fabric for upholstery, curtains, throw pillows, lamp shades, or anything else that doesn't run away from you before you can glue yards of fabric to it. I'm infamous for coming up with creative uses for fabric (some of which do not bear repeating). And don't forget to check out the accessories while you are there— fringe for your lamp shade, cording for furniture, beads to hang from the curtains, and so on. You may also want to visit your favorite department store to gather some ideas from the home department, such as curtains, tablecloths, and bedding. Just don't buy anything yet. File the ideas away in your head instead.

Remember to look for a large variety of samples. Some personalities just naturally gravitate toward one design, such as small prints, linear textures, or subdued colors. If you see yourself digging a rut, make a conscious effort to broaden your hunting range. If you are choosing all small prints, move to some larger ones. If you are choosing linear prints, move to some with more amorphous designs. If you find that you are only pulling from the blues and greens of your palette, then grab some samples of a contrasting shade, such as tangerine. Broaden your scope. You can always narrow it down later.

> *Go sample hunting with an open mind and an open heart.*

After you gather up lots of samples and ideas, bring them all to the table, along with your idea notebook or binder. Now pull up a comfortable chair, serve yourself a tall drink, and get ready for a planning session. Your AM Routine is a good time to do these planning sessions. But if not, it would be helpful to make sure the kids are tucked in bed, or at least transfixed in front of a movie. If you are a Starry-Eyed Dreamer then invite someone over to help you along. If you are a Creative Spirit or a Mother Hen, bounce your ideas off friends you invite over. MasterMinds may need someone who is a little more out there, in order to stretch their creative muscles.

Plan on Paper

Have you seen those cool presentation boards that all of the designers use on home shows? Well, this is the same thing, sans the heavy poster board. I use plain pieces of white card stock and tuck my sketches inside clear page protectors. This is not essential, though. You can draw your sketches on anything—plain pieces of typing paper, sketch pads, your dream journal, even odd napkins that are left over from your four-year-old's birthday party. Now with all of your colors and all of your samples, sketch some layouts of the room you are going to tackle. Get the measurement of the entire room, including the windows and doors, and draw the room out to scale. This helps if you want to try out furniture layouts on paper first. Personally, I am never this meticulous. I usually just sketch a rough square on the paper, draw in some windows and doors, and then start placing some of the samples on it to see how I like it. As you start to pull from your collection to build your design for the room, remember all of the important Fs—focal point, furniture, fabric, flooring, four walls, and fotos (Okay, that last one was a stretch. But, do you blame me?)

Focal Point

The focal point is (just like it says) the main point of focus in a room. This may be a given in the room, such as a fireplace or a huge picture window. Or perhaps it is a focal point that you create—a beautiful painting accentuated by lighting, or a large entertainment center. In my living room, I had intended for the focal point to be an antique piano, but instead, it has become an enormous choo-choo train that my son drags out everyday. A focal point helps center the room and also pulls the line of vision deep into the space. Don't lose sleep over the focal point. Just decide what you want to draw attention to in the room. Personally, anything that can draw attention away from the mass of books spilling out of the bookshelf is good enough for me.

If you don't have a focal point in a room, create one that says you.

When you decide on your focal point, arrange the furniture accordingly. Place the furniture so that people in the room can enjoy the view. A room, if it is large enough, can also have more than one focal point. If you do decide to go with more than one focal point (the Rubbermaid trash can and the Pabst Blue Ribbon neon sign), then arrange the furniture to accentuate both. For example, you may want the huge ficus in one corner of the room set off by two club chairs, and the sofa and loveseat in the center of the room facing toward the entertainment center. Go ahead and sketch out your focal point(s) on your paper, and begin to arrange the furniture around it. And since we're talking furniture . . .

Furniture

Nothing gives the room a breath of fresh air like rearranging the furniture. I am constantly trying new things around the house, especially with any emotional fluctuation or life change. I remember once when one of my best friends was moving away. I was upset about it, and rearranged the furniture in two rooms and painted a door purple with red polka dots (no, I'm not kidding). My husband finally got a clue and asked if I wanted to talk about it. So, if you feel like you are due for a change, furniture is a great place to start. Give it some serious consideration before you dive into the red polka dots—it took three coats of primer to cover.

When you begin to sketch out your furniture ideas onto paper, start with your largest piece first (probably your sofa), and place others around it. And be creative. Don't just stick with the old "push it up against the wall" trick. Try floating pieces out in the room. You may feel that it confines an area, but it really provides the illusion of more space. By floating pieces of furniture, you also provide more intimacy in your layout. Pushing furniture against the wall is fine if the room is small, or you are hosting a ballroom dance party. But if not, it makes for very poor conversation areas. You can have more than one conversation area in a room, especially if it is a large room and you have more than one focal point.

As you try out different arrangements on paper, make sure that you keep in mind the traffic patterns of a room. You don't want to direct the flow of energy in the room and then straight back out. You want to arrange the furniture so that there is a graceful flow into the room, creating the urge to hang out for a little while. Try not to put the back of furniture toward the entrance, although sometimes this cannot be prevented, especially if you are dividing the room into separate conversation areas. And make sure to include enough surface areas for everyone to conveniently place a cup or book. Coffee tables and end tables are perfect for this. However, I got rid of my coffee table in front of the sofa, and instead put a narrow sofa table behind it. The only thing the coffee table was doing was serving as a catchall for books and magazines, and getting in the way of cartwheels and wrestling matches. Now, if anyone sitting on the sofa needs to put down her coffee mug, she has to set it on the table behind them. It's a bit inconvenient, but the wide open space in the living room suits the needs of our family much better.

> *Furniture should be both comfortable and attractive.*

Another good idea is to work in flexible furniture that can be moved around from place to place. Ottomans work well, as well as small chairs or benches. Using flexible pieces of furniture helps when large crowds are over so everyone can have a seat and listen to Uncle Johnny talk about his ulcers. They are also helpful when the video games are on. The kids (or adults) can pull up the ottoman to the television in order to better battle the forces of evil.

Fabric

Now it's time to pull out all of those delicious swatches that you have been collecting. Hopefully, you have gathered up a wide range of colors, patterns, and textures. Put together the swatches that you have fallen in love with, and then start playing the "guess which one does not belong" game. Depending upon your style and personality, you may find that you have either too much variation or too little variation. If the whole effect looks more like what you would find in a dressing room at Disney World than in your living room, you may find that you have a little too much variation. Consider limiting your big, bold prints to one fabric, and use it sparingly. If you find you have chosen all bright hues, consider throwing in some neutral shades to ground them a little. And don't forget to throw in some nicely textured solids to provide visual rest stops. Go for variety, but in tasteful limitation so that you are not creating a visual circus. Even a three-ring circus only focuses on one ring at a time.

If you find that your color palette looks more like your dentist's office than your bedroom, than you probably do not have enough variation. Make sure that you have at least one medium-to-large print that contains your color palette, and pull from those colors for other smaller prints. If your colors are monochromatic, then consider pulling out a strong contrasting color from your palette for two or three accent pieces in the room, such as throw pillows or a border for your curtains. Don't forget about texture. And make sure you add some variety to your designs as well. If you find that you gravitate more toward floral prints, consider accenting with some linear ones. Or add some solids to your geometrics. Go for balance. Don't put your home on snooze. You're too exciting for that! And there are way too many cool fabrics out there.

As you begin to narrow your fabric selections, start with three—one main fabric (like the room in a nutshell), one smaller print with a contrasting pattern, and one scrumptious solid with a lot of texture. Put these swatches together on your room plan, and get an idea of the finished effect. If you love your choices (don't go with a fabric just because you think you should—love it or leave it) you can buy a yard or two of it and let the room try it on by draping it where it will go. After you settle on your fabrics, you can go for a few more, depending on the range of color, intensity of hue, and the size of the room. Start small and let it evolve. Give it time. Rome wasn't built in a day, and neither is your design scheme.

Flooring

Flooring is a huge part of your design, but one that many people overlook. If you are planning on replacing your flooring, there are awesome new materials coming out every other day. For a durable, yet cost-effective finish, laminate is a good choice. Natural materials, such as wood and stone, have enduring beauty and are also easy to work with (wood can be refinished, and stone can be repolished). Carpet is always nice underfoot, and the stain-resistant qualities today are better than ever (which comes in handy when your daughter gets ill in the middle of the night and doesn't quite make it to the bathroom). No matter what material you use, make your decision carefully. Do your research and ask around. Get some swatches and take them home with you to put with your colors and try out with your design plan.

> *Put splashes of style*
> *everywhere in your home—*
> *from the ground up!*

For the vast majority of us who are not planning on ripping up our floors anytime soon, it's nice to know there are still design elements that we can incorporate with what we already have. Throw rugs are excellent choices if you want to bring more color into a room, protect your flooring, or divide a large space into separate conversation areas. If you do go for a rug, make sure you get one that has a nonslip back. If not, you're going to be chasing it around all over the place. If you have carpet that is in good condition, but is a hideous color, you can always try dying it. One of my friends had great luck with this little trick. Her light beige carpet was in great condition, but after two little boys and an indoor/outdoor dog, it was never quite the same. She had it professionally dyed a deep khaki, which hid the stains and also revitalized her entire home, for a fraction of the money it would have cost to replace it. If you have one little spot that is terribly nasty, you may want to just replace that one segment. I have had to do this before. I was outlining some trees that I had painted on the wall and spilled an entire cup of black ink on the floor. Nothing in the world could get out that stain, so I finally just cut it out. I then cut a piece of carpet the exact dimension of the piece that I had cut out, and glued it down. I can't guarantee the results because we moved six months later, but it was still holding up perfectly.

With all the focus under your feet, don't forget about over your head. Ceilings are sometimes left out of the design plan, but they can often add a great twist to the design scheme. I usually paint my ceilings the lightest shade of blue on the palette, to open up the space and give it an outdoor, airy feel. However, if you want to bring in the space a bit, consider going with a warmer or darker hue. You don't always have to make the ceiling match the walls. Instead, you could paint it a shade that complements the walls, perhaps the shade of some of your accessories or the same shade as the walls, but with a higher or darker value.

Have fun with all five walls! And explore options with your flooring as well. But whatever you do with your floor, please don't be like my great aunt. She had narrow plastic strips running through her house, and you had to stay on the strips if you were walking on the carpet. Honestly, it was like being in a museum. I'm surprised she didn't rope it off. The only things I remember about visiting her house as a child are walking on plastic strips, sitting on plastic sofa covers, and being sent outside to play. No flooring is that special. The living is important, not what's going on underneath.

Four Walls

Paint color should probably be one of your last design decisions because it is easier to find a paint to match a room then find a room to match a paint. If you paint the walls first, then you are going to knock yourself out trying to find the perfect fabrics, rugs, and artwork to go along with it. However, if you find those beautiful objects that just scream at you, then you can easily paint a room around them. And painting a room is one of the easiest tricks in a book. A few months ago, my husband and I painted an entire room in four hours, and that was without a babysitter and doing all the edging by hand. Not only did it look great (from far away, it looked perfect), but we are also still married.

> *Let the mood of a room help you choose the color of its walls.*

When you begin to explore your color choices, keep in mind that you probably already have it. The shade you paint on the walls will probably be on one of the color samples that you first picked out when you matched all of the shades in your "one thing" starting point. You can look through all of those colors and find the perfect shade with the perfect intensity to play with the light in the room. Since color is the primary method used to create a harmonious flow through the main living areas of your home, you should join the rooms by using only shades from your color palette. When you find a shade that you like, tape it up to the wall for a day and try it out. And don't be scared to crack open a can of paint and swipe it on the wall. It is one of the easiest and quickest mistakes to correct. And what would life be like without mistakes? One time I painted a powder room in a stoplight shade of red that made it look like you had wandered into the wrong part of town. I would sit on the potty, scared to death that I was going to get caught up in a drug bust. After a week of retinal damage, I finally whipped out the primer and put an end to the hideous beast. Honey, nothing you can do, short of painting the wall with a Lisa Frank psychedelic unicorn, can beat that. Don't be afraid to make mistakes. They're fun to laugh about later.

Fotos

Yes, I know it's photos, but it didn't go with the other Fs. As you are designing your room, remember to pull out all of those photos and images you have been collecting. Attach them to your design plan with paper clips so that you keep in mind the effect you are going after. For example, you may have some pictures of architectural elements that you want to include in your design. As you work on your ideas, you can draw those elements into your sketches. Even if you can't include them right away, keep them handy for when you can. As you are developing your plan, these initial images that you were drawn to will help spur your imagination to come up with more design elements.

Color Outside the Lines

A formula doesn't create a home's design until you add an element of fun. You are an exciting individual, and you should bring some of that sparkle to your home. If something doesn't coordinate with your home's palette, but it makes your heart sing, then go with it. Let your design plans as well as your heartstrings guide you in your choices. Personalize your space with bits and pieces of you. When people come over, they want a glimpse of your life, not a tour through your coordinated home.

Time for Your Prescription

As you dive into the wonderful world of decorating, remember to take it slow and steady. Nothing great happens overnight (actually, I take that back. I have six great kids, but I think one of those was an afternoon episode). Give it time, and let your designs grow along with you. Sometimes we get so caught up in the process of designing our homes, that we just want the finished product. Don't get so caught up in the product, because then you miss out on all the fun of the process. Every time I have made a gross design error (and believe me, I have made some doozies), I can always trace it to being in a hurry. If you have to live with empty space for a while, then enjoy the breathing room. If your windows are bare, then enjoy the light. Things will happen as they happen, and if you try to hurry them along, then you may be stuck with something that you don't really enjoy.

Rx for MasterMinds

You are excellent at coming up with solutions and thinking in abstract terms, especially when you are solving practical problems. Here's you opportunity to think creatively just for the sake of creativity. Stretch your creativity muscles and think outside of the interior design manuals that line the shelves at Home Depot. You have a wonderful way of thinking, so let that same thought process apply to your home. As you collect pictures from magazines for your home design, make it a point to branch out of the house a bit. Go for photos that tug at something deep inside. Perhaps it is a black-and-white picture of an old oak tree, or maybe just a sunset over a tropical island. Once you nail down the feel that you want in your room, the rest is just putting together the pieces of a puzzle—and you win that category hands down!

Rx for Creative Spirits

You have a tendency to go in twenty directions at one time. Because of this mad-dash method, you frequently lose a bit of congruity throughout your home. Make sure that you develop the primary formula for the main living areas of your home before you go running off to purchase four gallons of Pepto-Bismol Pink. Once you have "that one thing," then you can run off with your colors and patterns and go as crazy as you like. Just make sure you have your formula down to put the design parameters around your mad dashery. As soon as you get your notebook together with your palette of colors and your swatches of fabric, you can work on as many projects at one time as you like. That's your style, and you're good at it. People may advise you to work on one thing at a time, but that would be like clipping your wings—utter torture. Get that formula down pat and then run with it!

Rx for Mother Hens

It may feel like rustling your feathers a bit to take some chances, but you're going to have to force yourself to do it. Just say to yourself, "There are no mistakes, just do-overs." As you collect your idea file, don't pass up on those designs that you love but the thought of implementing sends you reeling like a drunk sailor. Enjoy taking some risks every now and then. Go ahead and paint the ceiling chartreuse or lay some shag carpet that looks like Cookie Monster was skinned and stretched. It may be that one touch of whimsy that puts some sparkle in your eye. And if not, you can always do it over. Homes are very forgiving in this sense. So collect your ideas, and don't be afraid to implement the crazy ones. There are no mistakes, just do-overs!

Rx for Starry-Eyed Dreamers

Your home is such an expressive place for you. Everywhere you look there are bits and pieces of you and your family. The one thing that you often overlook is a focal point. Try to consolidate some of the smaller accessories into bigger focal points. Design one or two primary focal points in a room and then you can build your expressiveness around them. Perhaps you need a big bookshelf, or maybe a larger mantel. You have a beautiful spirit that likes to float around your home. Just give it a few points of reference to ground it a bit. And remember that you don't need to display every little thing. Experiment with the beauty of empty spaces and give your soul room to breathe.

Dream On!

When you get out that dream journal of yours, add one more F category to your design folder—the "feel" category. Go through those magazines and catalogs of yours and cut out anything and everything that gives you warm fuzzies. As you collect pictures to spur you on to designing your home, make sure that you leave the "yeah buts" behind. You know what I'm talking about:

"Yeah, but I live in an apartment."

"Yeah, but I don't have enough space."

"Yeah, but they may hate the color."

Every time you hear yourself saying "yeah, but" (whether out loud or in your mind) then stop yourself short. There should be no room in your life or in your home for any yeah buts! So, grab those magazines and catalogs and start tearing, cutting, and gluing. These pictures will not only serve to spark your design fire, but will also be a lot of fun to look back on over the years. Start dreaming and start collecting. Remember, the first step to reaching your dreams is to have the desire.

Chapter 13

Make It Sensational!

Now that you have your plan, and you know how to get it in motion, it's time to make your home sensual. And I am not saying that you need to put on your Barry White CDs and bring out the feather boas. When you create a sensual home, you are cooking up a feast for your senses. Your home's interiors should not only be pleasing to the eye, but also to your ears, nose, fingers, tongue, and let's not forget about that sixth sense, that gut feeling that we women are so good at (especially you Starry-Eyed Dreamers).

Vision

It's the first thing you notice and usually the last thing you remember. Our eyes are constantly at work, trying to take in everything around us. Visual effects make up the majority of home design, and for good reason. When we speak in our homey little circles, we love to toss around words like, color, lighting, and pattern. We depend on our two little eyes for so very much. So, let's spoil them rotten and give them a feast to dine upon.

> *Open your eyes to see all that your home could be.*

What a Vision!

In decorating a home, we always have a tendency to gravitate toward the visual sense because that creates the initial impact and causes the most dramatic effects. In the last two chapters, the main emphasis of decorating was on visual effects. But, by and large, the most important element you should incorporate into your decorating strategy is order. Without order, all of the paint, furniture, fabric, and accessories are a waste of time and money. Our eyes tune into chaos quickly. It draws more attention than that beautiful antique maple grandfather clock standing in the foyer. Let order be the element that ties together your interiors. I know, sometimes keeping order in your home is about as easy as scratching the back of your head with your toes. But remember that it is a constant pursuit. Caring for your home doesn't end when you finish hanging the curtains or painting a wall. It is a daily effort of picking up, putting away, wiping, washing, drying, and folding. When you are involved in these daily activities, you are doing more for your home than any purchase you could make. Instead of housework, keep telling yourself that you are beautifying. It makes all the difference in the world. Appeal to your visual sense by establishing and maintaining order first and foremost.

Once order is established in our homes (sometime after the kids go off to college), then we can decorate our homes with some delicious eye candy. The finishing touches that we add to our decorating scheme will quickly draw our vision. Resist the urge to crowd an area so that there is no clean sweep of vision. Leave enough open space so that your eyes have room to move around. I am guilty of always feeling the need to fill up a space. If two feet of wall are open, I am immediately looking for something to stick up there. This last time I redecorated my home, I packed away a bunch of artwork and made myself live with open space for a while. I figured if the wall really needed something, it would come to me eventually. It's true. I was much more selective about what I put up there, and love the arrangements so much more. The decorations on our walls don't just fill up space; they add richness to our environment. And the empty space that we have now is a calming element to our home (and our home can use all the calming elements it can get).

Accessorize, Accessorize, Accessorize

No home design is complete without those little visual touches to top it off. Accessories in a home are like jewelry. Your pieces of jewelry are the finishing touches that complete an outfit. That coral pencil skirt with the heather gray zip-up cardigan and striped tank just wouldn't be the same without that chunky silver bracelet and silver and coral hoops. But how do you choose what stays, what goes, and what you need to go out and track down? It's as simple as how you choose those bracelets and earrings. What do you love, and what feels right? These are the accessories that were just made for your home.

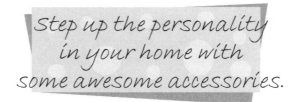

Step up the personality in your home with some awesome accessories.

Try to strike a balance between functional and pleasurable, and go for both at the same time if possible. The handmade ceramic plates that my children made are lovely to display within the cabinet, but we also enjoy getting them out on special occasions and using them. The lamps in our living room provide light for everyone in the room, but they also tie together elements in the room with the metal finish, the glass design in the center that echoes my beautiful set of glass candleholders, and the color of the lamp shade that matches our walls. Pick accessories that match your personality as well as your decor. You may be an ironstone-and-toile lady, or a burnished-metal type of woman. Find out what makes you smile when you see it, and what coordinates with your interiors. In my own experience I have found that when you collect those things that you absolutely love, then it will eventually all coordinate. You are a complex, interesting woman—let your home resonate that principle through its accessories.

The Art of Arranging

Well, now that you have your accessories you need to know how to display them. I have found that there is a certain art form to it. For example, the dirty socks lying on the bookshelf seems to detract from the living room decor, whereas the Ming vase does not. If you want to take it a step further, then there are a few things to keep in mind when you are displaying the jewelry of the room.

Arrange items so that there is plenty of variety. While you want the accessories to have coordinating elements, you also want them to have plenty of disparity, especially when it comes to size and texture. The variety in your accessories provides contrast and balance. Tall candlesticks look quite prominent next to a fat bowl. A shiny picture frame looks nice against a matte one. My husband's bald head makes my hair look especially full and vibrant.

Arranging items in odd numbers is also a little trick of the trade. It helps add uniformity without becoming repetitious and predictable. If you are using accessories to add an accent color, then go for three. We all know from watching *Schoolhouse Rock* that three is the magic number, so try it out with decorating. I have ruby red as an accent color in my living room. I used it in a chair, a piece of art, and throw pillows. Too many accent pieces begin to look more like a hodge podge rather than an accent. Keep it to three strong pieces for the most impact. Remember, Winkin', Blinkin', and Nod; faith, hope, and charity; Larry, Mo, and Curly—three is the magic number.

For Your Eyes Only

When you're adding those finishing touches, don't forget to leave your signature. Accessories are a great way to personalize your environment. Let them speak about you. My brother, Charles, is an amazing photographer. The main artwork in his home is his beautiful black-and-white-photographs. It is such a beautiful statement. I have a good friend who paints with oils, and she has walls in her home that are filled with her inspiring artwork. Another friend of mine is an avid quilter. She has breathtaking quilts on her walls that light up the room. For my husband and me, our kids are our life, and we have pictures of them hanging on every wall and resting in every nook and cranny. This is our signature. What is yours? What do you love and easily identify with? What do you want to surround yourself with? What exemplifies you? Perhaps you grew up next to the coast, and want to add seaside touches to every room. Maybe you are a hometown gal who would love to support your community by displaying the works of local artists. Find your signature, something that is all you, and put touches of it throughout your home.

> *Give your home your own personal touch with the things that say you.*

Your Own Private Collection

Collecting is big with a lot of people. You may be an avid collector of something, teacups, pottery, shot glasses from cheap resorts, whatever. I believe I have fallen into collecting children. They keep on showing up at my doorstep, so I just add them to the collection. My sister Regina has an interesting collection of small chairs. She came up with an unusual way to display them by placing them all over one wall in her house. It was all fine and well until her kids tried to sit on them. When you display your collections, remember that grouping them makes a much greater impact than spreading them out all over the house.

See the Light!

The right lighting makes all the difference in the world. It can set the mood for just about anything you have in mind. Basically, there are four types of lighting—general lighting, task lighting, accent lighting, and decorative lighting.

General lighting is commonly a big overhead light. General lighting illuminates a room, but overhead lighting can frequently be a bit too harsh. Personally,

I prefer to rely on lamps for general lighting. It is much softer and complementary to a room's design. My children could not possibly care less. I have come in their rooms to kiss them good night and found them reading books with the overhead light beating down on them. I run in and in a mad flurry turn on their task lighting, and flip off the overhead light, mumbling things about, "negative energy" and "bad karma." They usually don't even look up from their books, figuring mom is just in another one of her moods.

Task lighting provides light for specific uses, such as reading, cooking, or other activities around the house. If you prefer not to take up valuable floor space with surface areas, then you can use floor lamps, or mount a task light on a wall. I have always had good luck with this. Instead of buying lamps made specifically for wall use, I have always chosen outdoor lamps (the kind that you mount next to your front door) and wired them to use with an outlet. Add lamp cord switches to turn them on and off, and you've got a wall-mounted task light. I used barn lamps in my sons' room next to their beds. It goes with the whole cowboy/western theme. I have pretty little glass lamps mounted on the wall on both sides of my beds. I use transparent vanity bulbs in them, and they give off a very pleasant light for reading at night.

Accent lighting does just what it says—accents something. It is the Stealth Bomber of home lighting. You never notice it, but it sure does make an impact. Accent lighting is often hidden, such as track lighting, strip lighting, or recessed lights. But, it adds depth and personality because of what it calls attention to. You probably use accent lighting to call attention to artwork, collections, or other elements throughout your home.

Decorative lighting does just the opposite of accent lighting—it calls attention to itself. This type of lighting can be a lovely part of your room decor. Beautiful crystal chandeliers, antique glass lamps, little wrought-iron lamps with polka-dotted paper shades are all examples of decorative lamps. When you see these lamps at a friend's house, you wonder if it's okay to turn them on. Are they real lamps or fake lamps? Well, they can be real and fake at the same time! Keep plenty of these decorative lights around, and let them shed their light to call attention to themselves. There are so many interesting and beautiful ways to let your light shine. So, step away from the one, lone bulb beating down from the sky. No more bad karma!

> *Good lighting can make or break your home design, so try out all different kinds.*

Touch

We can frequently focus so singularly on vision that we forget about all of the other senses that compose so much of our perception. We depend more on our sense of touch then we even realize. If you have ever reached in the dryer for your favorite shirt and blue jeans then you know what I'm talking about. Touching makes a world of difference—a friendly word is nice, but a hug is ten times better!

Better Than Your Birthday Suit

When it comes to your clothing, remember that comfort is key. But let's not take it too far. The best way to get your home in shipshape, is to start the day by getting yourself in shipshape. Put on some clothes that feel wonderful against your skin and show off your best features. Get rid of everything in your closet that doesn't make you feel sensational, and replace it with clothing that fits the bill for both comfort and fashion (yes, they actually do exist). When you feel good, and you look good, it's easy to spread that same feeling throughout your home.

Snuggle In

Since it's usually pretty dark when we're sleeping (especially if our eyes are closed), it's more important to play up texture to get a good night's sleep, or a good night's whatever. Down comforters are always a good option because they have such good insulation properties. However, check the label and get one that is machine washable. If you don't then you're going to be stuck when your kids decide to bring you breakfast in bed, complete with chocolate milk and maple syrup. There are many down alternatives that are machine washable, and you can completely change the entire look of the room by replacing the duvet covers.

As far as your sheets go, don't get the cheap ones. Make sure your sheets are soft and luxe. Insist on a quality fabric, such as cotton or linen, and get the highest thread count you afford (threads per inch). Once you sleep on luxurious sheets, you'll never go back. Spending a lot of money on sheets is worth it because they last much longer and they feel much better. And since you spend about one-third of your life in bed, you may as well make it as pleasurable as possible.

> *Snuggle up with luscious sheets, and drift softly into slumberland.*

Pillows are just a matter of preference. If you are a stomach sleeper, you will probably want one that is squishy and soft, such as a feather pillow. If you are a back sleeper, you may prefer a pillow with medium density, with dense feather content or polyester fiberfill. If you are a side sleeper, you may prefer firm pillows that will support the alignment of your head a bit better. If you and your husband have different sleeping patterns, it may look as if the two pillows got in a fight, and one of them whooped the other. If you don't like the look of differently matched pillows on your bed, then buy two cheap pillows, cover them with shams or pretty fabric, and place them over the real pillows. This way, the pretty pillows are showing, and not the ones that look as if they played a bit part in a *West Side Story* street fight.

When You Just Gotta Go

Why not go in style? Play up the texture in your bathrooms. You could replace your toilet tissue with a softer brand, but I'm thinking bigger here. Place some soft rugs beneath your feet. And make sure that they have rubber backing, so you don't go slip sliding away. If you do go the rug route, wash them in the washing machine every few weeks or so, depending upon how frequently the shower or bath is used. This will prevent mold and mildew from taking hold.

Soft, thirsty towels are a must. If you don't absolutely love your towels then get rid of them or cut them up for rags. Big fat towels are so nice to cuddle up in after a shower. Or you can replace your towels with a soft robe to step into. I love the idea of robes, but I just can't ease into them. Every time I catch myself with a wet head, no makeup, and a robe on, I just can't shake the granny image. I've seen pictures of women who look sexy in a bathrobe, even with a wet head. I look geriatric. I'll stick with the soft fluffy towels.

Fantastic Fabric

There are so many fantastic uses of fabric all throughout your home. And there are so many fantastic fabrics to choose from! I could get lost for hours in a fabric store. And if it wasn't for six children who are pulling, grabbing, and hiding, I probably would. Consider all of the places where you can incorporate some luxurious fabric, perhaps a soft throw over your sofa or some throw pillows. Tablecloths are excellent choices, and they can really tie a room together. If you do go with a tablecloth, then know that you will have to wash them frequently, or just do what I do. Pull them off of the table when it's time to eat and then complete your cleanup routine by putting them back on. Curtains and drapes are beautiful accents to a room, and they can be in any texture under the sun. If you don't find what you like, you can sew some up lickity-split. Or take an easy out. Buy some place mats that match your tablecloth and pin them onto a curtain rod. It will make a simple and elegant valance, and no one will ever know.

> *Let texture play a big role in the drama of everyday life.*

Feel Your Way Around the Table

Let touch and texture play an important role at mealtime as well. Too many times, we fall into the paper plate trap. Convenience is fine as long as convenience is needed, but try to let mealtime be a time to fill hearts as well as tummies. Nice, thick plates seem to remind us to sit back and relax. If you are in need of new drinking glasses (and if you have children, you probably are), then pick out a glass with some heft to it. Take it out of the package and feel the weight in your hand. Is it something that your hand feels comfortable handling? Is the bottom heavy enough to resist tipping over? I love using sturdy stemware for water goblets at dinnertime, even with the children. We often fall into a habit of assuming we need to use the nice stuff for only special occasions. Every day is a special occasion, so celebrate life at every twist and turn. You can get good goblets at any department store, and it doesn't cost any more than drinking glasses. Match these up with some perfect plates, and turn plain old chili mac into an exquisite meal fit for any happy family (but this doesn't mean you can get the kids to eat it).

Napkins make a big difference as well. You don't need to fold a linen swan for each person's place setting, but supplying a cloth napkin is a nice touch that makes family mealtime that much more special. I have three dozen matching kitchen towels that we use as napkins. A little unorthodox, but it works. If you take this route, I highly recommend getting something you can bleach. I don't like using harsh chemicals. But kids and ooey gooey chocolate cake often call for drastic measures.

Hearing

Don't forget about filling your home with the beautiful sounds of family life. Beauty can take all different forms—everything from a gentle breeze blowing through a wind chime to a toddler banging a wooden spoon on a pot lid. Encourage all of the different instruments to play at once so that your can fill your home with an orchestra of life at its best. Sometimes silence is golden, but personally, I've always been fond of a good beat. No matter what the sound, if it makes a happy home, it sounds good to me.

Making Beautiful Music Together

The easiest way to fill your home with beautiful music is a no-brainer. Just fill your home with beautiful music. Find your favorite music and play it throughout the day. Branch out with some cultural music. You could even plan a theme night around a certain culture or geographical region and play music that is indigenous to the meal you are preparing. And how about the bedroom? This is a great place to add a little mood music. When Sinatra is crooning through the speakers, candlelight is flickering against the wall, and two glasses of wine stand at the ready, all you can do is hope you remembered to shave your legs.

Bring the Outdoors In

Some of the best sounds in the world can be found in nature (and I'm not talking about those "natural" sounds that occur so frequently—especially among my three boys). Find ways to let the lovely sounds outside drift in through your windows. Hang some melodic wind chimes outside your windows—they come in all kinds of beautiful tones. Putting birdfeeders outside will also draw those little singing minstrels from all directions. And what about a little fountain, strategically placed right outside your kitchen window so that you can hear the trickling stream. You can even place a little zen fountain inside and fill the space with the hypnotic sound. But be warned. The sound is nice at first, but after a while, it can begin to get on your nerves (and make you need the bathroom). If it doesn't, then you are more woman than I. Or maybe you just have better bladder control.

> *Listen to all of the beautiful melodies that surround you.*

I Love to Laugh

There is no better sound on this earth than a home filled with laughter! Lighten the load of those you love by finding ways to bring out a laugh. Perhaps you can plan a family game night once a week, and let your kids invite their friends over. Some of the best times I ever had growing up were when we got out the board games or played charades. Since we only had four channels on television and our video game collection consisted of Pong and Asteroids, we pretty much had to come up with our own entertainment, and boy, did we! Game night is a great way to regroup as a family and get a good laugh.

The Little Sounds of Living

Get creative and come up with little ways to add special sounds to your daily living. Jingle bells aren't just for the holidays. Put some bells on your front door, so that the cheerful jingle greets everyone who comes inside. Maybe you could sew a few to the border of a tablecloth or the corners of a throw pillow—the kids will really like using it as a throw pillow then.

Playing an instrument is also a lovely way of filling your home with music. If you don't play an instrument, then why not begin taking lessons? What have you always wanted to play? My sister Regina enjoys playing the dulcimer, the bodhran (an Irish drum), and the djembi (an African drum)—what a woman! Another sister, Christina, plays every stringed instrument on the planet. Another sister, Joanna, plays the piano. Me? I am attempting to master the kazoo and the triangle.

We have funny little sounds all throughout our home—the stuffed bear that whistles at you every time you walk by, the doorbell that makes monkey sounds when you ring it, and my children after they eat three helpings of my incredible black bean brownies ('nuff said). Find small ways to let your walls echo with happiness and cheer.

I believe my three favorite sounds in the entire world are that first baby cry in the delivery room, tiny feet running through the house, and "Daddy's home!" There is no better life than family life, and no more beautiful sounds than the living that takes place in a happy home. Tune your ears to embrace every little bit of it.

Smell

Surprisingly, the sense of smell is one of the keenest of the five. One whiff can immediately flood us with memories and take us back to a certain time period. The smell of a vinegar brine cooking immediately takes me back to my mama's kitchen during canning season. Panama Jack tanning oil takes me back to my college days. And Baby Magic baby lotion rushes me back to those tender moments when I was a new mom, slathering up my babies after a bath. If you think about it, there are so many smells with such special memories. Start creating some of those smelly memories within your home.

> *Our sense of smell can bring to life some lovely memories.*

The Scent of a Woman

Most people have a signature scent that they carry around with them. Whether it is Red Door, Dove soap, or Speedstick, there is a certain scent that people associate with you. My advice? Make it a good one. The science of scent is truly remarkable. Our natural chemistry works in such a way that the same perfume will smell differently on two different people. That's why it is so important to try on a scent before purchasing it. Those magazine adds with the scented strip have got the right idea. If you don't already have a signature scent, search for the perfect one. You will know it when you find it. If you have a certain soap that you love, use it and let the scent linger on your skin. If it is a certain hairspray that smells particularly nice, then spritz it daily—if not for the hold, then at least for the smell. Perhaps you have a great perfume. If you do, then spray some on your throat every day. Don't save it for a date night. Spoil yourself every day! Your children (even the littlest ones) will enjoy the aroma, and if you stick with the same one, they will always associate that beautiful smell with their beautiful mommy. Plus, it is absolutely pointless to save your perfume for special occasions because perfume and cologne have a shelf life just like everything else.

I never knew that cologne could spoil and turn rancid until one night when my husband was trying to set the stage for a little action. I was in the bathroom getting ready for bed, and when I came out into the bedroom there was a candle burning and a hideous stench in the air. I immediately remarked, "What on earth is that nasty smell?" and went to the window, threw it open, and began fanning the air. My husband looked a bit perturbed. He had come across the cologne that he had when we got married (twelve years prior) and thought he would surprise me with it. Needless to say, he did surprise me (and dampened the mood a bit as well). Do yourself and your spouse a favor. Don't try to fan the flame of passion with stinky old perfume because you'll probably end up fanning the air out of the window instead.

Follow Your Nose

I love finding ways to scent the air around our house. Pots of scented flowers are a great touch to greet people as they come to your front door (they will never suspect what actually lies inside). And I always have a candle burning when I'm home. Candles are a great way to add both beauty and aroma. Get a bunch in your favorite scent, and keep them stashed away. But don't save them, use them. And when you have a friend over and she comments on that wonderful smell, send her home with a candle as a gift from you. One word of warning when it comes to these delicious candles that smell of apple pie, gingerbread, and pecan pralines. If you burn these euphoric aromas, be prepared for the attack of the sweet tooth. Suddenly, you and every one in your home want to nibble on something delectable. And it is just cruel and unusual punishment to burn these when people drop in and you have nothing to offer except a pillar of wax. Burn these with glee. Just have all of the ingredients on hand to whip up a layer cake if the irrepressible urge arises.

Plug-in air fresheners are also a great touch to put in every room. These secret weapons are like the underground aroma squad—you have no idea they are there, but they're hard at work, just the same. I refill these babies about every two to four weeks, depending on how long they last and the stench they are attempting to mask. In my sons' room, I usually have to replace them hourly.

Kitchen Scents

Delicious smells drifting out of the kitchen definitely conjure up images of home. No candle can come close to freshly baked bread pulled out of the oven, or a simmering pot of stew on the stove. Take some time in the kitchen and cook up some recipes that leave deep, rich aromas hanging in the air. I would not get by two weeks without my enormous slow cooker. I cook vegetable soups and stews quite often, and the delicious smell wafts through the home all day long. It's so easy! Just get the dish started, and forget about it until dinnertime when everyone is chomping at the bit. And with the addition of programmable bread machines, you could literally spend just minutes in the morning preparing an entire meal that is cooked and waiting for you eight hours later. There was a time when I was able to use a bread machine, when my family didn't go through a loaf and a half in one sitting. Currently, I use my huge mixer and make five loaves at a time. It may sound like a lot, but when hands are grabbing at it from every direction, it's gone in no time at all.

> Cook up a storm in the kitchen and create a whirlwind of delicious smells.

And while you're at it, throw in something sweet as well. A pan of brownies or some berry cobbler takes little time to prepare, but smells so good and tastes even better! The smell of dessert will also have the little ones finishing all of their vegetables in order to get some (I am not beyond bribery). Even tiny efforts can scent up a kitchen. When I peel an orange, I like to throw the peels in a shallow pan with some water, cloves, cinnamon, and nutmeg, and let it simmer for awhile. The aroma is intoxicating! Try it at home, but just don't forget about it because the smell of smoking black orange peel is not that appetizing.

Fresh Air

I know it's not actually a scent, but fresh air really does smell good (unless you live next door to the water treatment plant or the city landfill). If the weather is agreeable, throw open some windows and let the fresh air flow in and through your home. It will not only increase the air circulation, but the positive energy flow as well. You can also strategically plant scented flowers, shrubs, or trees outside the windows so that you can scent your home from the outside in. At one house we lived in, there was a huge lilac tree outside the living room window. Every spring, that window would stay open so that the lovely scent could flow into the house.

Little Smellies

Find special little ways to stimulate the nostrils of everyone in the family. Pull a scented strip out of a magazine perfume ad and give it to one of your kids to use as a bookmark, spritz some soothing lavender water on fresh, clean sheets to give those precious children a nice-smelling trip into slumberland. Spraying some on your own sheets will also be a nice touch to pamper you and the one you love. Put a fresh bouquet of flowers on your kitchen table—you deserve it! Brew a pot of coffee, and let the smell invigorate you before you even pour it in a mug. Place some drops of vanilla oil on lamp rings. You could even have your lamps on a timer so that they light up and begin scenting the room before you come home from work or an errand. There are so many ways to add some aroma to your home. Get creative and start smelling up the place.

Taste

Okay, taste can only go so far when it comes to decorating your home. Aside from Willy Wonka's lickable wallpaper, where the shnozberries actually taste like shnozberries, you don't hear much talk of taste in the world of design. But the sense of taste goes a long way when it comes to decorating our lives and filling our homes with variety. We live in such a fast-paced culture, that we rarely take the time to really taste life. We are so busy living it, we forget to savor it. Taste is such a wonderful sensation, and probably the biggest reason why I can't eat just one chocolate chip oatmeal raisin cookie. If I'm not careful I'll eat half the batch (if I'm able to successfully hide them long enough from the kids—but they're awfully good at sniffing things out).

> *Fill your home with yummy treats, and watch the troops come running.*

Take Time to Dine

Some of the fondest memories of my childhood were created around the dining room table. While the day grew thin into the evening, we would spend long moments at the dinner table, laughing and telling stories long after the plates were scraped clean. Dinnertime was when we had some of our most serious discussions, intriguing conversations, heated arguments, and outrageous laughing sessions that caused iced tea to go up your nose instead of down your throat.

Don't let your fast lifestyle stretch into fast food as well. Make the day pause for your family. Put the homework aside, fold up the paperwork, and set out the nice plates. Dinnertime can be a wonderful ritual that makes the family regroup and touch base. I got an old barn table from a tag sale that has two extender pieces to go along with it. Since the table fits us fine without the extensions, I wasn't sure where to store the pieces, so I decided to paint on them and put them on the wall as artwork. I painted a little poem on them that I made up, with a verse on each piece. It reads,

> *Come to this table with a grateful heart, a hearty appetite,*
> *And plenty of time.*
> *Take from this table a bountiful feast for your body,*
> *Your spirit, and your mind.*

That's pretty much how I feel about dinnertime. With soccer, karate, basketball, club meetings, and every other thing under the sun, it's difficult to always find time to sit back and enjoy a family meal. There are always two or three nights during the week when the schedules are just too hectic. But as long as it is humanly possible, we light a candle, turn down the lights, put plates of delicious food around the table, and just enjoy being together. It doesn't always matter what you serve, because any food enjoyed with someone you love is truly delicious.

Get a special candle for your dining room table if you don't already have it, and let it be a visual reminder to indulge those taste buds family style. Children, as well as adults, love to dine by candlelight with nice stemware. Don't use your expensive pieces, because then you will get all crotchety when they drink from it. Get some inexpensive stemware that simply tells them, "You are important to me. I respect you. You are cherished." It's the little things that make the biggest difference. That soufflé can be a bit too dense, but no one will notice when the candles flicker, soft music plays, and a thin slice of lemon glistens in the water goblet. Your family comprises the most special people on earth to you—treat them that way.

It's All in Good Taste

Instead of just taking a moment to eat, take the time to taste. It makes so much difference. When you really focus on tasting food, you enjoy it more and you also become much more selective in the foods you choose. One reason for obesity is habitual eating. We simply eat because food is there and it is a routine behavior.

Instead of taste or hunger, we eat to feel the food in our mouths or the distension of our stomachs. When we stop and become picky about what crosses our lips, we eat less and we eat better.

We all have a set amount of calories to burn during a day in order to maintain our weight. When you know you are limited, you become much more choosy about the food that you eat. Why choke down a yucky piece of store-bought white bread when you can enjoy a slice of freshly milled, homemade multigrain bread? It's the same amount of calories, so why don't you go for the finest things and really take the time to focus and enjoy the succulence of it all. Yeah, those cookies in a box would be yummy, but not nearly as tasty as the fresh melt-in-your-mouth kind straight out of the oven. Save your calories for the most delicious morsels in life.

> *Treat yourself to the finest things in life— you are so worth it!*

Life Is a Party!

Even though it is not the most psychologically healthy perception, I consider food a celebration. Find ways to pull your family around the table by putting a little pizzazz into it. Once in our homeschooling studies, we were learning about ancient Greece. To top it off, I pushed the furniture against the wall in the dining room, we donned our togas (the littlest one used a crib sheet), and enjoyed a huge Greek feast, complete with reclining on the floor. It was so delicious, that now we have incorporated more Greek food in our daily cuisine. We just usually eat it at the table now, instead of off the floor (well, except for the toddler).

Theme nights are a great excuse for a party any day, and a chance to decorate accordingly. I try to plan one at least once a month. This encourages me to broaden my abilities as the family chef, and also increases the children's knowledge of other cultures and appreciation of other cuisine. How about a Chinese meal with indigenous music playing (you can get any kind of music you want over the Internet), and paper lanterns all around the room? Or Build-a-Burrito night with the music of a mariachi band in the background? You could even break open a piñata after you finished the flan. One time we enjoyed Viking Night, where I dumped all of the food out on the table, and we only used our hands! That sure is a strange spin on my nice plates, glasses, and flatware philosophy. The kids went bananas! So make up an excuse to do some out-of-the-box cooking. You don't need a reason to celebrate with delicious food—life is reason enough.

Fine Dining

Enjoying fine food does not have to be limited to that once-a-year swank party that the CEO throws. Get some classy cookbooks and enjoy experimenting with different recipes. Try some new vegetables, or even grow them yourself! Put a new spin on some old favorites. Go beyond the salt and pepper and try out some of the more exotic herbs and spices. Everyone in our family is either vegan, vegetarian, or of the "once-a-month-sneak-in-some-chicken-when-I'm-away-from-the-house" variety. If I was not experimental with food, we would either have slabs of tofu or bowls of pasta every night for dinner. As it stands, my family (even the kids) has adopted an adventurous perspective on dining.

I even had one of my kids ask a waitress if the chef could replace the sauce on her spaghetti with some extra virgin olive oil and a sprinkling of basil. It would have been fine if we were at a fancy shmancy restaurant, but I believe it was Shoney's. The waitress just looked at her as if she had sprouted horns. She then looked at me. Then she looked back at her. I finally chirped in, "How about a pat of butter?" Suddenly, recognition dawned in the waitress's eyes, much like the feeling of relief you feel when you are in a foreign country and hear someone speak your native tongue. If you do set out to broaden your children's palette, be prepared for the results. They will be the village freaks that everyone points at, whispering things like, "I hear he likes artichokes" or "Those aren't real meatballs."

Experimenting with food can have its ill effects, like when you conjure up that wilted spinach salad with capers and mandarin oranges. It looked good in the cookbook, but now that it is actually resting on your dinner plate, well, it lost a bit of its appeal. Your husband may give you a raised eyebrow or two. If that is the case, just tell him that you read somewhere that it is supposed to increase your libido, and then give him a little wink. He'll gobble it up in no time—capers and all. He'll even be licking the plate and asking for seconds, no matter how foul the dish turned out. Sometimes you just have to resort to drastic measures.

Broaden your horizons by trying something new on your plate.

The Sixth Sense

Even if you are not a Starry-Eyed Dreamer, you probably know what I'm talking about. We women are well known for our intuition. We can walk into a room, and instantly sense a bad energy or a good energy. You can tell when people have had a fight even if they don't say a word. We just have the uncanny ability to sense things. So what type of energy is circulating through your home? What do people immediately sense when they walk through your front door?

Welcome One and All

I remember in high school, my best friend and I would constantly hang out together, but her parents were real sticklers (remember Cameron in *Ferris Beuller's Day Off?*). Whenever I would go to her house, I would feel completely out of place, as if I had to be on my best behavior (which was difficult for me since my idea of a good time back then was dancing on the street during a stop-light or singing over the loud speaker in a department store). The energy in her house was not a very welcoming one. Then there was my house. Maybe it was because my parents had just accepted that I was obnoxious and learned how to tune it out, but my friends always felt welcome. My mom always had snacks on hand and was always willing to host any and all parties. She confided later that she would have rather had her children misbehave at their own home where she could keep an eye on things, than get into trouble somewhere else. Smart move!

I try my best to foster the same type of environment in my own home. I want all my visitors to feel welcome when they walk inside. I want my home to be a safe place to dream big and fail huge, to accomplish everything and make tons of mistakes. I want my home to be real life, with all of its color and activity, and not a place to show a false reality. Messes can be cleaned up, and mistakes can be learned from. Know that these will happen and let them. Welcome others

263

in your home knowing full well that dirt will be tracked in, wine will be spilled on the carpet, and salsa will get all over the sofa. Life is to be lived, and lived fully. Embrace it! Welcome it!

> *No home interior is complete without the positive emotion that wraps it all up.*

Feel the Love!

Create a feeling of warmth and love within your home by doing just that—loving it. Even though a home is a thing, it's okay to love it. When you pour love into your home, it pours it right back out at everyone living within it. People can walk in and feel the love and the positive energy oozing out of the walls, like melted chocolate oozing out of campfire-cooked s'mores.

One of my girlfriends, Amy, loves her home tremendously. She doesn't adore it, because then she would have a hands-off attitude. Instead, she loves it, and it loves her back. When you walk into her home, you feel completely at ease. You feel as if you stepped into a big fat bear hug. Her home is small, but from the front steps to the backyard, you feel as if she put out the red carpet just for you. Pots of flowers welcome you up the front steps, the melody of a wind chime greets you at the door. And her sweet smile and warm embrace are the best greeting of all. When you love your home, and truly enjoy living there, it will be as clear to everyone as the sun in the sky or the nose on your face.

There are many designers out there who can effectively blend a surrounding to suit all of the five senses, but there is only one who can master the sixth sense. The sixth sense lies in the spiritual realm, and when God is the designer, the interiors flow in a heavenly way. Let God pour His spirit through you and into your home. There is more power in His pinkie than in all of the cans of paint in the world. When we make God a permanent guest in our homes, we see only beauty and we hear only laughter. The food we taste is sweeter and the aromas are much more fragrant. And when we reach out to touch Him, He fills our home with His awesome love.

Time for Your Prescription

As you are decorating your home, keep in mind that no amount of paint in the world can mask an unhappy home. You can play up your home environment to appeal to every one of the five senses. But if you don't have the love and happiness, it's all meaningless. Your home is an extremely organic thing. In its own way, it breathes, speaks, and feels. You can hang the finest silk and sit on the most luxurious leather, but it might as well be spider webs and splintered wood if the love is missing. Your senses create your perception, but your perception is filtered through your emotion. Your first step in home design should be fostering an appreciation for where you are, and out of that appreciation will grow a beautiful home. I would rather spend my time in a messy home full of love, then a pristine home that lacked emotion. Your home is for living and loving—through the mess, the beauty, the failure, and success. If you love your home, it will love you back, as well as everyone who walks through your front door.

Rx for MasterMinds

You have the ability to zero in on one thing and forget about everything else going on around you. Fine if you are working on a bomb squad, not fine if you are designing your home's interiors. With your ability to focus on one thing, you need to remember to step back and take in your environment through all of the senses. Broaden your scope to fully embrace your environment, and make sure your environment is fully embracing you and everyone else in your home. Include one thing in each room that will feed all of your senses. Vision, of course, is the most evident. But think about melodic sounds, sweet aromas, lively textures, and something delicious to munch on. This will take a conscious effort on your part, but it will be well worth it.

Rx for Creative Spirits

Your attention span is not the longest one in the world (unless you are doing something completely intriguing—then no one on earth can pull you away). Because of this, find short and simple methods to play up the senses throughout your home. Your style responds best to quick changes that offer dramatic results. You have a ton of projects that you would like to do, but don't always have the time to get around to all of them. Instead of making a batch of potpourri, just plug in some air fresheners. Instead of building a solar-powered fountain outside the back door, purchase a few new CDs. Instead of reupholstering the furniture in the living room, paint the room a different color while staying within your palette. If you get around to the projects, great. But meanwhile, you can enjoy the pleasures of creating a sensual home in a snap.

Rx for Mother Hens

You enjoy your home, and you love to design it so that the space is playing to the senses. But remember that no orchestra is complete without the message in the song. As you are spreading out a feast for your senses, focus on playing up the most important aspect of all—love. Let the love that you feel for yourself and your family pour out into your home. Let the words be sweet, the thoughts positive, and the devotion honest and true. Remember that if your home is going to truly be a home, sweet home, it must begin with you. Take special efforts to lift up other family members with efforts on your part and encouraging words out of your mouth. Let your thoughts be laced with joy and kindness. The best way to satisfy the senses of family members comes from you. And it all comes around.

Rx for Starry-Eyed Dreamers

If sensual had a personality, it would be you. You are all five senses wrapped up in one. And the crown that you wear is that sixth sense of yours—intuition. Of all the personalities, you are by far the most intuitive of the lot. Don't downplay that sixth sense of yours. Instead, learn to trust it. When you enter a room, put out your emotional thermometer to test the waters. This will help you judge how you need to physically achieve balance by adjusting other aspects of your environment. For example, does the room feel frustrated or overwhelmed? Perhaps you need to clear the area visually by putting away some clutter. Does it feel tired? Try increasing the emotional volume by putting on some perky music. Does it feel stagnant? Circulate some positive energy by lighting some candles and filling up the space with a warm, delicious aroma. Let your heart be your guide, and you will seldom go wrong.

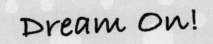 

Dream On!

Gather round while we play a game of "know your senses." Get out your dream journal and think for a while of all the things that appeal to your senses. In big, bold letters, write down the headings See, Touch, Taste, Hear, Smell. Now underneath every heading, let your imagination lead you to write down all of your favorite things that most please these senses. For example, some of my favorite things are:

See—a sleeping baby, vacuumed carpet

Touch—clean cotton sheets, warm spring rain on my skin

Taste—chewy brownies, soft pretzels with mustard

Hear—laughter, rolling thunder at night

Smell—clean laundry, flavored coffee beans

And that is just the beginning! Close your eyes and imagine those things that make your senses come alive. Write them down, and let your list go on and on. After you finish, you have an entire library of stimuli that you can draw from to put a spark into your life. Spoil your senses and wake yourself up to a full and vibrant state of being. Nothing gets that creativity going like a sensual kick in the pants. Pamper yourself by dishing out some sensual stimulation every day. In more colloquial terms, stop and smell the roses—literally! Seek out and surround yourself with those things that you love to see, touch, taste, hear, and smell. And take the time to really experience it. If you enjoy the smell of your sweet little baby after a bath, then don't just take a passing whiff. Close your eyes, hold her sweet toweled body close to yours, and inhale the delicate aroma—capturing the scent as well as the moment. We are all just by-products of our experiences. So make these experiences glorious in every way!

Part 6

Live It!

Chapter 14

Room by Room

Now you know the formula for the art of home—de-clutter it, organize it, clean it, and decorate it. You've got the recipe to make one heck of a home, so now you can start cooking. Step by step, room by room, you can begin creating that masterpiece today.

Entrance and Foyer

It's that smile, that wave, that first handshake. It's that looking glass that leads you into wonderland. The entrance to your home says so much about you, and sets the tone for everything throughout your home, so why not put your best foot forward? After all, Alice would have never been tempted to step into Wonderland if that looking glass had not sparkled and shined just so.

De-clutter It!

The entrance to your home has got to be one of the biggest rest stops in the house. It's the first place people want to shed their shoes, jackets, backpacks, purses, and anything else that may be in their hands at the time. It can easily become cluttered if you are off your guard. Every once in a while, put your entrance through a fire drill, and remove things that do not need to be hanging out. Try to look at your entrance as a visitor would, and remove items that detract from its appearance (It's easy to get used to things once they have been hanging out for awhile.).

Front porches are also infamous for becoming the local hang out for the unused, unwanted, and unneeded. Clear out the porch or front steps so that the beauty of your home can come shining through. This is also helpful when the delivery person is bringing you a package. He won't feel like he is doing that run-through-the-tires army drill all the way to your front door.

Organize It!

I am jealous of anyone with a mudroom, so let me just go ahead and clear the air right now. If you have a mudroom that you are not currently using, please drop it off at my house. But no matter what you have, whether it is a mudroom, a laundry room, or a front- or backdoor, you need to strategize around the items that are constantly being placed there. We have a coat closet where we store all of our outdoor clothing. During warmer weather, I keep our hats, gloves, and scarves packed away in the top of the closet and have one jacket for each person hanging on the rod. For the shorter set (the four youngest), I have a hanging rack mounted to the side wall at a perfect height for them to hang up their own jackets. When it is cooler, or even downright cold outside, I keep one jacket and one coat for each person in the closet at the appropriate height. I also have a rolling cart with three drawers in there that holds hats in one drawer, scarves in another, and gloves in the third. This works splendidly because it is clearly labeled and organized, and it is easily accessible for even the youngest children. They get them out. They put them away. Easy!

You may also need to consider organizing around other items that are dropped off at the entrance, such as purses, bags, and shoes. If you have the room on a close wall, you could create your own drop-off center with a cubby or locker for each family member. This works very well because each person is responsible for her own belongings. You could also slide a bench up to the wall to make it that much easier to put on or take off shoes. Just be warned—having a bench right there is like begging for people to dump stuff on top of it. If you don't have the room to mount something to the wall, consider a large basket or plastic box for each person. You could even put these on a couple of wide, sturdy shelves and leave the top free to use as a seat.

> *As long as dirt exists,*
> *coming in and going out will*
> *always be messy.*

Clean It!

At least once a week, you should put your entrance and foyer through the scrub and shine. Start outside and shake off any mats and move them aside. If they are too large to shake off, then sweep or hose them off when you do the rest of the front. Attack the front door and make sure that those spiders aren't beginning to claim your house as their own. Don't feel guilty about sweeping their webs away. They were probably looking for something to do anyway. You are just keeping them from getting bored with life. Start at the top, over the door, and work down until you are sweeping off the front steps or front porch.

Now you can get your all-purpose cleaner or oil soap spray, and clean off all of those lovely mud-pie fingerprints that you never really noticed before. Spray it all over the door, let it sit for a minute, and then wipe it all off. If it's not perfect, let it go. It's better than it was before, and that's all you're really after. Good lasts longer than perfect. Perfect is gone before you even have the chance to put the cleaner back in the caddy.

Once you move on inside, you may have already noticed that your front, side, or rear entrances need to be swept about ten times more often than the rest of the house (especially when the weather is nice). Don't wait until the dirt has found a way to travel throughout your home. Catch it when you see it. You don't see those guys with the brooms and dust pans waiting until the food court shuts down to sweep up the french fries (okay, maybe you do). But, my point is get the dirt as it happens, just the small spots here and there. It will be hard to resist the urge to sweep the entire floor. But, if you can train yourself to spot clean, it takes just seconds and you dramatically reduce your workload. Now you can go enjoy some french fries (not off the floor, please).

Decorate It!

Entrances are so much fun to decorate because you are giving your visitors a sample of the delights that lie inside. A wreath on the front door is always a nice touch, and you can modify it for the seasons. But think outside the wreath as well. Maybe you could hang a wall basket with a pretty plant spilling out, or some decorative kitchen tiles. Draw your visitors to the front door by painting it a strong color that stands out from the rest of the house, such as black or red. And resist the urge to paint the mudroom entrance or the garage door the same color, because then it will lose its focus. Instead, consider going with your shutter or window trim color, or the same color as your house, but a shade darker or lighter. If you have a large enough area near the front door, such as a porch, consider putting a bench or a couple of rocking chairs there to do the old Mayberry "sit for a spell" routine. This cozies up your entrance. I'm not saying you have to strum, "Red River Valley," but it's a nice touch just in case. And, who knows, if you have your guitar, and the breeze is just so . . .

Another good idea is to supply ample pots or other devices to plant year-round arrangements. Pansies and flowering cabbage look great during cooler months, and spring and summer are open season for just about anything that strikes your fancy. And don't think you have to just plant in pots. Rusty wheelbarrows and wagons with appropriate drainage look great, as well as a pair of old rain boots by the front step. Use your imagination and give it a touch of whimsy.

> *Let your home design pour out of the doors and spill outside.*

And extend the whimsy to other decorative items as well. One of my neighbors has a big carousel horse on her front porch. It is an adorable accent to the white wicker chairs and tea-serving cart. During the winter, my mother-in-law keeps a worn-out runner sled with a pair of old skates propped up against the front wall of her house. It looks so cute that it's all you can do to keep from belting out a chorus of "Sleigh Ride." And a neighbor of mine has a baker's rack on her front porch that she decorates. The coolest of all her arrangements happens on Halloween when she covers it with flickering candles in all shapes and sizes. Trick-or-treaters are especially spooked by the effect.

As you walk into your home, try to create a design element that greets you. Introduce the colors of your home with a painting, wreath, or other decoration. It's kind of like giving your guests a sample platter. But it's a good idea to give your visitors a taste of what is in store with all of your palette colors displayed in a focal point right there in the foyer. It could be as simple as a skinny pine table against a blue-gray wall holding a bright yellow candle, a green ivy topiary in a deep blue-gray pot, and a glistening red vase holdig a bouquet of daisies. There! You've introduced yellow, red, green, and two different values of blue-gray. Put out the sample platter, and reel them in.

Living Room

If you are like me, the living room is for living, not for showing off, whether you call it a den, a family room, or whatever. It's the room where everyone likes to hang out. Let this room embrace all of your family.

De-Clutter It!

Living and clutter coexist. Therefore, you are going to have to de-clutter this area quite frequently. Children, especially, have a tendency to want to drag things in here and leave them. If it doesn't have a home, and you want it to stay in the living room, then make a home for it. If it doesn't belong in there, then get it out. I will constantly pick odds and ends up and throw them in the trash. I'm really bad about that. That's probably why my son's robot is missing half of his head. On more than one occasion, my kids have peeked into the trash can after we have tidied up to make sure none of their precious belongings have been tossed in. I figure that if it is that precious to them, they would be able to keep up with it. Oh, well, I guess I figured wrong. I'm sure that robot thinks so (but I'm not sure he can think with half a brain).

Old magazines and videos are also a big clutter problem in the living room. If I really want to keep something out of a magazine, I tear it out and file it away. But I have come to the realization that if it didn't pop out and grab me, then I can probably go on living a productive life without it. Try to toss magazines that are a few months old so that you can make room for fresh, new material. Don't beat yourself up about wasting money. You flipped through it. You enjoyed it. Now let it go. It served its purpose. As for the old videos, I usually just pass these along to someone else or throw them away if they are not in very good condition. When your youngest child is eleven years old, there is really no need to keep those Barney videos around (unless she is a closet fan. And if that is the case, I would keep them around solely as blackmail.). Gather up the ones that you no longer watch and let someone else enjoy them.

> *Your living room is meant to be used for living, not for storing.*

Organize It!

There was a time when I actually relegated the toys to the toy room. Then, after the eighty-fifth time I picked up the toys and moved them out of the living room, I finally got a clue and just organized around the activity that was taking place. We like to hang out as a family, and I had been discouraging it by my myopic organizing stategies. So I picked out a bunch of their favorite toys (the ones I spent every evening picking up) and brought them into the living room. Since I didn't want it to look like a daycare center, I grouped the toys and put them into pretty baskets that are placed on a bookshelf (Tinker Toys are in one basket, baby toys are in another, Matchbox cars in another, etc.). Now they feel free to dump out a basket and play with the contents. I still spend a great deal of time picking up toys, but now I don't have to lug them all the way to the playroom.

Television viewing often takes up a large amount of time in the living room, so you may as well organize around it. We keep our video collection alphabetized and grouped by category, such as children, drama, comedy, and holiday. The movies are labeled at the top with the first letter of the title, and the labels are color coded to their category. This makes it so we can easily locate them and put them back. We also keep a copy of the listing in page protectors that hang from a hook on the inside of the closet door. When a friend is over, it is quick and easy for them to look over the list and choose a movie. When we get a new one, we just write it in. When the list looks as if someone has written his memoirs on it, it's time to update the list in the computer and print out a new copy.

Clean It!

When everything is neatly organized in your living room, cleanup should be a snap. But, for some reason that goes beyond my limited understanding, there are always those days when it looks as if you had a visit by a wrecking crew, rather than a few friends over after school (or maybe that was a wrecking crew). When you stay on top of it, the mess will rarely get the best of you. But, you also don't want to be one of those screeching shrews that follows the kids around pointing and yelling, "Put that back!" The last thing you want to become known as in kid circles is the lady who chases you out of the house. Strive for balance. Treat your home as you do a close friend—with honesty and respect. Be honest enough to live a real life that is full of messes and mistakes, and be respectful enough to put forth the effort required to care for it appropriately. Even though it is just walls, windows, and a roof, your house can be your friend. As I've said before, if you love it, it will love you back, and it's one hundred times better than a pet rock.

> *Treat your home with love and everyone will love living in it.*

When you're cleaning, attack those high places first with your lambs wool or feather duster, then work down over anything hanging on the walls. Your oil soap cleaner should work well for cleaning any wood furniture. If you prefer polish, then go that route. But, sometimes polish can leave a residue. Keep this in mind and buff thoroughly. If you have any plants, you should put them outside and hose them off every few weeks, or if the weather is not cooperating, stuff them in the shower and rinse them off. After they dry completely, you can go the extra mile and spray them with some orange oil-based furniture polish (Orange Glo). This makes them shine beautifully, and it smells great (and with all the diapers I go through, my home can use all the good smells I can get my hands on).

The last thing you will do is vacuum the floor. I try to pick up every little thing off the floor before I vacuum, but every now and then I miss something. Don't tell my mom, but sometimes this "accidentally" gets kicked under the furniture. Like I've always said, go for the appearance of perfect, not the real thing. Cleaning in this manner works fine until you have a guest over with a seven-year-old boy who likes to slide on his belly and investigate underneath the furniture. I tried to tempt him away from the living room with a box of cookies, but he got to the sofa before I could intervene. All we heard from the kitchen was, "Wow! You wouldn't believe what I found down here!" I then cringed as I heard him pulling everything out (dust bunnies included). Trying to redeem any dignity that remained, I calmly walked over, checked out the area of contamination and said, "I worked hard to kick all that under there, and I would appreciate it if you stuffed it all back when you are done." My friend seemed to appreciate my candor. Remember, no one expects you to be flawless, and when the curtain comes down it's actually a relief for them to find out you are not.

Decorate It!

Make your living room a comfortable, relaxing room to live in. Hard, stiff furniture is great if you have no feeling. For those of us who have sensory nerves, go for furniture that seems to have a narcotic effect. Your sofa will probably be one of the most expensive pieces of furniture in the house because of size and function. But it's usually the centerpiece of the room, so go for quality. If you are lucky enough to have inherited a great one from somewhere, but the design is not you, then consider slipcovering it. But do yourself a favor, and sew up a tailored one that has separate covers for the body and the cushions, or hire someone to do it. It is really quite easy to do—just place fabric over it, pin it at the seams, and sew it together. If you are inexperienced, then by all means, don't go for a pattern or texture that you have to piece together. Go for simple solids or patterns that work in any direction. But whatever you do, don't be tempted to buy a slipcover that fits over the entire sofa, unless you just love high maintenance. Short of nails, tacks, rubber cement, and grape jelly, no contraption exists on the market to keep that piece of fabric in place. I've tried. And even if my kids didn't enjoy jumping on the sofa, it would never stay in place (okay, so maybe the jumping didn't help matters).

Arrange your furniture so that you open up the flow into the room, and have one or two intimate conversation areas. Any coffee tables or ottomans that you have should be no higher than the height of the seating on your sofa or chairs, and any side tables should be no lower than two inches below the arm of the sofa, and no higher than thirty inches or so. But these are guidelines. If there is a little give or take here and there, don't sweat it.

> *The science of design is whatever has the right chemistry for your family.*

Pull out some accent colors and splash them around the room. If you don't already have the perfect artwork to put on the walls, why not create it yourself and incorporate the kids in the process? You could buy some canvases in the size that you want, perhaps one large one to operate as a focal point or a series of smaller ones to adorn an entire wall. Paint the canvases in a colorwash of your strongest accent color so that you will have a good contrast against the wall. Then use the other colors in your room and a variety of different values to paint a picture on it. If you are hesitant to try your hand at it, then your children will be more than happy to. Just give them the colorwashed canvases and a variety of different paints, and stand back. These will make prettier pictures than you could ever purchase, and much more significant. You may even find a new hobby or career. If your kids show that they have a real talent, perhaps you could begin taking orders from your friends and start making them earn their keep.

Dining Room

The dining room is a wonderful place to extend your home design, whether you go for the more traditional look of a polished mahogany table with a matching buffet and china cabinet, or you are the more rustic pine-with-benches-pulled-up-to-the-side kind of girl. Let your dining room speak as much about you and your family as the rest of the house by giving it some pizzazz, some zest, some *je ne sais quoi.*

De-clutter It!

It's happening everywhere. With the increase in people working from home, the dining room is beginning to double as the home office. The table is buried underneath piles of papers, books, and a laptop, and the nice china just gathers dust. If you find that you doing more working than eating in your dining room, then why not just turn it into your office? Don't try to live under a canopy of "shoulds." Who says you should have a dining room? If your family enjoys eating in the kitchen, then choose your own floor plan. If you have no need for a formal dining room, just turn it into something else. But, the first thing you need to do is get rid of the clutter.

Don't let the table serve as a rest stop in your home. If you find that it is beginning to be a drop-off point, then you need to do the old throwaway, give-away, put away, and store away routine. Clear the area so that you can actually enjoy a meal there. But, if you prefer to eat in your kitchen, then turn this area into whatever your beautiful heart desires. Bring it into the design of your home and enjoy the space in whatever way you choose.

It's your space
so make it fit you.

Organize It!

If you do find that you are using the room for a purpose other than dining, then figure out what that activity is and organize around it. If it is functioning as your home office, then pass the table along to someone who can use it and trade it in for the perfect workspace. If you need more room for the kids to play rather than to eat, then clear out the room except for some exceptionally soft chairs and an entire storage wall full of toys. If you don't trust the kids, then you may want to consider padding the walls and anchoring the chairs to the floor. If you are one of the rare few who actually uses the room for dining purposes, then eat up!

Clean It!

If you are fortunate enough to have a gorgeous chandelier in your dining room, then make the most of this focal point. Weekly dusting should be enough to maintain it, but clean it thoroughly at least once a month to make it sparkle at its best. You can place a plastic tarp, dropcloth, or trash bag over your dining room table (or whatever happens to be underneath the chandelier at the time), layer a pile of towels on top of it, and spray the chandelier generously with nonsudsing ammonia. When it is finished dripping off, step back and enjoy the sparkle. You can clean any hurricane lamps by removing the glass shields and washing them in warm water with a few drops of detergent. A nice touch that not many people know about is putting halogen bulbs in your chandelier. The light is cleaner and brighter, and really shows off your best features (which we learn how to do from the first time we get a hi-cut swimsuit with vertical stripes).

Hopefully, no matter how much you need to dust your dining room, you will probably never have to do as my mother did when I went through my secret agent phase. As a young girl, I was determined to stop crime in our suburban neighborhood by dusting for fingerprints in the dining room (someone had taken my sister's geography notebook). I had gone through three-fourths of my mother's Johnson's baby powder before she came in and caught me. The entire dining room glistened in white like a scene from a Currier & Ives greeting card. I didn't uncover any crime rings, but I did learn early how to use a dustcloth.

Decorate It!

Having a buffet in the room is a nice touch when you are hosting parties and enjoy putting out a spread. It is also a good focal point for some bold accessories or holiday decorations. A china cabinet is nice, as well, but don't fall into the ho-hum of the china cabinet, buffet, and dining room table suite that you see in all of the Sunday paper furniture store fliers. If you do have such a set, maybe you could change things around a little bit. Put the china cabinet in the kitchen and fill it up with some awesome pottery, or maybe stick an old dresser in the dining room to cozy it up a bit. If you do keep the china cabinet in the dining room, then why not throw in few homemade plates or the "udder buddy" creamer shaped like a cow among the nice china. It's the touches of whimsy that intrigue us and keep us on our toes.

A nice centerpiece really shows off on a beautiful dining room table, and if you feel that creative urge strike, go for something with a little more personality than a silk flower arrangement. My mother keeps a huge ironstone soup tureen on her cherry dining room table. The simple contrast in form and value is beautiful. For holidays, I have an antique french fry cutter that looks just like an old sled if you prop it on its side. Three little stuffed elves ride on it in the middle of the dining room table for about a month until I tuck it back in into storage. How about a basket of plastic fruit, only with sequins glued all over them? Or a grapevine wreath lying on the table with a big fat pillar candle in the middle? Maybe you could use a simply beautiful understated plant, and stick some exotic silk flowers into it for a cool effect. There are many ideas for a centerpiece, so get those creative wheels turning.

When it comes to dining, don't save your fancy wares for fancy occasions. Every meal should be a way to celebrate being together. The little touches can add so much to a meal, and even make your less-than-appetizing meals seem delicious. How about pudding served in champagne glasses? Fine china with left-over pizza? I've even been known to feed the kids beanie weenies in our crystal parfait glasses. Sometimes it's not so much what we're eating, as much as the perception of what we're eating.

Kitchen

Hands down, this is the most popular room in the house, and I'm not saying that just because I love to chow down. No matter where you try to hold your party, the entire crowd always congregates in the kitchen. If your home were a body, it would be the heart. It's the starring role in your house performance, so give it the star treatment. It will be awesome! And you don't have to pick out all of the green M&M's.

> *Your kitchen does
> a lot for you,
> so show it some love.*

De-clutter It!

Without even realizing it, we can hold on to kitchen stuff for an eternity. It just keeps getting pushed farther and farther back in the cabinets. Every year or so, you should put your kitchen cabinets through a deep cleaning. I remember a few years ago I found an electric casserole slow cooker that could only hold about a quart of food. This worked fine for me in the first few years of marriage, but what in the world would a family of eight do with a contraption this small? It wouldn't even hold enough ketchup to satisfy my kids when they eat one serving of french fries. However, it was doing a great job gathering dust. Out it went. There are lots of other things that find their way into our kitchen and never get out. Here are a few items that you may have hidden away:

- bottoms without lids (if they need them)
- lids without bottoms
- free plastic cups that come with kid meals
- worn-out tools (the rusty can opener, for starters)
- specialty cookers that you never use (rice cooks just as well in a microwaveable casserole dish)
- fifty-one duplicates of measuring devices
- ugly dishes that you never eat from
- twelve oven mitts when you only use two
- dull, cheap knives
- coffee mugs, coffee mugs, coffee mugs
- rusted and scratched-up cookware

A kitchen is one room where it is very important to have good quality tools and equipment. Preparing meals for a family is one of the greatest honors and responsibilities, and you deserve to have a well-equipped kitchen. By keeping and using only high-quality tools, you are making your time in the kitchen more efficient and effective. And by using only dishware and flatware that you love, you are making mealtime even more pleasurable. For the price of those fifteen dull knives, you could have purchased three that perform perfectly. And that beautiful stemware is just taking up space in the back of the cabinets while you drink from those ugly, plastic cups. Don't hold on to shoddy equipment hoping that one day it will miraculously perform better. I remember having about five casserole dishes that were old, scratched, and rusted. I kept using them, but I wasn't enjoying them. I finally got rid of the whole lot and bought two perfect glass casserole dishes. They cook evenly, and cleanup beautifully. Now I enjoy using them, so I cook with them more often (much to the chagrin of my children when I make spinach, shitake, and red pepper lasagna).

If you are frustrated with an item, don't put it back in the drawer, throw it in the trash and get one that you love. You earned it. Clear out those cabinets and keep (or get) only what you use and what you love. Maybe you could clear out as much as possible, have a yard sale, and use all of the proceeds to hold a kitchen shower for yourself. Start making your wish list now.

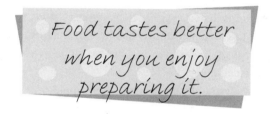

Food tastes better when you enjoy preparing it.

We even have tendencies to hold on to food that we will never eat. I remember visiting my husband before he was my husband. I walked into his bachelor pad kitchen and opened his cabinets, looking for something to eat. There were two boxes of macaroni and cheese and a can of beef consommé. I laughed hysterically and began interrogating my fiancée as to why on earth he had a can of beef consommé in his cabinets. He pleaded the fifth.

We got married, and as our lives united, the can of beef consommé found its way into our humble little home.

I got pregnant. We moved to a slightly larger apartment. The can of beef consommé moved with us.

We had our first child. I got pregnant again. My husband got a new job across the country. The can of beef consommé moved with us.

We had our second child. I got pregnant again. A Boy Scout troop came to our door collecting cans for a soup kitchen. And so the beef consommé exited our life, almost as mysteriously as it had first entered.

Do yourself, your family, and your pantry a favor. If you have no plans on eating it, then get rid of it. So what if it has a shelf life of twenty years (that should be your first clue as to its health benefits). If you haven't used that envelope of powdered seaweed pesto mix in the past six months, then chances are, you won't.

Organize It!

The best way to organize the kitchen is just like you organize everything else, by function. Keep your cookware in one spot, your stemware in another. And make it convenient for you by storing it as close to where you use it as possible. Keep the cookware near the stove and the stemware near the refrigerator. I keep all of my measuring supplies in a basket in the cabinet, but I use my measuring spoons so often that I just hang them from a hook in the wall. And you can group your pantry items in categories that are similar to the grocery store. Keep your cans together, baking supplies together, cereals and breakfast items together, and the like. This not only makes it easier to locate, but it also helps you figure out when you are running low on supplies.

You may also want to organize around other people who use the kitchen, especially the four-feet-and-under set. On the floor of my pantry, I have a big basket that we call the snack basket. It is always full of individual snacks for the kids, and they are welcome to help themselves to it after school. Usually it is sandwich-size zipped bags that little hands can manipulate. I buy huge bags or boxes of snack food and then fill up a bunch of little bags. I also will make an enormous batch of trail mix and prepare individual servings. The kids love this, and enjoy choosing whatever they may want. Every now and then I tuck in some snacks that the kids especially love to surprise them (like packs of chocolate-covered soy-nuts—I have strange kids). The basket usually looks like a snack-food version of the Halloween candy collection. Try organizing your kitchen to allow the little ones to function as independently as possible by keeping things they use on their level.

A well-organized kitchen is a blessing (especially around dinner time).

Clean It!

Cleaning the kitchen sometimes feels like an hourly task, so make it as easy on yourself as possible. Try to keep the counters clutter-free to make cleanup a snap (no wiping around stuff). And the best trick of all is to clean as you go. Don't wait for the headache of cleaning up after you have prepared a meal. Instead, make cleaning part of each step in the process. Open a can, rinse off the opener, toss the can in the trash. Peel and chop the onion, sob as if there is no tomorrow, throw the debris away, wash off the cutting board. I'm still waiting for that sous chef to show up at my door and give me a hand in the kitchen, but for now I'm cleaning as I go.

Every year you may also want to empty the cabinets and pantry shelves and wipe them off thoroughly. I have no idea how it happens, but crumbs, dirt, and other grossies find a way to get behind objects and set up camp. Foil their little campout like a torrential downpour, and clean it up. Don't wait for the bug infestation. The last thing you need to deal with is one of the ten plagues.

The microwave can also get pretty nasty, especially when you forget about the cup of coffee you are warming up and it bubbles up and over the side of the mug, or you underestimate how much rice expands and it flows out of the casserole dish, or your child is cooking a veggie hot dog and it explodes all over the place (not that we have ever done that, of course). Make it a habit of giving it a quick cleaning every other day or so. Spray some cleaner and nuke it for a few seconds to loosen up any grime, then it's a breeze to wipe it out. And when your son microwaves a blown-up balloon to find out if it will increase molecular activity to the point of explosion, the cleanup will be ten times easier if it wasn't grimy to begin with, I promise (not that we've ever done that, of course).

Decorate It!

This ain't your mama's kitchen, or at least it shouldn't be. Your kitchen should say just as much about you as the rest of your home. Make it a room where everyone wants to hang out (because they will whether you like it or not). Incorporate design elements throughout that tie it into the rest of the house. Cozy it up a bit with splashes of color and artwork. Include some photos in your kitchen, but don't just stick something on the fridge—add some class to it. Get some perfect frames that coordinate with your kitchen for pictures of the loved ones you cook for.

You can also change your decor without breaking the bank. If you have appliances in good condition but they don't coordinate, consider resurfacing them. It costs a fraction of what you would spend on new ones. You can even do it yourself by covering the face with a piece of stainless steel cut to the machine's measurements. If cabinets are in good condition but outdated, they don't have to be replaced either. Paint goes a long way (just make sure you use gloss or semi-gloss for easy cleanup). You can also replace hardware or add decorative molding to the edges of the cabinet doors. You may want to splurge in a few awesome touches, such as an amazing tile backsplash or some funky modern lighting. Or how about cabinet doors with glass insets? If I were to ever do this, I would go with one or two cabinets instead of the whole lot. If I did them all, I would be forced to always keep my glasses and stemware perfectly lined up—way too much pressure for me!

Style up your kitchen and add a little panache to your pancakes.

Your kitchen can be functional as well as beautiful. I applied a series of cork tiles to the inside of one of my cabinets, which I use to keep track of important pieces of paper. It remains hidden while the cabinet doors are closed. And my kids love to display their latest accomplishment on the fridge (as all kids do). In order to prevent the bulletin board effect, I have five magnetic clips that I keep on the fridge, one for each of the older kids. That way, they can display one thing at a time. When they want to put something new up there, the old one goes tucked away in their file. Actually, with as many kids as I have, even with only one item up there at a time, it still looks like a bulletin board. One day, my fridge will be cleared off. But tissue paper flowers only last for a short season. For now, I will let them brighten up my kitchen.

Bathroom

De-clutter It!

The bathroom can easily become a host to a lot of clutter. I think every Secret Santa in the world has given bath salts or exquisite lotion as a gift, and girlfriends like nothing more than to present each other with cute little soaps. We love these gifts! Not that we actually ever use them, but boy, do we love them! Once when I was cleaning out my bathroom, I put all of my nice soaps (the kind that were just too cute to actually use), and I put them all in a small basket in one of my cabinets. Then I figured, I deserved to use them. And, one by one, I did. I wouldn't put soap in my bathroom until they were all gone. I don't think I ever smelled better in my life! The ones that were great, I used to the very last sliver. The ones that were just so-so were used a bit and then tossed. I also used all of the lotions with the same principle in mind. The great ones were used, the others tossed. If you have a collection developing in your bathroom, why not treat yourself to your own mini-spa and use them? If you just love the cute packaging, then put them in a pretty vanity tray and place them in the bathroom when guests come. They won't use them either, but it's a nice touch.

We also like to accumulate makeup. It's good to weed through it every once in a while for two reasons—bacteria can quickly grow and pose a risk (especially in eye makeup) and styles change quickly. Makeup fashion changes on a dime. Matte becomes gloss, gloss becomes sparkle, sparkle becomes iridescence, then we're back to matte again. And colors change just as frequently. Gold is the new black, then peach is the new gold. Staying on the cutting edge of style means sticking with the tried-and-true base products that have proven their quality, and adding special items here and there to show that you actually can find your way through an *Allure* magazine. When it comes to de-cluttering your beauty supplies, it's out with the old, in with the oh-so-new.

> *Clear out the odds and ends
> that you never use and lather up
> with the good stuff.*

Organize It!

As usual, group your stuff by function, and contain it as much as possible. Keep your makeup in a basket or plastic bin. You probably don't need a rolling trunk unless you're a makeup artist, or very insecure. If you do have a bunch of makeup, sort it into the essentials that you need daily for a quick prep, and then into the extras that you pull out for that hot date (and I'm not talking about a trip to the grocery store). Try to contain the little bottles and tubes so that cleanup is easier and when you open up the medicine cabinet, it doesn't rain Bath & Body Works.

Keeping your shower organized is also important. You don't need seven different shampoos, unless you have seven different heads. And limit your bath soap or body wash to one or two products. Storing your razor in the shower is fine if you enjoy shaving with rusted blades. If not, then keep them clean and dry in the cabinet. It not only makes your razors last much longer, but it also helps lessen that razor burn that is especially bothersome around your bikini line—ouch!

Clean It!

Cleaning a bathroom regularly is a must. The dusting and polishing can go for a few days, and the vacuuming can wait until the weekend, but the bathroom? One hour left unattended, and there are only two words that can describe it—pee yoo! The canisters of cleaning wipes are a must to keep under the sink. If you practice daily wipe ups, then there is no real down and dirty cleaning that needs to take place. Every day, whether you see dirt or not, practice taking a few seconds to quickly wipe off the counter, the back of the toilet and seat, and then toss it on the ground and wipe around the bottom of the toilet and other messy spots with your foot. Yes, it's unconventional. Yes, it works. By attacking the itty bitties every day, you're not facing the monster messes on a weekly basis.

If you have a shower door, then practice the post-shower nude squeegee. I hear it's soon to be an Olympic event. The daily wiping off will prevent mineral deposits and soap scum from accumulating. Vinegar also help get rid of this as a result of its high acid content. If you have a shower curtain and liner, then you already know that mold and mildew hath no greater love. Taking it off and washing it in the washing machine with hot water and bleach will make it look as good as new. You just have to deal with the mess of unraveling it and having water splash everywhere. You could also buy el cheapo liners, and replace them once or twice a year with more el cheapo liners. If you have tile in your bath with grout that gets mildew minute by minute, then may God have mercy on your soul. This is a pain to clean, but it's nothing a grout brush and baking soda can't take care of (or cleaner with bleach if it's especially stubborn).

> *A clean bathroom makes you feel clean all over.*

Because of the moisture and warmth, your bathroom loves to harbor germs and bacteria. And odor is a result of bacteria. Air fresheners are a nice touch to put in your bathroom, but regular cleaning will get rid of the odor instead of just mask it. The children's bathroom can get especially funky. If you have little ones who bathe in the tub with a collection of bath toys, then you are already aware that these can easily harbor their own form of pond scum. Every few weeks, you may want to throw them in the dishwasher to clean off the muck, and the heat of the water will kill off the germs. If you have any boys in the family, perhaps you could enroll them in archery lessons so that they can develop a love of proper aiming technique. If not, then we're back to the daily wiping around the toilet area. But do your best to keep your bathroom as tidy as possible, so that when you take a shower, you actually feel like you're getting clean.

Decorate It!

Bathrooms can be fun areas to decorate. They are not so huge that you have to open up a home equity line just to give it a facelift, and they are not so small that they make no impact. It's the perfect size to test out some new decor ideas. You can even have a theme room. How about a botanical bath or a party potty? Give your powder room plenty of personality by painting it in an accent color. You can even try your hand at some faux finishes. If you don't like the effect, you can spend a few hours and get rid of it. Dress it up with some seasonal towels and a groovy soap dispenser. You can add a special touch by throwing in some reading material for those people who enjoy camping out (or hiding from the kids). I am convinced that if it weren't for indoor plumbing, *Guidepost* magazine would not even exist. If you go the reading route, just make sure you throw in a can of air freshener as well.

For your own private bath, maybe you can create your own exotic spa. You deserve to be pampered, so don't wait around for anyone to do it for you. Pamper yourself! No matter how small your bathroom is, you can give it a luxurious feel by incorporating some simple design elements. Thirsty towels are always nice, especially if they all match and have a sumptuous texture to them. If you have the room, install a towel warmer. They don't cost much at all, and it feels so good to wrap yourself up in a warm, dry towel after a nice long bath. You can even use these to dry sweaters or pants that cannot be tossed in the dryer. Adding some special touches here and there will make your trip to the shower feel as if you are retreating to an exclusive spa (just try to ignore the kids beating down the door).

Home Office

These rooms are becoming more and more standard in homes today. It seems everyone and their sisters are doing some work out of the house. You want this space to function as an office, but you still want to incorporate it in the entire home. What to do? What to do?

De-clutter It!

Keep your office hours, just as you would if you were going in to work. When you begin work, prepare your workspace accordingly, and when you quit work, clean it all up. We can often take advantage of the home environment by not clearing out the clutter that amasses as a result of our work. If we were going in to the office, we would probably be required to leave the area relatively clutter-free at the end of the day. Give your home the same amount of respect. Instead of just putting items down, put them away where they go. If you work daily out of the home, then you may have to do a weekly de-cluttering of all of the paper. Keep the surface of your work area as cleared off as possible so that your office adds to the design of the house, instead of detracting from it.

> When it comes to
> the home office, go for more
> "home" than "office."

Organize It!

If you are going to get any work accomplished at home, it is vital that you keep it as organized as possible. Keep work files separate from home files (you wouldn't want to pierce that corporate shield), and make your files as broad as possible. You don't want to thumb through forty different file folders to get to the one you need, so try to consolidate as many as you can. Having in and out baskets are essential, as long as you don't let that in basket look as if you have been out on maternity leave for the past month. No organizing strategy in the world will help you if you don't make it a habit of staying on top of your game.

Clean It!

Cleaning your home office requires the same amount of effort as the rest of the house. So, do the top-to-bottom dusting and follow it with a good cleaning and polishing of whatever needs it. Don't fall into the trap of separating your home office from the rest of the home just because it has the word office in there. Your entire home needs to flow, and that includes all work spaces. If you use your home office frequently then it is even more important to make daily habits of straightening up the papers, getting rid of any piles, and creating clean open spaces on surface areas. You want it to be a pleasant place to work. If it isn't, then you won't want to balance your checkbook, then that check will bounce, then you will get all frustrated, kick the dog, yell at the kids, and burn the casserole—all because you didn't feel like dusting furniture!

Decorate It!

Just because you work out of the home doesn't mean you need to make the space feel like a corporate office. Out with the ugly blinds, the water cooler, the office geek that waits on baited breath for the doughnut and bagel cart to come by. Make your home office blend in completely with your entire home decor. You can go with some office furniture that coordinates with your home or you can use a heavy oak kitchen table with a wicker chair and a barn lamp. That's the great thing about having a home office. It's your home, so design it any way you want. Create a work space that comforts you and inspires you. If you make it a place where you want to work, then you will get far more accomplished. Even a CEO can appreciate logic like that.

Your Bedroom

Now is the time to design the room that dreams are made of, literally. There is nothing quite like drifting off to sleep (or doing other activities) in a room that is most perfectly you. So get ready to roll up your sleeves and create your own private version of cloud nine.

De-clutter It!

Don't fall into the trap of using your bedroom as a catchall just because you have the option of closing the door and shutting it off from the rest of the world. Your bedroom is your own private throne, so show yourself the respect and admiration you deserve by keeping the queen's chambers free of junk that could weigh you down. Closets are one of the biggest clutter headaches on the planet. I'm not too sure, but I think that we get the word, "closet," from the Latin word for "clutter." Anyway, it's about time to open up that closet and air it out a little bit.

Your closet does not need to be a place where you stash trash. If you don't wear it, then get it out. Save that shelf space for those sexy strappy slingbacks

*Cleaning out the closet
eventually spreads throughout
the entire room.*

that you were eyeing at the store. Throw out the wire hangers. They belong at the cleaners, not in your closet. I'm not saying you need to invest in cedar hangers for all of your clothes, but at least go the plastic route. They cost pennies, and they make your closet look so much nicer and better organized. Display your shoes and purses on shelves, and keep the out-of-season ones safely stored away in boxes and clearly labeled. Nothing belongs on the floor, except maybe a laundry basket if this is the area where you change your clothes.

If your closet needs a major overhaul, there is no better time than the present. And no matter how bad a condition it may be in, nothing can even come close to the closet that my two sisters and I shared when I was a young girl. Yes, three girls, one small closet. Clothes were not really hung up. It was more like they were suspended in a pressurized vault. We had sliding doors on the closet that were often knocked off their runners by the sheer mass of what lay inside. And to this day, I have no idea what the floor even looked like for the mountain of clothes that were piled upon it. One night, my two sisters and I, three seemingly intelligent girls, sound of mind and body, made the collective decision to strap on canteens, Girl Scout mess kits, and backpacks and go on our own expedition—into the closet. It could have been too many readings of *The Lion, The Witch, and The Wardrobe,* but we were going to see who could enter one end of the closet and make it to the other end, still alive and breathing. Did I mention it was one o'clock in the morning?

I was the first to go in. After many bumps, bruises, and a close run-in with a denim jacket, I felt my way to the other sliding door and exited the beast of a closet. It was now Joanna's turn. We could only suffer alongside her, as we heard the sound of muffled grunts and groans, and the sound of her falling, only to rise again. Finally, just when we thought we had seen the last of good ole Jo, she made it out the other end alive. Then it was Christina's turn. There were hugs, there were tears, but we finally broke apart and let her go forth. It wasn't long before we heard her pause, and we thought all hope was lost. Then came a sound that we had never expected. From the bowels of the closet, we heard Christina's now weakened voice.

"Oh no!" she cried, as the entire length of the hanging rod loosened its hold and crashed down upon her, sending a resonating quake through the quiet house that sounded as if we had felled a tree. My father rushed in with sleepy eyes and hair in a blaze of bedtime fury.

"Girls, what's going on in here?" He hollered. He threw open the closet door, only to see Christina pinned to the floor with mountains of clothes beneath her, mountains of clothes on top of her, and a canteen, Girl Scout mess kit, and backpack strapped to her body.

We sheepishly said what any child would say, "um . . . nothing."

Like I said, nothing could be as bad as that. If you do have an insurmountable closet or bedroom, strap on your mess kit and go exploring a bit before you clean it all out. You'll never know what you may come across.

Clean It!

One of the most effective things you can do to set the tone for cleanliness in your room is to make up your bed as soon as you get out of it. It's that button that puts you in ready mode. This one action can be the impetus that starts your day going in a positive direction. When your bed is made, you are more motivated to keep the other surfaces neat and clean (plus, you have a place to fold laundry).

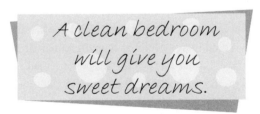

A clean bedroom will give you sweet dreams.

Weekly dusting and vacuuming are also important in this room because of the amount of time you spend there. A couple of weeks of neglect will have you sniffling and sneezing as if it were mid-May at the botanical gardens. And if you bring any cups into the bedroom, then make sure that you take them back into the kitchen. The last thing you want your bedroom to look like is the bus tray during happy hour.

Decorate It!

Your bedroom is a great place to veer off your home's palette, and choose any decor that brings a sparkle to your eye, or other body part. With the main living areas of your home, you are pretty limited to stay within your color palette, unless you are going for that *Alice in Wonderland* effect, where every room is a doorway into another world. Interesting, but it doesn't help much with flow and transition. You have the freedom to do anything you want in your room, so let freedom ring!

A bed-in-a-bag is fine, but don't go for the room-in-a-bag as well. Give your room some verve, some panache, some mojo! Add a bit of the unexpected. Instead of a bedside table, why not stack up a couple of old trunks? How about a taste of the exotic with some mosquito netting around the bed? And who says you need to place the head of your bed against the wall? Why not go for a diagonal placement, or place it smack dab in the middle of the room? You can use this placement to create your own private princess lair with a headboard that mysteriously becomes the back of a secret writing desk when you walk around it. Go for some colors in your room that make the hair on the back of your neck bristle (but in a good way), and splash them all over the place. Maybe a deep purple velvet chaise against a bright chartreuse wall, a satin harlequin print all over the bed, and lavender linen draped around the windows. Mmm, it's enough to make your mouth water.

> *Give your bedroom a balance of yin, yang, and yippee!*

If you have the room, carve out a little spot just for yourself—a place where you can sit with a cup of tea (or a favorite beverage), and just catch your breath for a minute. Put a basket there with a few of your favorite magazines or books and a chair so luscious that it reaches out and pulls you in. This will be your time-out corner. When you know you are about to blow a fuse, it's time to end the round, ring the bell, and go to your corner. Make this a spot that calms your mind and renews your spirit.

And when you decorate your bedroom, keep in mind that you are probably sharing it with someone, namely your husband. Pink and frills are lovely for an afternoon tea party, but it doesn't do much to fan the flame of passion. Give him a bedroom that both of you can enjoy—together. First and foremost, a messy room isn't a big turn-on. If you're planning on turning up the heat, then turn down the mess. Decorate your bedroom like you mean business, and create an entire atmosphere of pure seduction. Dress your bed with those delicious sheets that wrap around your body like a second skin. Light the candles, scent the room, cover your body in something tasty, and let the action unfold (it will probably begin with one of the kids getting out of bed for a drink of water).

Kids' Rooms

They start out so pretty and perfect. A beautiful, pale wall with a delicate crib placed just so. A rocking chair in the corner, a changing table with tiny little white diapers stacked neatly in the bottom, and maybe even a little rocking horse with a sly smile on his face. A sly smile that seems to say, "You just wait. Give it a few years, and you won't even be able to see the carpet. That rocking chair over there is going to have the arm broken off of it and boogers wiped all over the seat. The closet is going to turn into a secret fort. And me? Oh, sure, I may look pretty now. But just you wait until that sweet little boy sleeping in the crib attacks me with the permanent markers. Just you wait."

De-clutter It!

Ah, the nurseries. They never get cluttered. Those babies are so darn cute, that we can't bear to contaminate them with anything remotely resembling clutter. But when the kids get older, clutter begins to take on a whole new form. Suddenly, it becomes home to acorn collections, paper clip jewelry, bouquets of dandelions, and bows made out of bubble blowers and rubber bands with birthday candle arrows as ammunition. It happens. And it's all beautiful. So, how do you decide what stays and what goes? Easy. You don't. They do.

If you gravitate more toward the MasterMind or Mother Hen personality, it's going to be hard to loosen the reigns far enough to give them freedom over their own domain. And if you identify more with the Creative Spirits or Starry-Eyed Dreamers, then it will be difficult to know when you need to get in there and encourage some clearing out. But, it's all about balance. You want your children to have the room to express themselves, but also have the room to live, breathe, and grow. All of our kids are allowed to have a junk drawer in their room. Eventually, all of their odds and ends wind up in this abyss. When it is too full to cram anything more in there, it is time for some clearing out. I usually have to be the one who lays down the law here. Together, we sort through some stuff, and the child decides what should go and what should stay, with some friendly help from me. Some things are just too precious to part with.

> *What may look like clutter to you, is priceless to your kids.*

But, as far as clutter goes, I can tell you that it is a given with children. They are constantly in pursuit of discovering themselves and the world around them, and collecting, creating, and admiring is all part of the beautiful process. Give them the room and the freedom to make messes, and give them the skills and the wisdom to clean them up. There's no secret formula to know when to step in and when to step back. It's just a matter of stopping for a moment and seeing through their eyes. As a mother the only map we are ever given is our own overwhelming love for our children. Parenting is for the most part a lesson in learning how to feel your way through.

Organize It!

The best way to ease up on the clutter is, of course, organizing around it. Kids do everything in their room, from tea parties on the rug to jumping contests on the bed. Organize around their activities so that their stuff is as easy to put away as it is to get out. In addition to at least one off-limits junk drawer, a child needs something to hold special toys that he keeps in his room. My daughters have a dresser that is specifically designated to hold toys. My sons have bins in their closet for the same purpose. I would not ever recommend toy boxes. They look cute in the catalogs, but lids can easily fall down on little fingers, the surface is impractical because you can't place anything on it, and it becomes a pit of clutter where everything gets thrown. A child has to practically empty the contents in order to find one specific thing. A drawer system makes more sense because it is easier to access, and the surface can hold items as well.

Provide good reading light for your children while they are in bed. And some place to put the books after they have finished reading them. I try everything possible to keep up with books, but I am convinced that there is some black-hole principle at work within my home. I have paid so many fines to our local library, that I think by now they should have a Keeley wing. Organizing will help you keep up with things, but I'm not making any promises.

Kids also just need a place to call their own. Sometimes, a child just needs to retreat for a little bit, and it would be nice to have her own safe corner of the world to climb into. When I was a child, I had a pecan tree. It had the perfect branching that fit my little body like a glove, and I could sit in that tree with a book for hours during a lazy summer day. The Swiss Family Robinson had nothing on me and my pecan tree. Give your child a haven. If you have the room, it would be nice to add a little sofa or table and chair. If not, then you could always plant a pecan tree in the yard!

And while you are organizing their rooms, please keep them in mind. You may have to make some alterations in order to accommodate their abilities and foster independence. Lowering the rod in a closet or putting the majority of clothes in the bottom drawers encourages little ones to dress themselves and put away their own clothes. And limiting their bed linens to a simple fitted sheet and comforter or duvet will enable them to easily make their beds by themselves. It may not look pretty, but it's one less thing you have to worry about.

Clean It!

Even though children seem to be in their most natural state when they are covered in some type of filth (especially in the summer), they still need clean sheets to curl up in, clean floors to play on, and clean air to breathe. One of the best gifts you can give your child is a love of order and the discipline to create it. Help your child clean her room by working alongside her. She needs gentle direction and smart moves to model, not a "no more wire hangers!" lecture. You want to be a dear mommy, not "mommy dearest." Help her put order in her space by putting everything in its place, and then teach her to clean her room appropriately.

Try not to turn it into a "me-mommy, you-child, do as I say" thing. Instead, help her to see that a clean room is a way to bless herself with an area that she is proud of and happy to live in. Comments such as, "Wow! It's beginning to feel great in here!" go a long way.

> *If a kid can kick a soccer ball, she can clean a room. Just be proud even if she doesn't score.*

When your children do attempt to clean their rooms, you may have to duct-tape your wrists together to keep from going in there and doing it over. Let their efforts be enough. It may not be done as well as you wanted, but it probably was done a lot better than what they wanted. Your job is to build skills and encourage growth, not to create perfect little housekeepers. But if they are already perfect little housekeepers, could they come over and play with my kids for an afternoon?

When you are cleaning the baby nursery, remember to go for friendly cleaners. If you really want a nice smell in there, then burn some essential oil on a lamp ring, but don't fill the air with any aerosol sprays. Polishing the furniture with oil soap spray is perfectly safe. And as for their laundry, there is nothing special about baby laundry soap. Any detergent that is free of dyes and perfumes will fit the bill perfectly. If you want a fabric softener, you can use white vinegar in the rinse cycle or buy some softener that does not contain perfume. For cleaning the big toys, make your own safe cleaner by dissolving a few spoonfuls of baking soda into a spray bottle full of water. If you have a teething baby, make sure you regularly clean their teething toys by running them through a cycle in the dishwasher. But, be warned, you can take all of these precautions, but they will still pick up the dog's rawhide bone and chew on it when you're not looking.

Decorate It!

Here's where you get to create a world of enchantment. There are so many great theme ideas for children's rooms. The most important thing is to build the room around the child instead of trying to fit your child into a room that looked good in the book but just does not fit his personality. Get some books out of the library or home improvement stores, and look at the photos together. Keep a mental collection of the ideas that your child fell in love with, and try to incorporate them into a room design. Just keep in mind that this precious time when your child is young is so fleeting. I know you have some great ideas for his room, but remember that it is his room. Give him the freedom to express himself in its design (within limits, of course).

> *When it comes to home design, let your kids express themselves— to a point.*

Keep in mind that kids will come up with some pretty wacky stuff. Recently, when I was redoing my daughters' room, they were torn between red and black. I just sent them back to the drawing board. I reserve the right of having veto power over any or all of their decisions. After looking through some magazines they finally came up with a floral idea using periwinkle walls— perfect! That was a year ago, and they are sick of it. We've already got some plans on the drawing board with café au lait walls and white, hot pink, and leopard print accents. My three boys also love to share a room. They currently have a Western-themed room, but the two oldest are beginning to grow out of it. Because they love doing puzzles, we had a puzzle room in the works. One wall would have a huge crossword puzzle with their names and special words in the blocks. Another wall would have the clues for the up and down columns. And puzzle accents would be all through the room. We were just about to put the plans into action—and then they saw *Lord of the Rings*. Does anyone out there know how to paint a hobbit?

The Family Car

Let me just go ahead and clarify something, my car, or should I say, my great blue abyss, is far from pristine. I would love to keep every little thing in its place with no crumbs or dirt on the seats, but the truth of the matter is that life just doesn't always work that way. Reality for me is a trunk full of more gear and supplies than the entire overhead compartment on a 747. Usually about six seconds after I come to a complete stop objects finally quit rolling around on the floor. And there are probably enough food particles stuck in the creases to feed my family for a week (which is a good thing just in case we are ever trapped in our vehicle). Okay, so maybe it's not that bad. Or maybe it really is!

De-clutter It!

I have to do this every single week, or else I have no room for the kids to sit. If you are finding that you are doing more hauling of clutter than kids, then it's time for a clean out. Whenever I have to de-clutter, I take two plastic bags to the car. One if for throwaway, and the other is for put away (usually that's about all you will need). Even the youngest kids can help out with this task, because it's pretty easy. Once you toss away all of the trash, then you can bring the other bag in and put it away. If it is a lot, then go by one of the tried-and-true methods that you have come up with to get you to put it away. Maybe you can grab some during TV commercials, or just do five items at a time. Or maybe you can do what I do, since the kids made the mess, they clean it up. If a child is able to bring something to the car, then they are able to bring it back into the house and put it away.

Organize It!

A well-organized car is such a blessing. The last thing you need to worry about when you have a crying baby, a chattering adolescent, a dentist appointment to make, and a trip to the grocery store to fit in, is where to find a tissue after the toddler just sneezed a Go-Gurt all over his face. A family car needs to be equipped with enough supplies to fill anticipated needs and to handle emergencies.

Car emergencies happen all the time, and always when we least expect it. Be prepared by keeping a plastic tote in the back of your car with a city map, pocket atlas, flashlight (with spare batteries), tool kit, a can of flat-tire repair fluid, and jumper cables. And always, always, have a spare and know how to use it. Don't be the helpless damsel in distress who sits on the side of the road waving your hanky. Self-reliance is very, very sexy. Anyone who can change a tire in a pair of heels has my vote for woman of the year.

As far as personal needs and emergencies, always have a well-stocked first-aid kit on hand. The prepared first-aid kits that you can purchase seem like a good idea at the time, but they turn out to be inconvenient. When you run out of supplies in these kits, you can never replace them because they are all in little trial sizes. Just make your own instead, and include the items that you know from experience you will probably need. And don't forget to throw in things like tweezers for splinters and some Tums for the Boy Scout spaghetti dinner. You can keep your medicine kit in anything. Plastic craft or sewing boxes are a good way to organize items, and because everything is compartmentalized, you can tell when items are running low and need to be replaced.

> *The family car is your home away from home— keep it well stocked.*

For other emergencies, it's good to think ahead. If your job requires the need to wear stockings, keep a spare pair in the car, along with some clear nail polish to stop any runs before they stretch into a hideous stripe of exposed flesh that resembles an exclamation point with your big toe sticking out at the bottom. If you have little ones that are in diapers or are potty-training, remember to keep plenty of diapers and wipes on hand. And wipes are convenient all the time, so keep some handy.

You will also have your fair share of trash in a car, so keep a little trash can or bag handy. And contain all of those other odds and ends that you need to carry around with you. My girlfriend Caroline has a perfect little lined basket that she keeps on the floor of her car. Inside it, she keeps all of her car supplies—tissues, wipes, car charger for her cell phone, sunglasses, hairbrush, and all of those other things that you could just kick yourself when you leave at home.

I always try to bring some type of snack along with me. This way, when errands begin to pile up, I can just grab the snacks and start throwing them toward the back of the van until the snarlings and gnashings of teeth die down.

Clean It!

I have found there are two types of people in the world—the ones who are out every weekend, washing, waxing, and vacuuming out their cars, and the ones who drive around with "wash me" written on their back windshield. Somewhere, in the happy world of balance, lies a place called happy medium. You can keep your car clean without being meticulous about it. If you do have a new car and are meticulous about it, just take one good road trip with kids in tow. You will return purged of perfection, just like your two-year-old purged that bag of nacho cheese Doritos back at mile 224. My brother and his wife came to visit me in his new car with their two kids. As they packed up to return home, I saw my brother pull out the Handi Wipes and wipe off the bottom of his kids shoes. My heart went out to him—oh, the poor, misguided soul! Last time I was at their home, his wife, Michele, and I went to the mall. I'm not sure, but I think I caught a glimpse of a Burger King cup in their car.

About once a month, I wash the car and then head over to the gas station to fill up the van, vacuum it out, and reward myself with a big fat cappuccino. Yes, I know that real cappuccino cannot come from a machine like that. Actually, I don't really want to know what the concoction is that I'm drinking. All I really care to know is that it is reward enough for me to wash the van and vacuum it out. Plus, it's caffeinated.

You may also want to keep canisters of wipes in your car to give it the quickie wipe off. These are a great idea for maintaining the interior of your car. Remember, if you strive for perfection you will be constantly fighting unnecessary battles. Go for good. If you're driving around heads of states, that's a different thing. But the purpose of a car is to get you from point A to point B, safely and pleasantly. Once this is accomplished, all of the superfluous time you spend perfecting your car could be spent much more constructively elsewhere. Take up knitting (but not while you're driving)!

Decorate It!

Okay, so aside from the air fresheners hanging from the rearview mirror and the Chihuahua bobbing his head in the back, there is only so much decorating you can do with the family car. In my van, I have a male hula dancer shaking his groove thing on my dash. It's a tribute to my husband. If the urge strikes, go ahead and whip out the washable tempera paints and use your car as a canvas. Don't worry. It will wash off. I am still threatening my oldest daughter with painting our car in flowers and rainbows. The thrill of embarrassing her in front of her friends is almost irresistible.

Time for Your Prescription

It's fun to put each room in your home through a makeover. But life is never like we see on television where they get everything done in twenty minutes and someone says, "Okay, you can open your eyes now!" Great things take time and effort, and you may as well go into with your eyes wide open. Know that it can and will get frustrating. The curtains you ordered don't look right with the wallpaper. There are more bins than shelf space. Your brooms and mops spend more time as horses for little cowboys instead of cleaning tools. Real life is far from ideal. But that's the fun thing about it. The joy is in the living, the failing, the starting over, and the pride of accomplishment. When you begin putting your home through boot camp, things won't always turn out right. But they will eventually evolve into just the thing that your heart was after all along.

Rx for MasterMinds

Time for you is quite a subjective concept. You get started doing an activity, and the next thing you know it has reeled you in like a shopping mall on the day after Thanksgiving. You like to begin projects and you don't leave it until it's good and done—very good and done. But when it comes to doing home interiors, you need to make sure that you do the job, but only good enough to allow you to move on to the next phase. If you get stuck going for perfect, then you're never going to be satisfied, and you'll never move on. To make sure you move from one stage to the next, set a schedule and stick to it. Do the job thoroughly, but when time is up, then make yourself move on to your next scheduled activity. Perfection isn't the success. Progress is.

Rx for Creative Spirits

You are a shining star, ready to light up the night with all of your accomplishments. But sometimes, your tendency to bite off more than you can chew just leaves you with a bad case of indigestion! Don't try to take on the world. Some things just work better when you do them in sequence. You may want to cover the walls in that beautiful shade of apple green, but force yourself to do the majority of de-cluttering first. Let the paint be the goal for the dirty work you have to do before hand. You know what special touches you want to add to the home, so use them as motivators to do the necessary work that you would rather avoid. Those decorative touches will look even more beautiful when you have done your prep work.

Rx for Mother Hens

Okay, lady. Now is the time for you to take a chance or two. Have fun with your home and don't get caught up in the right way or the wrong way. Some things just have to evolve. And allowing yourself to feel the freedom to take a decorative risk or two is a step forward no matter what the result. And remember that your family is a unit, so the best outcomes occur when everybody works together. Enlist the troops and respect their freedom. It may take a bit of adjusting on your part. But family is far more important than standards. You want to go for *family*, not *fantasy*. So keep in mind the kind of house that you would like, but don't let that become more important than the home you love. Any effort that results in family harmony is a success no matter how you look at it.

Rx for Starry-Eyed Dreamers

You have no problem going with your gut instinct. As a matter of fact, that is your primary mode of decision making. So when it comes to your home, feel free to follow your heart. But even more important, make sure that you are taking action. You can sit around and ponder all day without taking any steps toward meeting your goal. So go with your gut, but *go!* Find a place to begin in a room, and just start there. A little bit of action has a remarkable way of pushing us into doing more and more. The hardest exercise in the world is just pushing in that workout video and pushing the play button. But once you start, the rest of the course seems to chart itself out like magic. Don't wait until you hear a gunshot from the starting block. Just put your blinders on and take off!

Dream On!

Step into my office, and have a seat on the sofa. Let's talk about your childhood. What are your first memories of home? My friend Kimberly has fond memories of waking up to warm oatmeal in pastel-colored metal bowls. My husband remembers reading comic books in bed with his dog curled up at his feet. I remember sitting on a sofa watching my mother curl her hair every single night. What are your memories? Write them down in your dream journal. Hopefully, you have some fond ones. But if there are some harsh memories that you have locked away, then write those down as well. There is healing in recognition. And sometimes the best balm for an unhappy childhood is to open the memories and let the light of God bathe the wounds.

For the good memories, try to find ways that you can build those into your home today. To this day, when Kimberly is having a difficult day or feeling a bit blue, she whips out the oatmeal to feed her spirit. Sometimes adding a fond walk down memory lane adds some of the best design touches to your home.

And the bad memories are just as important. These are the memories that you need to make a conscious effort to replace with something that emits a positive energy. If dinner times were filled with arguments and discord, then this is one area that you can consciously build into a time of family unity by dining together, preparing delicious meals, and perhaps having a family devotion. Take the pain that is held in your heart and use it as a cornerstone to build memories of happiness and joy. Write down next to each unhappy memory a way that you can turn it into source of positive energy in your home. All it takes is recognition, will, and the grace of God. He can do miraculous things through our lives when we open up and let Him.

Chapter 15

The Best Career in the World

Let me just go ahead and grab my soapbox and let the world know—home management is the best career in the world! What other job out there do you get to be surrounded by those people you love most in the world? And what other job out there leaves more of an impact on those around you? Managing a home is a career in which you feel the thrill of victory and the agony of defeat, sometimes less than five minutes apart. It's unpredictable, never boring (unless you just want it to be), and keeps you challenged 100 percent of the time—kind of like a professional sport! Like any athlete, your performance is a product of passion and effort. As a matter of fact, it has as many highs and lows, as much sweat and energy, and as much enthusiasm and raw grit as anything you find on a Gatorade commercial.

For the Love of the Game

You can tell the athletes with a passion from the athletes who are in it for the fame and fortune. One is saying, "Give me the ball, Coach" and the other is saying, "Show me the money!" When Michael Jordon was at the height of his career, he was taking the minimum salary with the Bulls in order to free up more money to acquire players. Of course, he wasn't in the poorhouse by any means. Hanes, MCI, Ballpark, and Nike, along with about twenty other companies, were seeing to it that he had a roof over his head. But the point is, he was in love with basketball. It was obvious by how he played the game. He wasn't always making a million dollars every time he smiled at the camera. There was a time when no one knew who Michael Jordon was—just a kid who knew how to handle a ball. But because of his passion, he was practicing jump shots when most were negotiating contracts. He didn't choose basketball because he loved money. The money came to him because he had a love for basketball.

If you're not aware of it by now, there's not a lot of money to be found in a career in home management. If you're looking for the big bucks, then look somewhere else. You've got to foster an environment that will increase and perpetuate your love for what you do, because that's all that really matters. It's funny how we get about money. We let it place a value on our work, when actually that reality is far from the truth. When we have a true passion for what we do, then life conforms itself to fit our perception. People value us because we send out the message that we are valuable. We are happy because we choose to be. We are respected because we respect ourselves.

I've never gotten a paycheck for cleaning windows or painting a room, but I have felt the deep gratification that comes with a job well done. No one has ever paid me to care for my children, but when I witness one of them taking their first steps or learning how to cut with scissors for the first time, I wouldn't trade places with anyone. Home management is not a lucrative career, but it is more valuable and more desirable than any job on this earth. We are creating environments that can make or break a person. We have the power to infuse others with positive energy, or drag them down.

I doubt you will ever get a tip for waiting tables in your own home. But do you really need $8 to make you feel like a better person? Look around you. See the sparkle in your child's eyes as he reaches for his dessert. Hear the laughter around the table. You put it there! It was your dedication and your passion for what you do that built these people and this moment. God placed you here for a remarkable career that no paycheck could come close to encompassing. So dive into your career and enjoy all the benefits that come with a job well done.

When you are playing a sport for the love of the game, the money and fame will come in its own time and in its own way. When you are creating a home that comforts, fulfills, and inspires, and you're doing it out of love and passion, the blessings will come in their own time and in their own way. Don't demand the compliments or run through a "poor me" routine. Just know that deep down inside you are creating a better world right where you are, and work at it with all of your soul and strength. The blessings will eventually pour into your life, and in such magnitude that you will hardly be able to contain it all!

The Nancy Kerrigan Effect

All sports have their fair share of spills and setbacks, and home management is no exception. Just when you think you are in the final stretch, you trip over a hurdle and go for a spill, right in front of every single spectator. This comes with the territory. Expect it. Embrace it. Wipe yourself off and move on. At least you're gutsy enough to enter the race in the first place!

I remember watching the '94 Winter Olympics. Nancy Kerrigan and Kristi Yamaguchi were the hot tamales of American female figure skaters, but Yamaguchi's final performance blew Kerrigan off the ice. As a matter of fact, Kristi was so good, that when it was time for Kerrigan to go in the rink and show her stuff, she was so threatened by Kristi's stunning performance and so frustrated by the turn of events, that she completely flubbed up her entire routine. Every time she went into any type of spin or stunt, she would land in a spill. It got so bad, that by the end of the performance, the announcers weren't even calling attention to it. They didn't have to—she was doing a fine job herself. She dug her grave deeper with each passing second until finally, the agonizing routine was over. She summoned up any remaining dignity, bit back tears, and left the rink.

I can't even count the times I have felt like the day was just one disastrous performance. Every time I tried to gain my footing and get back into the game, I would end up flat on my face, humiliated and angry. Sometimes, we put so much pressure on performance, that we set our own traps for failure. We stress ourselves out completely by trying to be mommy of the year or homemaker of the month. Home management is not a show-and-tell competition. We're all in this game together, and no one is going home with the gold. Every now and then, you just have days that start out bad and get worse every minute. I don't have to go through the routine, because I'm sure you (if you're human) are already too familiar with it. A million and one things are going wrong, the house looks like it should be condemned, and you haven't even had a chance to take a shower! And it seems like the more we try to get things under control, the more out of control it becomes. These days happen as sure as night follows day. You can either learn to embrace it, or live in the agony of trying to create a life that is just an illusion.

Nancy's problem was that she was so singularly focused on performing perfectly, that she forgot to enjoy her performance. When we get so caught up in doing everything right, we are just setting the stage for failure. Forget the stress of perfection, and just enjoy the days. What's the point of doing what you're doing if you're not having fun doing it? Burn the white gloves, and befriend a few dust bunnies. I know this appears to contradict everything I stress about cleaning, but for many personalities, way too much stress is applied to home management. If you want to be Mr. Clean then put on a tight white shirt and shave your head, but it's more important to make your house a home instead of a showplace. Let your family feel the pleasure of living, and not the pressure of living within your standards. Let them maintain their own rooms, to a certain health standard. I've even heard of some women so focused on keeping an immaculately sanitized bathroom, that they insist that any male individuals pee sitting down. Are two drops of urine really enough reason to strip them of their dignity? Anyway, we all know that dominating the toilet via a vigorous stream of urine is just a leftover trait from their bow and arrow days as hunter/gatherer.

A home is where you let your hair down, not stick it under a hair net. Relax! Some days go perfectly. You could take footage of the day and air it on the Home and Garden Channel. Then real life hits and hits hard. Go with the spills and know that it won't last. The crazy days are just as much a part of your beautiful life as the perfect days. It's all in the same package. As soon as you get all of the kids buckled in their car seats, someone is going to need to go use the bathroom. When you put in new carpet, someone is going to track in mud. When you buy brand new drinking goblets for the kitchen, one is going to come crashing to the floor. It's life! You can either get angry about it and set yourself up for another spill, or you can just go with it and keep a smile on your face. Either way, you are not going to change what happened, so you may as well deal with it in a positive way.

To this day, I couldn't tell you a single thing about Kristy Yamaguchi's performance, but I can tell you that as tortuous as it was, Nancy Kerrigan stuck it out to the very end. And that's the same attitude that we need to have. We will have days that are full of spills, but we need to get right back up on our skates. The last time I looked, there was no finish line to our job as home managers. Yeah, sometimes it will get easier, and then there are those days that leave you flat out on the ice with a bruised ego and a freezing fanny. The most important thing we need to remember is that we are in it for the long haul. Take the spills as they come, and quit comparing yourself to others. The most critical eye on you is your own. Look at yourself through loving and forgiving eyes, and it will be so much easier to just flow with the music.

If I recall correctly, Kristy may have won the gold, but Nancy got to go to Disneyworld and star in a parade. Personally, I would take the parade over the pedestal any ole day. It's too difficult to stand up on a pedestal all the time. You're sure to fall off sooner or later. At a parade, you can just relax and have fun. You only go around once, so why fret and bother with perfection? As Frankie says, "Relax. Don't do it." Quit worrying about the impression you are making on the world, and focus instead on the impression you are making on yourself and your family. No matter how crazy the day is going, you will never have this day again. Don't throw it away by getting mad and frustrated over things that don't amount to a hill of beans. So what if there's crayon all over the wall? So what if no one has a clean pair of matched socks? This is life, not a competition. Take your fall, laugh, wipe yourself off, and get back to your routine. The twists and turns and flips aren't the important things in life. Sometimes it's just a matter of keeping your balance.

Stay in Training

The more you train, the better you get. If you don't know how you are ever going to get your home looking good or the laundry caught up, just realize that it all begins with little steps of effort. Even tiny steps or steps done incorrectly make a difference. It's the effort that makes the difference, not necessarily the accomplishment. Athletes need to constantly stay in training so that their bodies develop the habit of playing the game. With the level of competition in the NFL, the players need to stay in training throughout the calendar year. The Super Bowl may be the final chapter for the season, but the book never closes. Players get a few weeks off, and then they are right back in training. Their level of performance is directly related to their investment in training. If they want a good season, they better expect to train hard.

After giving birth to Klara, my youngest child, I decided that it was time to get in shape. After my sixth child, I was a little more "booty" than "licious." It could have been the melodic "swish, swish, swish" of my inner thighs when I wore corduroy pants or perhaps it was when I caught sight of my flabby arms waving back at me in the bathroom mirror when I was changing a light bulb. Or maybe the straw that broke the camel's back was when I was asked if I was pregnant as I held my three-month-old baby in my arms. Anyway, I got inspired, bought a workout DVD at the store (I just read the back of all of them and got the one with the shortest workout), and even purchased a new tank top and yoga pants. I set the alarm, got up in the morning (thirty minutes late, but still), and put on my new exercise clothes. Looking in the full-length mirror was not a great start to the day. I felt like I should have had an "Eat more Chikin" sign around my neck. But I prevailed, put on the DVD, and started working out my tired body.

When I first began, I was wondering when the grace and balance that I used to have would kick in. Instead of saluting the sun, I felt like I was doing a drunk hippo weeble-wobble dance in front of it. Twenty minutes into the workout, and I felt like my body was a gigantic slumbering bear that I was attempting to wake from a deep, dark, comfortable hibernation. Every movement brought some type of resistance. I started on the abs portion, and instead of my body responding to the exercises, I was greeting by a quivering, quaking mound of flesh that refused to do what my brain was telling it to. With each squat my knees sounded like Pop Rocks candy, and the entire workout finally culminated in a "step-right, kick-left, alternate arms with five pound weights, twisty thing." By that point, I was just happy to still be alive, so I was doing more of a "Curly shuffle, wave at the television kind of thing." I had abandoned the weights back at the halfway mark when I could no longer lift my arms over my waistline. The next morning, I remember sitting on the toilet and wondering if it would be more embarrassing to call my husband in to help me stand up, or just be content to crawl across the floor with my underwear around my ankles and use the tub as support.

Oh, the things that happen to our bodies when we refuse to keep it in shape! And it happens to our career as a home manager also. We can often fall into the trap of believing that one day things are going to calm down and we will be able to catch up on everything we have been putting off. But it just doesn't happen that way. It's the daily efforts and the daily exercises that keep our homes in top shape. The laundry is just going to keep getting backed up, and the garage is going to get more and more cluttered. The little minutes that you spend in productive activity throughout the day, are keeping you in top shape to manage your life and handle all of the obligations that come your way. It's the old plate-spinning trick. You never know how many you can spin until you start spinning. And when you keep spinning, you become better and better at it. Sure, they'll crash to the floor every once in a while, but that's my next topic. The point is, keep the efforts flowing and continue with the little steps that maintain your home and get you further toward reaching your goals.

As I've said over and over, it's not the huge marathon makeover sessions that matter. It's the little endeavors that put you ahead of the game. It's picking a few things up as you walk through a room, throwing in a load when you have a few minutes, organizing some papers while you watch a television show. This is your exercise routine. And if you keep up the daily effort, you are training your mind and your body to be able to perform more efficiently and effectively. Suddenly, you have more free time on your hands because of how you are training yourself to manage it. Stick to the routines and discipline yourself to go through all of the motions.

No Nosebleeds Allowed!

Managing a crazy household sometimes takes so much gut strength that you feel like you're going to pop a stitch or two before it's all over. But you strain, and you strive, and you eventually accomplish what you set out to do. Sometimes it's just trying to get the kids bathed and into bed that's about to drive you bonkers. But whatever it is, you know that your shift isn't going to be over anytime soon, so you have to hang in there and dig down deep to find that strength and drive to get you over that next hump. Stay in training, but know when you need to be put on the injured list.

One evening, my husband was doing some mindless flicking around on television and he stumbled across a strong man competition. I was mesmerized by it, drawn to it like flies to horse poop in a Fourth of July parade. Suddenly, I found myself sitting beside him watching these men pull cars, haul huge metal balls, and other strange things that I had previously believed were limited only to Dr. Seuss books. As I was watching, there was one man who was lifting something extremely heavy over his head. I don't remember what it was, probably an elephant or something. Anyway, he was straining so hard that blood started streaming out of his nose. Now, you've got to understand something here. If he is straining so hard that blood is running out of his nose, then you know that something is going on with the rectal region as well. As far as what may be happening down there, I don't even want to venture in that direction. But, after it was over, he just wiped his nose and moved on to the next event. He was walking a bit peculiar though—like a mixture between Johnny Bravo and a gibbon.

I may just be a bit delusional, but I believe that blood coming out of your nose is probably cause for alarm (unless it's just a harmless side effect from the steroids). But if your body is telling you enough is enough then you would be smart to listen to it. Sometimes we women run our beautiful bodies down into the dirt running after kids, cleaning the house, being a chauffeur, preparing the meals, and anything else we can cram into our days. With proper planning and preparation, it can all go quite smoothly. But then there are those little chapters of life when things get particularly hairy, and almost nothing could prepare you for the strain. Perhaps hubby has to be out of town for a few weeks, and you are left running the home (and everyone in it) all by yourself. Or maybe you're on your own anyway, trying to do the work of two people. It could be that you are caring for little children as well as older parents. Or maybe schedules are just getting crazy, tempers are flaring up, and you feel pulled in a thousand different directions. It's okay to drop the plates every once in a while. Life is real, and if you are really living it, then expect a few drops of blood out of your nose every now and then. Just don't be so quick to wipe it off and jump back in the event. You may just need to put down the load you're lugging around, and withdraw for a while.

This is not a strong-woman competition. No one is out there doling out prizes for the home manager of the year. And even if they were, we would know full well that it was just one big setup (kind of like most of the reality shows out there). The only perfect mom I know is Caroline Ingalls from "Little House on the Prairie," and even she went a bit loony and tried to cut off her leg once. I guess she had baked just one too many pies. Home is where the masks are stripped off and what you see is what you get. It's one big perfectly imperfect package. Listen to your body and your mind. It will tell you when enough is enough. Learn when to step back, put down your load, and take a breather. The work isn't going anywhere, and, believe me, it will be there piled up when you get back in the game. But, you will be refreshed and refocused. And your efforts will be much more productive.

If you don't draw the line somewhere, then no one will. You've got to learn when to cut yourself some slack. If you feel constantly run down and run over, then maybe you need to delegate some work, hire some help, or readjust your standards. Or something really drastic—just secure the little ones, throw duty to the wind, and grab ten minutes for yourself. As far as delegating some work goes, the success of a family is determined by the extent to which they are able to work together. The more we share the work, the less work there is to share. You don't have to scrub the sink every day. If your kids are old enough to spit toothpaste into it, they are old enough to wipe it out. And who says men can't help out with the laundry? Even if he's colorblind, he can pretty much tell how to separate lights from darks. And if you do solicit some help from him, make sure you let him know what to do with a brand new red sweater. To this day, I still have a drawer full of pink dish towels. If you feel guilty about not doing all of the work yourself, then consider it a process in education. Every person, children included, should know basic homemaking skills (yes, even boys). You are helping them by teaching them how to help out around the house, even if it's not up to your standards. And speaking of standards, if you're feeling strained and run down, maybe you need to readjust yours a bit. Don't see the dust as dust. See it as a way of building up the resistance of your family's immune system!

And don't forget that you have options. When you feel as if you are going to bust a gut, then you may need to resort to hiring some help. It could very well be the best money you've spent in a long time. I was completely reluctant to do this. I always saw spending that money as a complete waste when I could always do it myself. But, here's the kicker—when mama's got blood running out of her nose, then nobody in the house is going to be happy. When you push yourself too hard, you are taking everyone with you. Spend the money if you have to and consider it an investment in the family. When things get just too harried around the home, and I have a million obligations, I will often call in the troops. If a deadline is looming, or a new baby comes into the picture, you can guarantee that the last thing I am going to be doing is mopping floors. I love to clean, but I love to do other things also. When you have a thousand different directions to take in life, consider which one will be most in line with your long-term goals, and go after it. Sure you can do everything—just not all at the same time.

When you do feel the veins in the side of your face beginning to pop out, you need to do whatever is necessary to step backstage for a minute and gain your composure, even if it means just closing your eyes for a moment and breathing deeply. I remember one particular nosebleed segment of my life. I had a rapidly approaching deadline, my toddler had been up from 4 AM to 5:30 AM trying to convince me to go downstairs and turn on the Wiggles, the girls had pulled out all of my tea trying to find the perfect one for their tea party, and the boys were busy making an arts and crafts mess in the dining room. Finally, my toddler was down for a nap, and I got comfortable in a rocking chair to nurse the baby. The combination of sleep deprivation, a baby in my arms, and a rocking chair had the same effect as two ounces of Dewar's and *The Abram's Report.* I was sound asleep in less than five minutes. The kitchen needed to be cleaned, the boys' mess had to be corralled, but I desperately needed to relax for a minute or else they were going to have a screaming harpy for a mother. The baby nursed for about fifteen minutes and then fell asleep also. After I had been resting for about thirty minutes, with a sleeping baby in my arms, a breast imprudently peering out of my shirt (after six kids, my breasts don't peek, they peer), mouth open, head back, and drool pooling up in the corner of my mouth, my daughter came over and woke me up. I knew my nosebleed segment was drawing to a close when she said, "Mama, I can help you out with dinner tonight because you kind of look like a grandma sitting there." Okay, time to wipe the nose (or the mouth) and get back into the next event.

Feel Your Heartbeat

In the 1980 Winter Olympics, the USA hockey team went to Lake Placid, New York, to battle the Soviets, who had never lost a single game—never! Out of forty-two games, they had forty-two wins. The USA team was made up of a bunch of unknowns who were thrown together to battle it out on the ice against teams from all over the world. The odds were against them even coming close to beating the Soviets. When the USA team had its first exhibition game against the Soviets, the Soviets whooped it (to put it nicely). The combined skills of the various American players could not even come close in comparison to the training and the abilities of the Soviet players. It was an uneven match. But the Americans had a secret weapon. They had the drive, and they had the determination, but most of all they had passion. Losing to the Soviets was not just unwanted, it was unacceptable. The Americans were willing to take whatever risk necessary, and make their bodies perform whatever feat needed to win against the Soviet team. The combination of passion and skill leveled the playing field for the teams, and the USA team took the game. The skill didn't win the game as much as the passion did.

317

You have got to feel passion for what you do. You've got to keep pushing the envelope and challenging yourself. Set impossible goals, and if you have enough skill and enough passion, you will reach them. The skill part is easy. It comes with practice and learning. It's the passion part that is the kicker. It's so tempting to slip into a half existence, to let the days run together in such a way that you can't tell one from the other. You've got to push yourself to create something new. Take on new projects. Pull some tricks out of your hat. Perform magic throughout your home. Live with passion. My kids always get the same response whenever they come to me and say, "I'm bored." They always get the lecture of, "You may as well say you are not creative. But since I know you are, you are just content not to challenge yourself." Then I usually give them a chore or two to keep them busy. Needless to say, they don't often complain of boredom! No matter who you are or what your personality, you are a creative person. Your home can be a challenging environment. This is your life to create—make it passionate!

You often see athletes checking their pulse rates. They use this to moderate their activity level. If it is too high, they may need to take it down a notch. But if it is too low, then they know they need to kick it into high gear. Check your pulse. Are you trying to take on the world, or are you content to just let the world pass you by? You have more power and more choice in your career than almost any other one on the planet. You are creating an environment. Push yourself to go the limit.

My daughter had to make a phone call one time, and she was a nervous wreck before she had to do it. She said that she didn't want to make the call. I then asked her if her palms were sweaty. She said they were. I then asked her if she could feel her heart beating. She said that she could.

"Good," I told her. "That means you're challenging yourself."

When it comes to managing your home are you living in a way that makes your palms sweat and your heart race? Try something new. Start something impossible. Set completely unrealistic goals. You will surprise yourself at how you can instinctually respond to challenges when you bring passion into the picture. Courage is performance in the face of fear. Live with courage! Live with passion! Live in such a way that you can feel your heart beating. Live it—just the way you are.

Time for Your Prescription

You know your personality, and you know how you work best. Now make it work for you. You have the power to create your own realities. As go your thoughts, so goes your life. So make those thoughts some good ones. The fulfillment that lies within your career as a home manager is predominantly dependent on you. Whatever you believe about yourself becomes you. Respect what you do and honor who you are. And remember that whatever you are going to get out of life depends upon how much you are willing to put into it.

If you are looking for the best way to improve on your home management skills, then invite God into your home. There's just something about hosting the holiest of holies that keeps you on your toes. And when His spirit pours through your home, the rooms are prettier, the food is tastier, and the voices are sweeter. And the positive energy is so strong that it is nearly combustible. If you are living for yourself or your home, then the housework will always be a chore. But if you are living for God, then managing your home is a pleasure indeed.

Rx for MasterMinds

You love to think things through and you move with caution through life. But there's a time and a place for everything. Sometimes the scene calls for some delicate tiptoeing, and then there are other times when nothing fits the bill like a cannonball off the high dive. Keep in mind that you only go around once, so make it count. As a home manager, you have every good reason in the world to move with composure and a bit of trepidation. But there are times that call for a little more boogie in your shoes. Don't forget to take some chances every now and then. You'll never know if you never try.

Rx for Creative Spirits

You have no problem living a full life. As a matter of fact, you love nothing more than being the star of the show. But remember to give enough credit to your supporting cast. As a home manager, you have the power to greatly enrich and enable the lives of those you love. Use this power to the fullest by being the force that fuels their dreams and breathes some life into their spirits. And make sure when you lead the troops with your amazing style that you are conscientious enough to remember the follow-through. You always start off with a bang, but frequently allow the fire to fizzle out. Practice some of that stick-to-itiveness that will allow your dreams to become reality. With your passion, you are already halfway there.

Rx for Mother Hens

As a home manager, you have truly found your niche. You have amazing skills with coordination and logistics. And people are never sorry when they depend upon you. But as you are filling every need around you, remember to fill your own as well. You may end up scraping the bottom of a dry well if you don't make a conscious effort of fueling your own tank every now and then. And everyone will be better off, because when you have joy in your spirit, it's easier for you to let it spill out into the lives of others. And as hard as it may be for you, try to remember to loosen your grip on life every once in a while. Not everything in life and in you can be predicted and controlled. Sometimes you just have to let go and believe in a bit of magic.

Rx for Starry-Eyed Dreamers

You live with integrity as the cornerstone of your existence. And you, of all people, have no problem following your heart through life. But all the self-actualization in the world won't put results in your lap. Sometimes, you need to put some feet to your dreams. Don't wait for life to come to you. Instead, take the initiative to reach out and grab it. As a home manager, you are the heart of the home that beats strong and true. Now summon up the strength to go where your passion leads you. You are passionate about your home and your family. Show that passion by investing your sweat equity in making that home all you know in your heart it can be.

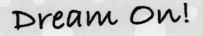

Dream On!

Get out that dream journal, and never quit dreaming!

Index